Born on the
Battlefield Too

Born on the Battlefield Too

The Reality of Spiritual Warfare

JOHN HENRY JAMES 3RD

authorHOUSE®

AuthorHouse™
1663 Liberty Drive
Bloomington, IN 47403
www.authorhouse.com
Phone: 1 (800) 839-8640

Published by AuthorHouse   03/06/2015

ISBN: 978-1-4969-7314-6 (sc)
ISBN: 978-1-4969-7313-9 (e)

Print information available on the last page.

Scripture quotations marked KJV are from the Holy Bible, King James Version (Authorized Version). First published in 1611. Quoted from the KJV Classic Reference Bible, Copyright © 1983 by The Zondervan Corporation.

Contents

Israel, Judah & Dorian

For My Sons:
They were Born on the Battlefield too…

Israel, Judah & Dorian

&

My Sister Tracey N. Hayes & Niece: Lela

*"Now I know that the Lord saveth His
anointed; He will hear him from
His holy heaven with the saving strength of His right hand."*

Psalm 20:6

Prologue

The War Zone

"Who shall separate us from the love of Christ? Shall tribulation, or distress, or persecution, or famine, or nakedness, or peril, or sword? As it is written, for thy sake we are killed all the day long; we are accounted as sheep for the slaughter; nay, in all these things we are more than conquerors through Him that loved us. For I am __persuaded__, that neither death, nor life, nor angels, nor principalities, nor powers, nor things present, nor things to come, nor height, nor depth, nor any other creature, shall be able to separate us from the love of God which is in Christ Jesus our Lord."

Romans 8:35-39

These passages in Paul's letter to the church in Rome, along with Ephesians chapter six, are perhaps my favorite versus of scripture. It has given me great joy and strengthened my resolve as a soldier for Christ in both my natural and spiritual walk. The premise is one of having simply made up your mind!

Think about it; that doesn't sound like such difficult task or even tremendous accomplishment, but nowadays, making up ones mind can be comparative to climbing Mt. Everest! Making the decision to follow Christ and leave the past behind is the basis of Christianity! This simple or *not so simple* idea of making a decision will define you. Once done, there will be all sorts of things that can and will stand in your way to move you; turn you around and attempt to take you backward. We can strive to understand the strengths and weaknesses of our enemies, but we must remember that the battle is not ours, it is the Lord's and all that is required of us is to 'stand'.

What then can come between you and Christ? What weapon can prosper against you?

I have to begin by letting you know that it has been extremely difficult to transition this book from thought to page (13 years to be exact). Then again; so also was the first! It appears that my lot in life is such that God will not allow me to publish anything that I have *not* personally experienced. Can I also add that the journey to this book has been frightening, painful and arduous?

The subject matter of the following pages will bring to light answers to questions that each of us has asked ourselves at one time or another. For others it will confirm their highest beliefs and expectations. For others still – their worst fears. This is the second book in a progressive series of spiritual warfare material and like "***Born on the Battlefield – the Art of Spiritual Warfare***," it is intended to inspire the reader to live a victorious life while here on earth.

This book was being written in the back of my mind while the first was in the publishing stage. Well, to some degree that holds true, but the full truth is that God reveals *what* He will and to *whom* He will, when He will, what it is *that* He wills, at different points in time. So the best and finest way to put it is that I believed that I would write this book… I simply did not know when or how.

It was done in 2001; one year after the first book, but now in 2014, thirteen years later, and after having lost the whole manuscript to a very untimely computer crash, you are about to embark on the journey that I have lived for the past thirteen and a half to fourteen years.

The notes for this book were being compiled at a furious rate as the Spirit of God gave me direction. I simply put the information on a table in the back of my mind like puzzle pieces. I could only decipher parts of the full picture at times. At others, I could see whole sections of the puzzle falling into place. It is only now in God's divine wisdom and planning that He has given me the ability to release this book.

The "...Reality of Spiritual Warfare" picks up where "...The Art of Spiritual Warfare" ends. This will unlock the door to what you may already know, but have never equated to your spiritual walk. It will challenge you to be more radical in your faith and force you to recognize the face of the enemy in your daily life. You are now leaving your comfort zone and are about to enter the *War Zone*.

Author's Desk:

"This book should be used as an assistant to your and with our Bible as a compliment only as I was informed by pastor James Smith of Emmanuel Church International"

Introduction

My War

Why am I qualified to write this book? I have no recognizable title [Other than the *two* that every man receives upon salvation; which are Brother or Sister and Minister of the gospel], no degrees of noteworthiness, no denominational pedigree. I have however been made to practice what I am preaching and have the experience that has been tried and tested and I still <u>stand</u> and am *'persuaded.'*

My books come after long and tedious wars with the enemy, the world, and with myself. I am in effect working out my own salvation with much fear and trembling, hence the title – "Born on the Battlefield."

The Lord, while giving me both the anointing and talent to produce books on spiritual warfare, is very adamant about the **reality** of ministry. By this, I mean that with a decent vocabulary, today's technology and an in depth study of any subject; anyone can write a book. I happen to know people that have written books about subjects that they have no experience in. I, however, have to minister the truth in this book to and about, those persons who God has placed in my path. Therefore, I can understand the necessity of what God allows in my life and the purpose for which he created me.

If you don't know Dear Reader, that you will have to **suffer**; for what you say that you believe; then you don't know my God! If you can understand that God so loved the world enough to give His *only* begotten Son, then it stands to reason that He would allow us to *"make our callings an election sure."* This is simply to say that God is expecting 'something' out of us – and why shouldn't He? The price to purchase back mankind was heavier than most of us would care to dwell on or go into depth about. Think about this; if we sin from the time that we are old enough to do so; call it 'stealing a cookie' off of the kitchen table when we are 2 years old, and during the course of 80 years, have committed nearly every other sin imaginable, then we must at least look at the fact that Jesus took on all of that, for everyone, in the whole world, all in one day; on one cross; and in one human body and then went to hell to preach to those who were there... We **owe**! We could never repay anything *that* grandiose, but if we think about the sins of one single man over the course of a lifetime and multiply those by everyone that *has ever* or *will ever* live and who has previously died, and then multiply that by say 6 billion – you b then will begin to scratch the surface. You *will* **suffer**!

In 2004, I was privileged enough to travel to Africa (Kenya) for missionary work and was able to minister about what I had already experienced and written about in *that* first book. In 2005, the enemy attacked my family and took my middle daughter Monique away from us and in 2008 he came after my wife (remember that this book had already been written and was slated to go to publishingMy wife has been constantly and consistently attacked by the enemy and I have had to endure this reality - and always will.

Needless to say that it has been very difficult to keep the family together. After ten years; my oldest daughter Tamara, the oldest girl, is in the Air Force; Dorian, the oldest boy, is going into the Air Force; Nelijha, the youngest girl has graduated from High School and is working and Judah and Israel are doing well, we have grown in mind body and spirit; we have achieved tenure in ministry, we have purchased our first home, and the other children are a daily blessing to us as we watch them grow and mature in Christ. Monique is out on her own and doing well and now has a solid church family with her own daughter Kaylyn; which make me a grandfather!

My beautiful wife now has a steady job, sings on the church choir, has an amazing dance ministry (Alabaster), and is a true worshiper in every sense of the word. She is also a wonderful wife and mother, but only through faith, prayer and one heaven and hell of a war! I will not give my wife's testimony for her; she tells better stories than I do and her personal experience makes her stories credible and believable to those that God leads her way.

As I pen this as my introduction to the second book in the 'Born on the Battlefield' series on spiritual warfare, understand that life is not always as dramatic as what is portrayed in "The Exorcist" or in movies neither is it as flashy as today's televangelist 'witchdoctors' make it appear.

The enemy is subtle, and his tactics are equally as subtle. What we have allowed in the modern world of Christendom, is to allow the gospel to become *watered down* and the children of God to be taken advantage of by motivational speakers calling themselves pastors and by people preaching *another* gospel. The fundamentals and simplicity of our gospel are being diluted as we enter an age that should be the apex of our ability to communicate the gospel to the entire world.

I have seen firsthand the power of God in action. I have stood in a courtroom facing the possibility of five years in prison and watched as God moved on my behalf, in the presence of thirty or better witnesses as God held the judges tongue and prevented him from pronouncing a sentence that would most assuredly have destroyed my family and the work of God in us. There were more than a few persons that got saved on *that* day as the bailiff shook my hand and I left the courthouse a free man.

I have seen the love of God move the hardest of criminals to tears; one man (calling himself 'Country') in particular who was a confessed arms dealer and murderer, a member of the Chicago gang called the "Disciples". The weight of sin and the death of his mother brought him to my door in tears one mild and brightly lit summer day, where he accepted Christ sobbing on his knees in the doorway of my townhouse. I have had spiritual experiences that would surely cause many of you Dear Readers to doubt my words, but nevertheless, I place God in no box!

I have seen more delicate demonstrations of the power of God as His power has risen up in people to minister and speak the gospel in power, to their own astonishment, later realizing that it was not *them*, but rather the Holy Spirit speaking through them. I have seen the words of the gospel touch people's core, as that pierces the darkness of their heart and illuminates their spirit and minds. I am a witness to true healing, true deliverance, true peace and also to the truth of that gospel at work in the lives of those who *truly* believe.

Among all these things that I have mentioned and made remark of, I have only seen true believers fight and be able to stand on the Battlefield.

There is not one of God's children who did not face controversy in scripture. Male or female; young or old, they all fought their own personal wars. Some fought against themselves and their character flaws; some fought against their environment and the cultures around them; and some fought the powers of Satan directly, but they ALL FOUGHT.

A Christian without a war story is either a babe in Christ or a watered down version of what their full potential ought to be. As harsh as it sounds, if you're still a benefit to the enemy, then he has no reason to war against you. For me to outline the details of my personal war(s), would take another book entirely; one which I have not yet been given permission to write. Suffice it to say that the pages that follow are a portion of what I have learned, experienced, and would like to share with you.

Without prolonging the following study, let's deal with this 'Reality'.

War!

The Dimensional Theory of Realms

This chapter will prayerfully give us a slightly different take on how to look at where we should begin in our thought process, where we are in relationship to what is around us, and where we could and should be aspiring to progress forward too.

Forgive me Dear Reader if you begin to feel at some point that I have taken you back to school, but it is really all about what God says; so don't kill the messenger!

> *"Study to shew thyself approved unto God, a workman that needeth not to be ashamed, rightly dividing the word of truth."*

2 Timothy 2:15

War \wo(ë)r\ **(a)** A state of usually open and declared armed hostile conflict between two or more opposing companies, states, kingdoms, or nations **(b)** A struggle or competition between two opposing forces; or for a particular end.

The term 'war' has come to mean many things, but rarely does it carry the weight, impact, or magnitude of what it formerly represented. In today's society, and by today's standards, the word *war* has come to denote discomfort, dissatisfaction, disease (dis-ease), and anything else that dares to raise its ugly head against the safety and security of our comfort zones. We have a war on drugs, a war on teenage pregnancy, a war on alcohol, a war on certain diseases; we even have a war on *war*. We have wars between corporations and between television networks; wars on being overweight, wars on being underweight, wars on stress, and wars on anxiety. There is a war on a person's right to choose and concerning whether that choice is ours. For every cause, there seems to be a counter cause that is ready to go to war against it. Right here should be the marker in the annals of modern thought; we have excluded God from our society and with no marker for 'absolute' truth, there seems to be a societal problem in the overall determination between right and wrong. Is it wrong to engage in a sexual relationship with the same sex? Is it wrong to abort a child from the womb? Is it wrong to think that nothing is taboo as long as we do not harm our fellow man?

Less than fifty years ago, the answers to these questions would have been obvious and 'absolute' to the common man and there would have been a majority answer for each one of those questions across the board. Today's society has morally eroded to the place where these once commonly agreed upon truisms have been watered down to the point of confusion concerning their answers. The behind the scenes war is one between God's truth and the enemy's truth. If you doubt this then remember that God is not the author of confusion and so many people are truly confused today and fight a war about being able to simply make a decision – about anything!

By definition the word itself means: *struggle between two opposing entities that are at odds with one another.* "So, what war is Joe Public fighting from day to day? Is it the rat race of life? Is it man vs. himself?" These things may be relevant issues, yet they actually do not scratch the surface to what lies at the heart of the real battle. The reality is this – Joe Public is born into sin; must adhere to the fact that the enemy is bigger; stronger, more powerful; more cunning; has more forces and Joe Public who must wage spiritual warfare for his very own *soul and spirit*, from the day of his conception! But, God... Now I wish to be very specific when I choose certain words and terminologies. Since I am not pro-choice, when I use the term conception, I mean the moment that sperm fertilizes egg. When that miracle occurs, the second that it occurs, the enemy has already openly declared war. If you stand in opposition to this thought then ask yourself, "Why it is that so many abortions (1.16 million yearly in the United States) occur? Why are millions of potential lives, each year in America, prevented from reaching maturity? Why are there such debates over what the woman's rights are concerning this issue when the answer or power does not lie in the legal system, but rather in moral consideration?" Simply put, the enemy knows that he has prevented 1.16 million lives from being able to accept salvation; 1.16 million people who could potentially spread the gospel of Jesus Christ; 1.16 million people that will fulfill their God created purpose and 1.16 million people that could change the world.

Further, the problem is that while the enemy has declared war on every man and every woman, very few men and women actually understand that they are engaged in this war. It is ironic that the war between America and Iraq mirrors this point. The Muslims worldwide who openly oppose the American way of life have declared Jihad (Holy War) on the United States. Why do we continue...in fact our government insists that we are fighting against terrorists? No, we are not! The Muslims have told us what they are doing from the beginning and what they believe. Acknowledging this fact, for us, means that we will have too, number one, take a spiritual stand and number two, risk being politically incorrect. A very simple observation may be that more and more once professed Christians are converting to Islam and after 911; it has now become trendy for men to wear beards as do the Muslims, without me having to acknowledge trends.

Almost all of us fight the wrong battle. We fight a perceived battle that is more diversionary than realistic. We are consistently occupied and consumed by *"...the cares of this world." (Matthew 13:22/ Mark 4:19/ Luke 8:14 & 21:34)* This entrenches us ever deeper into the muck and mire outside of the real battle. Therefore, our focus is distorted when it should be concentrated and we never actually or fully see clearly our true enemy or his plans. The incredible thing about this war is that it is raging in three separate realms and that it transcends space and time. It is being fought in the ***physical realm***, the realm in which we live. It is being fought in the each one of our minds or the ***mental realm*** where our emotions and way of thinking are involved. And it is also being fought in the ***spiritual realm*** where God and Satan; angels and demons exist.

At times the war is impacted by events that happen within the ideals of time and space and at others it is not. The physical effects of warfare can be measured by space and time, while the effects of spiritual warfare can only be measured in terms of victory or defeat.

The effects of mental warfare can be measured, in certain instances, by both. If I have a physical victory over something, the effects are calculable; measurable. I could be healed from an affliction derived from the enemy or from sin and be healed in my sinful flesh. There is then a measurable triumph in that I have regained my health and strength. If I achieve a spiritual victory, in that I defeat a problem in something that is standing between me and God, then I have won yet the physical aspect can only be measured internally in my spiritual relationship with my creator. A win in the mental realm can cause me both physical and spiritual elation and/or change in that I am measurably elated over conquering an issue that has been stressful and so I smile and am more apt to show signs of open relief in my posture, conversation, body language, and so forth. At the same time, there is no mental obstruction to hinder my prayer life, my praise life, or any other aspect of my internal spiritual communication; however the enemy will attempt to trick us into believing that he has that kind of power. He does not.

There are principles that govern each realm both together and apart from one another. Certain principles transcend the barriers between realms while others remain confined. What may work in the realm of the mind may not work in the realm of the spirit or in the physical realm. Sometimes, it is necessary in one realm to achieve victory in the others. Ideally, in terms of Christian growth and maturity, we seek to be well-rounded in scripture and to understand the governing principles of each. A good way to begin learning how to integrate the three together would be to look for God's promises and other things that He says He will do both for us now and in the future and look for the little words 'if' and 'as'. This usually means that we have an obligation or an expectation or need have to do something; to believe something in order to receive a promise or benefit. This usually entails mental and spiritual preparation before gaining a spiritual reward, triumph, insight, blessing or promise. This by no means says that we move forward by works, but there are good works and bad works. By doing this we can begin to exercise the things that will prosper us in warfare and know about the things that will *not*. They are different for each person and we should allow God to train each of us as soldiers, as He wills, in order to get the best results. Remember, that the 'Salvation Army' is not just a thrift store.

I had a recent opportunity to listen to a speaker in Annapolis, Maryland at a woman's conference. The subject matter touched briefly on spiritual warfare, but the term that she used stuck out in my mind. She used the phrase "4th dimension". Not an unknown term as far as science fiction or quantum reality is concerned. She used the phrase to describe the realm of the spirit and *that* is what intrigued me. To explain dimension is a matter of high school science and arithmetic, but we must first have knowledge of the preceding three dimensions in order to propose an accurate theory of the fourth. Once we form an idea about the fourth dimension we may gain insight into the spirit realm and better understand of how to engage in spiritual warfare or the fourth realm.

ZERO DIMENSION:

Zero dimension is defined by a point in space and/or time. It cannot be depicted accurately because in order to do so; in order for our three dimensional minds to perceive it, we must give it dimension. We must accept it as a concept. In 'science', points are used to plot graphs, make measurements, and denote various changes in certain systems and so forth. In 'time', points are used to make note of events remarkable of change or remembrance. For spiritual warfare and for the purposes of building our spiritual arsenal we will call zero dimension our 'point of reference' or *faith*. This is our anchor, our constant; it is immovable, immutable, absolute, permanent…!

Mankind consciously or unconsciously longs to find this anchor in life. Without it, he inevitably senses imminent chaos or will blind his senses to the impending, inevitable end of life without it – death (physical and spiritual). We must define this point in order to determine any other point or dimension. In the Christian life this point is our faith in God. Without this initial point; this immovable, unchanging, element in our existence, we cannot fully or rationally depend on ***any*** other thing. If our reference point is our job, our spouse, money, or success, then we should recognize that these things are *all* subject to change. They are not static and they are not eternal. If we have faith in ourselves, in our abilities, or even our own personal realities, then we should also recognize our *own* propensity to change. What we are establishing with 'zero dimension' is dependency, loyalty, authenticity; something we can trust. Without it, what can we ever hope for?

Science and mathematics lend themselves to establishing such characteristics through theories and equations, however, as mankind continues to learn and discover, we continually find that we are repeatedly no closer to absolutes of any kind. Science requires that we must first establish something that we understand to be *fact* and then begin to theorize and draw conclusions from those facts. This is only a way to build upon what we already know not a definitive conclusion to what we first surmised as fact.

Take the theory of the earth being flat for example. Man believed that the earth was flat and began exploration based on what he knew, at that time, to be factual. Building on that foundation, he began to venture out and found the opposite to be true – that the earth was in fact round. This did not prove or validate what he once believed as accurate. Mathematics requires that we form a point of reference before we proceed in the forming of equations. We may begin with numbers and use such basic arithmetic as addition, subtraction, multiplication and division; all found in scripture. However, what can be said for numbers and equations that were incalculable, even with technology as vastly different as it is today, say as opposed to 100 years ago? Search the internet for any number greater than 1trillion and compare the ideas. At certain junctures in mathematics, we begin to depart from what is supposedly known and we begin to hypothesize and theorize.

Unfortunately, as touching math and science, my perspective on the situation is not a particularly popular standpoint. The sad truth is that even Christian advocates in both science and math do not strictly adhere to keeping God completely within the equation. Creationists and numerologists handily straddle the fence when outlining their theories and neatly leave God out as an absolute. There has been no consistent or significant proof for any modern scientific theory. We have no scientific explanation for the creation of the universe; no defined idea for the age of the universe; no concrete evidence for how mankind was formed; no evidence of what happened to the dinosaurs; we don't know what's above us or beneath us; and no explanation that has been given makes any sense without the inclusion of a 'divine creator'. That fact in and of itself should force: scientists, geologists, mathematicians, archeologists, etcetera, to redefine their viewpoints on almost all of modern scientific theory. If we recognize God and 'divine creation' as a reference point and begin to formulate theories and opinions based on that as fact and belief, we may begin to achieve results that could possibly lead to incredible realizations. More simply put, we could simply ask God about what He has created and for what purpose. Imagine modern science seeking the answers to questions about healthcare, space exploration, technology, the human mind and other such things from the one who can ultimately answer all of these questions and more! What if mankind was intended to explore the vastness of God's universe beyond the confines of earth as a testimony to the greatness and glory of God? We were never meant to die, death is a result of man's sin nature, what if as an eternal being, we were intended to explore the wonders of the stars and the endless universe that God has created? Did God create this all for nothing?

Without God in our aspirations to become great on earth, we can really only achieve a semblance of greatness; an appearance of true intelligence. This is why we must first establish a 'point of reference'. Once we have this point, then we can begin to move in any direction we so choose and upon meeting resistance or failure we can return to that which we truly know as fact and begin again. We must confirm a defined point so that when all else in life fails; when all else proves to be unstable, we can remain secure in *this* one thing…*"For I am the Lord, I change not…"*

Malachi 3:6

11

We will call 'zero dimension' point A

POINT A.
[Faith in God]

THE 1ST DIMENSION:

The first dimension is defined as a *line* or *distance* between two points. We can depict this graphically as a physical line on paper to be representative of a starting and ending point; the ending point not necessarily being the final destination. Let us refer to the 1st dimension as our '*vision*'. This is where we are at a particular point in space and/or time with relation to where we wish to be or to where we are going. In truth, we should derive our 'vision' from our point of reference, so the first dimension should represent where *God* wants us to be. If our 'point of reference' (A) is representative of God, then the direction of our line (*distance from point A to our end point*) should be represented by yet another point in space or reality that we will call point B. While point B is our endpoint, we will remember that it is not our final destination, simply the distance between the two points. We will call point B 'God's divine will'. This is His purpose for our lives where the line or distance traveled between the two points is signified by the Word of God. The goal is to make our vision identical to God's will. Point A (God) is where we start with the goal being to arrive at point B (manifest vision) via the shortest distance possible; that being a straight line (Word of God).

If our reference point is something other than God, then point B can represent any number of variables. Should that be the case then B can represent God's permissive will, in which He allows but does not necessarily condone our present actions or present course... The worst case scenario is that B will represent an unknown position in our lives that has originated from a reference point that is not eternal. Let us suppose that our initial reference point (A) is money. Our destination (B) is determined, not by God's will, but rather upon present economic projections; the Dow/Jones Industrial Average, The NASDAQ, the S&P, and so on. If point A is our spouse, then we are subject to inevitable human failure at some level or another and our destination becomes dependent upon something that is tragically indeterminable. Our vision must originate with God as our point of reference and progress toward an established point that has been ordered for us by God. Only then can we be reasonably sure of point B before we have left point A. Why only reasonably sure? There are outside factors that may hinder or slow our progress while moving between points. Free will, sin nature, demonic forces, time, chance, and the character of each individual can impede our progress and delay or prolong our vision. These factors can prevent our course from being straight or unhindered and often do. It may be that it is not the right time for our vision (Ecclesiastes 9:11). It may be that the enemy is hindering our vision as in Daniel's case (Daniel 10:12-13) or it may be that we are hindering our own vision as in Sampson's (Judges 14:1-3, 16:1&4). God may allow your vision to be prolonged if it is in His best interest; for our own or if prolonging it allows someone else to receive salvation (Acts 8:26-39). Whether or not we are in a close enough relationship to God to comprehend that vision will ultimately determine the journey that occurs between points A and B. God says about the journey that, *"Where there is no vision the people perish..."*

Proverbs 29:18

GOD OR WHERE WE BEGIN/ A._____. B/ WHERE GOD WANTS US TO BE

THE 2ᴺᴰ DIMENSION:

The second dimension is a plane that consists of two complimentary or opposing sides, a front and a back. Let us refer to this dimension as '*thought*' or the relationship between our minds and our spirits that are eternal. In life, our flesh and our spirit oppose each other for dominance while our minds remain the source of fuel that each one feeds off of for strength. The mind can be trained to feed depending on a great many factors. Within this is the key for dominance of both the spirit and the flesh.

Before we are saved, our spirits acquiesce to the carnal desires of the flesh, while our sin nature drives us to crave earthly aspirations such as sex, money, power, fame, self gratification, status and much more. These aspirations give our flesh temporary pleasure and our minds momentary peace, but this is not lasting peace; this is not lasting joy. When we receive salvation, we have a new spirit placed within us and we receive the gift of the Holy Spirit of God neither of which can be satisfied by the desires of the flesh or the carnality of this world. Our new spirit man craves the things of the spirit and the will of God. The Holy Spirit becomes; renews our conscience and directs us away from carnality and toward the things of the spirit. Since the flesh is still alive, it will wage war against the spirit and the Holy Spirit of God (Romans 7:1). This is a battle that the Christian will fight for the duration of their earthly existence *and* a battle in which the enemy will seek to take advantage. God however, renews our spirit, yet we must renew our own minds.

When preachers today preach that you must do <u>more</u> to receive the Holy Spirit, this is a new gospel; another gospel; the preaching of works. Galatians 1:6 says **"...I marvel that ye are so soon removed from him that called you into the <u>grace</u> of Christ unto another gospel."**

Research how many times and how many people were filled with the Holy Ghost before HE was officially given to those who already believed before the advent of Christ and even before the Spirit of God was given in the book of Acts. [Sampson, David, the prophets, Zacharias, John (from the womb) and the disciples were all filled with the Holy Spirit before HE was officially given to all in the book of Acts. Old Testament and New Testament; hence two witnesses.] The Holy Ghost was given as the Comforter to sanctify/set aside those that believe, not for man to make sport or profit from those ignorant of the Word of God.

The Word tells us that we receive the gift of the Spirit when we 'believe' and that Gods power and that alone is what keeps us. Never let man misuse scripture or twist scripture where they ask, "Have you received the gift of the Holy Ghost?" The unpardonable sin is to not believe that God sent his Son!

Romans 12:2 says, *"…be not conformed to this world, but be ye transformed by the renewing of your mind, that ye may prove what is that good and acceptable and perfect will of God"*

Paul outlines this fight in Romans chapter 7 and 8. The first step is to realize and recognize immediately what is happening. This is how young Christians are overcome early in their walk with Christ. This is a matter of recognizing the battlefield of even that you are on one. The enemy and the flesh begin to war with young saints the moment after they accept Christ as their Lord and personal Savior. Our minds must be constantly and consistently renewed throughout the course of our Christian walk so that our relationship with God is maintained and our thinking becomes agreeable with our new spirit. Whereas, when we were in the world we nourished our carnality. When we become new creations in Christ Jesus we must nourish our spirituality. Why? Romans 8:6 and 7 states, *"For to be carnally minded is death; but to be spiritually minded is life and peace. Because the carnal mind is enmity against God: for it is not subject to the law of God, neither can be."* When our thoughts are lined up with the will of God, then our lives can be led by the Holy Spirit who ministers to and guides us. This is an essential part of living a balanced life.

In geometry, we can represent a two dimensional object with a square; four equal or balanced sides. The front face of the square will represent the mind and the back face shall represent our spirit man. We already have point A and point B, but the next dimension does not incorporate only a point C as one would imagine, but a point D as well. To add only point C would merely add another point of destination, but rather we must add another aspect to what we have previously incorporated. We are also confined to the same plane meaning that while we have integrated another aspect we are still only moving in a direction that is only parallel or perpendicular to our reference point.

By representing the mind/spirit relationship as a geometrical square we can imagine two sides of an object that cannot be separated. This is the scariest part of not being saved; the fact that our minds and spirits will be alive in hell if we do not achieve and maintain our salvation. While point A remains static; points B, C, and D, and the line between them, can represent any characteristic of either mind or spirit that helps too balance and connect them all. Should these points represent fasting, reading the Word and meditation, the *mind* is renewed. When these points represent prayer, praise, and worship the spirit is fed and matures. The mind and spirit can coexist harmoniously if we, *"...cast down imaginations and every high thing that exalteth itself against the knowledge of God, and bring into captivity every thought to the obedience of Christ..."*

Romans 10:5

THE 3ᴿᴰ DIMENSION:

The third dimension is the dimension in which we exist and can be represented by moving off of or away from the two dimensional plane by adding, not another point, but rather another plane. In the second dimension we used lines within a plane to denote length and width. This dimension consisted of a starting or reference point; the distance or journey from one point to another; and the relationship linking or connecting that journey and the subsequent harmony or disharmony depending on outside stimuli and the strength of our relationship with Christ. In geometry, three dimensions can be represented by length, width and the addition of *depth or breadth as the scripture says*. Let us then call this added point E and cause it to represent how well we move from our reference point, to our destination point(s) and also to the level of success that we achieve while on this particular plane.

The third dimension is actually the *physical* dimension; the dimension in which God created man to live in and where he exists. This is the tangible and visible and can be drawn as a six sided box or cube. This is also the dimension *to* which our five senses react and the realm, plane or dimension with which man is most familiar.

The third dimension is composed of a zero, first, and second dimensions and so, we being third dimensional entities, are comprised of the same. Physical man is made up of his principles, beliefs and or reference points in life; his vision of his life's goals and the balance or lack thereof between his mind and spirit. These things have a prominent effect on the physical man as a whole. What must be recognized is that our third dimensional environment has an impact on our physical man and these stimuli can ultimately influence the other elements of our total composition. Worldly stimuli such as where we live, what we do, and how we cope with our surroundings; spiritual warfare, time, chance and the way we think, all have a profound impact on our relationship with our creator. These third dimensional effects can be the basis for our losing sight of our reference point. Our vision can become skewed and the balance between our mind and spirit can become emaciated. Our goal should be one of becoming like Christ in that while He was provoked by these same stimuli, he did not allow them to blur the vision of His reference point.

I speak to Christ's humanity, in saying this, and not to His Godhead. The fact that He maintained His vision and direction, during His time here on earth, is a testament to His mortality because being God in the flesh *was* His reference point. Christ was tempted in every way by the world, His flesh, and the enemy and yet He never sinned. When the enemy comes against our lives with strongholds, temptations and various traps, how will we measure up? When the world places before us stumbling blocks, trials and different tests, will we ultimately stand and remain? These are questions that we must ask ourselves and finally be pleased with the answer. In aspiring to be like Christ we are told, ***"For whom He did foreknow, He also did predestinate to be conformed to the image of His son..."***

Romans 8:29

It is a wonderful thing to realize that while we are here on earth we shall be in a constant state of being conformed and molded into the image of Jesus Christ. Later, we shall be transformed into the image of our risen savior in heaven as He is, **"the firstborn of many brethren..."**

Romans 8:29

John Henry James 3rd

Even Jesus tells us that the world will hate us because it first hated Him, but we are to handle each situation we face in the third dimension as He did. The Holy Spirit is, after all, The Comforter, when we feel as if we cannot persevere. We cannot become overwhelmed or dismayed by such outside forces that we are caused to lose focus of God. This can cause us to become casualties of war and God wants us victorious, not only for ourselves, but for the benefit and end that others might be saved. We are in fact, already victorious, but exist in our third dimensional state as having achieved no great note worthiness with regard to our vision or the path we take to move between points. This is why point E in our Christian walk causes our three dimensional box to remain the same size when it was designed to expand, with regard to our reference point. As we gain a greater understanding, knowledge, and relationship with God, our vision can grow as well as the steps that we take along any guided path to achieve His vision for our lives. We then begin to experience a greater balance between our minds and spirits as we become confident in the security of our salvation and grow in His grace. We have greater visions and less friction in obtaining success (point E) as we reach a level of maturity at each point.

Science and math were never my strong points in school. However, I have learned to love them as a Christian. Not that I presume myself to be good at either, but I am however intrigued. I recognize a very simple fact about each one and that being that while scientists and mathematicians base everything both seen and unseen on these two ideas, they have no reference point with which they can establish true fact. Ideas about space, gravity, energy, number sequences, mathematical theorems, quantum physics, chemistry, and anatomy, all beg the presupposition of a creator and require inevitably His final resolution to give their theories credence. When the bible says that, *"...there is no new thing under the sun..."* (Ecclesiastes 1:9), I take that literally. All of the thoughts and ideas that scientists have had in the past have already been regarded. The technology may be advancing, but the reference points for these technological advances stem from antiquity and a creator.

18

I have had a considerable amount of fun in studying this material and relating it to spiritual things. It seems very natural that we use the same terms in science that we do to describe our lives such as points and levels (planes) the same way that the Word uses mathematical terms such as addition, subtraction, multiplication and division. It seems ironic as well that mankind does everything in his power to erase the truth of his creator even His existence while living within HIS creation. An old saying goes. "Everyone wants to go to heaven; no wants to die." God tells us about heaven and hell and how to gain the first and avoid the last, but man, in his arrogance, seeks to bypass his creator and do things his own way. This will bring me to the fourth dimension; the realm of the spirit.

THE 4TH DIMENSION

The fourth dimension is the realm of the *spirit*. Referenced in the Word by the words 'north' or 'height'. Admittedly, the research of this particular portion of our study has taken me into places that I had not intended to go. In the physical realm; the idea of the fourth dimension is a mere concept and mathematicians have varying ideas on its laws and principles that allow us to, at the least, conceptualize that realm.

Man has tried to represent his idea of the fourth dimension by such ideologies as 'Alice in Wonderland', The book 'Flatland' and even 'Alice in Wonderland or 'A Christmas Carol'. These are all unassuming and viewed as a child's tale for the unassuming patron, while in the spiritual realm, however, God gives us truth and laws and principles of which we will look at later in our study. Even the representation of such ideas is difficult because it is a dimension both above and beyond our own dimension. So I must limit what I believe about the fourth dimension unless the information encompass another book entirely. Suffice it to say that I will take 'artistic liberty' with both the physical and the spiritual aspects of this part of the study if for no other reason than to awaken your thought processes and imaginative juices as it were.

Imagine, if you will, what we have previously outlined as the representation of the third dimension – a six sided cube. Now, as in the idea of doubling a square and forming connecting lines to achieve a cube, we will double our cube and connect the lines. In a cube, two squares share one line, whereas in a fourth dimensional cube (hypercube or tesseract), every three squares share a line. The only problem is that in three dimensions it is hard to depict this in a drawing. Some mathematicians draw two cubes partially connected, while others draw a cube within a cube, and others still, two cubes that are skewed diagonally from one another. This inevitably led me to wonder about the representation of other four dimensional objects and the theories surrounding them. What I have found, in my opinion, is further proof that man is hopelessly and eternally lost without God. All ideas and speculation on fourth dimensionality lend themselves to eternity or the idea of endlessness – the *spiritual* realm. The fourth dimensional cube incorporates the idea of a cube that is in many places at once by the shear complexity of the design. The idea of the fourth dimensional triangle tends toward an infinite number of spaces and an infinite number of objects. The concept of a fourth dimensional sphere is that of a sphere that expands infinitely and so on with the other ideas about the fourth dimension.

The fourth dimension, in relation to our study, is that point which we shall call point X in which we cross over from finite to infinite. It includes our reference point, point A (God), our journey or vision, point B, our mind and spirit, points C & D, our growth and success in the temporal realm, point E and finally our ending place in the eternal and forever. Whether the culmination of each successive point causes us to spend eternity in heaven or hell, each one of us *will* arrive at point X.

What is it about the spiritual realm or fourth dimension that is so puzzling and exciting to the human mind? For starters, it is uncharted territory and the unknown and undiscovered always intrigues human curiosity. Unfortunately, the only way to glimpse the fourth dimension is by crossing through the veil of death and afterward there can be no report of ones findings; no compilation of that research. Or is that true? The spiritual realm is there; the Word of God tells us this. The bible, however, leads the way and has concrete findings and assurances concerning the subject. Other writings are mere conjecture and draw much of their speculation from the Holy Scriptures. Any doctrine or religion that claims dogmatic truth and complete spiritual assurance pre-Christianity post Christianity or otherwise will never predate the Adamic Dispensation. An example would be The Code of Hammurabi. Written in 1760 BC, it predates Christianity, but we must simply remember that Christianity is a fulfillment or realization of Judaism which began with Abraham approximately 2500-3000 BC and the word Christian was merely a term of identification for the non-believers of Antioch. Matthew and Luke both place Abraham in the direct lineage of Adam as a precursor to the pure bloodline of Christ and no human law can predate Adam.

"And when he had found him, he brought him unto Antioch. And it came to pass, that a whole year they assembled themselves with the church, and taught much people. And the disciples were called Christians first in Antioch."

Acts 11:26

All we can really know about the realm of the spirit comes directly from the Word of God and the resurrection account of Jesus Christ and those five hundred plus persons in the New Testament who bare witness to His return from beyond the veil of death and saw His ascension. So what is the truth and what is fiction? I have a few outside examples if you will indulge me Dear Reader?

The first being a movie that I saw where two actors were discussing the possibility of fourth dimensional beings. They themselves are standing on a busy city street and one man gives this example to the other.

"There could be an accident several blocks away from where we are presently standing and we would never know a thing about it. We could not hear the screech of tires, the impact of the cars or the screams of those involved in the collision. A window washer atop one of these nearby buildings may however, be able to see us, the accident, and a great many other things from his vantage point. The point being is that his perspective is different than ours. To us, he

would then appear to be 'all knowing' because his vantage point has allowed him to gather more information than we ourselves could from our own perspective which is presently limited."

I thought this beautifully appropriate for inclusion in a book on spiritual warfare. This is very indicative of how the enemy deceives us. He operates in a realm that is outside of our vantage point and so he takes advantage of what? Of information. What he can see, what he knows, what he has access too as a consequence of being on a *higher* plane of existence enables him to plague humanity, seemingly to no end. This short conversation in a movie tells us that we have at least certain considerations about how the fourth dimension operates. [Fiction/Non-Fiction]

My next revelation about the fourth dimension came from the book called 'Flatland'. This is an imaginary tale of fictitious characters who are two dimensional that have no concept of the third dimension. These persons have normal everyday lives, as we do, and yet there world is completely void of the dimension of height. The directions *up* and *down* are completely foreign to the inhabitants of 'Flatland'. They move about from east to west and from north to south. They move both forwards and backwards and have even worked out certain difficulties that even we can imagine and with which we can identify. They have restricted vision because their perspective is two dimensional and anything greater is a three dimensional concept. The story revolves around the main characters Mr. A. Square (resident of the 2nd dimension) who is visited one day by Mr. A. Sphere (a resident of the 3rd dimension). Mr. A. Sphere attempts to explain the concept of height to Mr. A. Square which proves to be an effort in futility. From A. Mr. Sphere's perspective, he can see all of 'Flatland' at once. He cannot only see its inhabitants and their day to day activities, but he can see their very internal organs. Remember, he is on a plane that they cannot themselves see or even know about so A. Mr. Sphere takes Mr. A. Square out of 'Flatland' to show him the unknown dimension of height. This works only in part and does not fully convince Mr. A. Square who has the arduous task of trying to explain his journey to the flat world around him upon his return.

Although this book was written by a Christian mathematician (Edwin A. Abbott – whose name happens to have two A's in it or A^2 the mathematical way of saying "A Square") and is salted with Christian ideology all the way through, I found a very simple and very profound mistake after reading it. While it is undeniably the author attempts to explain his spiritual beliefs while incorporating his mathematical theories, he has neglected to grasp the fact that in order for Mr. A. Square to be carried into the 3rd dimension, he would have had to be *transformed* (physically) in some way in order for him to be able to see what Mr. A. Sphere was seeing. All things being equal, the idea of perspective again comes into play. Mr. A. Sphere, was of a different realm and this afforded him a different viewpoint/perspective of a dimension that was lower than his own. 'Flatlanders' could only comprehend the directions that I mentioned previously, while not being able to fathom the direction of *height*. The rational conclusion is that when we consider the spirit realm (4th dimension) we must ask ourselves whether or not a similarity can be drawn by placing ourselves in the position of Mr. A. Square and spiritual beings on the same level as Mr. A. Sphere? It is only from a perspective or *direction* that we cannot yet comprehend that the fourth dimension exists.

Paul has understood the limitations of our perspective by writing, ***"For now we see through a glass darkly; but then face to face: now I know in part; then shall I know even as also I am known."***

1 Corinthians 13:12

I believe that this is the concept that Edwin Abbott was trying to convey through mathematics. This book is a conceptualization of the spirit world that alludes to the Christian difficulty of trying to explain what should be accepted by faith to a world that cannot understand the concept of the spiritual. We can acknowledge the spiritual as invisible and intangible, but invisible and intangible only to us three dimensional beings and only before the advent of Christ. We now have direct access to and power to move in and out of this realm through Jesus Christ.

Ephesians 2:14 says that, *"For he is our peace (completeness) who hath made both one, and hath broken down the <u>middle wall of partition</u> between us…"* That middle wall of partition is what prevents us from bridging the gap between dimensions. The bible tells us that we now have access to God in the fourth dimension through the blood of Jesus Christ.

One of Satan's ultimate deceptions is to keep us ignorant of our own potential and power. It is the dominion that was promised to Adam in Genesis 1:28; stolen by Satan in Genesis 3:6; and regained and given back to believers by Christ in 1 Corinthians 15:22, 42-57. Let us remember that Eve was in Adam and was not created until Genesis 2:22. Adam changed the woman's name to Eve in Genesis 3:20 after she had eaten of the tree of the knowledge of good and evil. Adam named her as he did everything else because they were both called Adam by God. By defeating death, Christ nullified the effects of sin on all that will believe on His name. Remember, mankind was given complete dominion and rule of the third dimension. Satan needed to trick Adam out of his authority in much the same way that Jacob deceived Esau. Adam was to keep and manage the Garden of Eden with his helpmeet (wife) Eve. This was power in the first, second, and third dimensions Adam had an established reference point; a clear harmonious vision and complete access to the fourth dimension whereby he communicated and fellow-shipped directly with his creator. His dominion over the third dimension was stolen by blocking his, or man in generals, access to the fourth dimension through sin. Since sin separates us from God, and God dwells in the fourth dimension, our link was severed and we lost: our reference point, our vision, the ability to have an unimpaired journey, the balance and harmony between our minds and our spirits, which equates to a lesser success as we move through life and finally, our dominion over the third dimension.

I have previously stated that we will use zero dimension to represent our faith in God, but by no means do I demean God to dimensionality. I use it only to illustrate the point that we are fearfully and wonderfully made as human beings. To accentuate the fact that we are multifaceted in the way that God has made us and that, as in math and science, there are several dimensions to our composition. We should never limit ourselves to being the product of simply one of those aspects. Complete reliance on one aspect can mean the exclusion of another when it clearly takes a synchronization of all to achieve what God has intended for us.

We cannot become entangled in our thinking, our goals, our struggles, our balance, our trials and temptations, or even our third dimensional limitations. Jesus *broke* third dimensional laws in mans dimension; not as God, but as showing man what was possible through faith in God – the reference point. He turned water into wine (transmutation); He fed five thousand people on one occasion and four thousand on another (manifestation); He walked on water (anti-gravitation); He walked through walls (permeation); He regenerated body parts (regeneration) and much more! We have the same power to do these things and much more. Jesus Himself said so. Through our reference point we have the power to access the fourth dimension in order to make the *invisible* visible in the third. Through faith we regain our dominion. Why is this necessary to manifestation in the third dimension? ***"Faith is the substance of things hoped for the <u>evidence</u> of things not seen."***

Hebrews 11:1

Zero dimension and the fourth dimension both have to do directly with God. We start with zero dimension as faith in God to establish that anchor point from which we shall not drift. By the time we understand our access to the fourth dimension through Jesus Christ and begin to utilize that access, we are wielding spiritual power. This is why God is the Alpha and the Omega; the beginning and the end.

Our objective is to achieve a well rounded plan of attack concerning our spiritual battle here on earth. Once we understand the elements that we are composed of we can alternate between them and even manufacture formulas that will help us too achieve victory. Let's try to understand the book of Hebrews in relation to the creation and journey of man.

God obviously uses faith; *beyond our understanding*; but faith nonetheless. If He did not, then he would not have placed such an emphasis on it as a prerequisite to our perfection and ultimate transformation.

> **For when God made promise to Abraham, because he could swear by no greater, he sware by himself,**

Hebrews 6:13

So if we take the idea, conveyed in our reference point, we understand that God Himself is immutable; unchanging. The first and second dimensions are a culmination of God (The Father), Jesus (The Word), and The Holy Spirit(The Comforter) who act in unison and harmony and have established a vision. The power to make the invisible visible lies in the harmony of all of these mechanics working together and the result is ultimately manifestation. In every dimension seen or unseen but for this study, the third dimension in particular, the focus is on those things that our senses perceive. (Man, plants, animals, elements, planets, suns, moons, stars, etc...).

Faith in God + Spiritual Power (Vision + Thought) = Manifestation/ Realization
0D+4D (1D + 2D) = 3D

D = Dimension

This is my simple yet awkward attempt at mathematics! In math, one always does what is in the parenthesis first. So by adding His thoughts and vision together a harmony is achieved between The Mind, Word, and Spirit of God. We then multiply the three remaining portions of the equation together. God is His *own* reference point and He is omnipotent. The result is as stated and seen all around us every day. Manifestation of God's vision. (Forgive me mathematicians)

Think about what the bible says concerning our faith growing (Romans 1:17). Think of what Jesus says about us doing more than what He did (John 14:12). Think about what scriptures tell us about establishing a vision and renewing our minds (Proverbs 29:18 & Romans 12:2). This is all a reiteration of the formula and of how the battle is won.

Let us never forget that God created the physical laws and principles that govern the third dimension in which we live. He is the perfect scientist and mathematician. In order to understand or at least value what God has done we must begin to dwell on heavenly things. Operating in the power of the spirit realm [4D], which is a higher or more perfect dimension than the third dimension, God speaks (Word of God) into absolute nothingness. The mind of God (God the Father) and the spirit of God (Holy Spirit) are also in perfect harmony [2D] and move from point A to point B to achieve the vision [1D] with their tri-unity and omnipotence as the only possible reference point [0D]. Where there was once nothing, there is now another realm/ dimension; a physical dimension [3D]. I have spelled out a simple personal theory, but imagine this happening at the speed of thought. This is the shear power and ability of faith in action. It takes no movement only thought. The people of the Hebrews chapter eleven are not credited with planning, but rather with acting according to what they believed.

As Christians, we have only begun to scratch the surface of tactical spiritual warfare. The concepts of dimensionality, mathematics, time, and space may not be intriguing to many of my readers, but these are factors in our human equation that we must all operate within. Satan has a very good grasp on the mechanics of each one of these sciences and our continued ignorance of our own environment is what allows him to keep his advantage in this war.

Here is an example. *Mankind has studied time travel, quantum physics, astrology, astronomy, the chaos theory, the decay theory or second law of thermodynamics, and anything else you would care to name in relation to time. A minute few have focused their efforts on God's time table n relation to humankind. The ones that do focus specifically on end time events. Yet, we must factor in Gods words concerning them in Daniel and Revelation. Satan, however, has focused on the: seconds, minutes, hours, days, months, and years that go into making up the human life. He has focused so intricately on distraction and misdirection so that we miss opportunities, pass by chances, and become entangled in activities that keep us from our purpose. The bible tells us that,* **"...of that day and that hour knoweth no man, no, not the angels which are in heaven, neither the son, but the Father."**

Mark 13:32

Satan does not know it either, but what he does know is that his time is close. So he has taken time to study and learn what man does with the time that he is given. He also knows what things added or subtracted from a persons life can give them difficulty in moving from point A to point B or any point.

Can you see Dear Reader where the focus lies? Does the fact that we do not know ourselves and how we exist in our own environment say anything about how we have presently been fighting our battles? God's word to us is so rich and so deep that the answers to questions that haven't been thought of lie within them. The Bible is knowledge *to* us and for *us*. God is a good Father and will never deny us wisdom (James 1:5), especially concerning His word. In later chapters, we will see how the enemy has trained his earthly army. We will see that Satan has given his minions knowledge about human character and behavior. Yes, they have had thousands of years to perfect their reconnaissance, but would not an omnipotent, omnipresent, omniscient God provide *His* children with at least the means to do battle against such an enemy?

When we learn to use the instruments that God has given us, to speak in faith and actually expect God to honor our words then what can stop us? Scripture tells us in first Samuel 3:19, that God did not let words of Samuel the prophet fall to the ground. This means that every word that he spoke was honored by God.

I believe that Satan tried to use the principle of faith to overthrow God and take over heaven. He (Satan) has spiritual power. He was second in power only to the Godhead and with that power sought to usurp his creator. The phrase, "*I will...,*" denotes faith and belief in a personal vision. If we look at Isaiah 14:12-14 we hear Satan utter the five fatal "*I wills*".

- *I will ascend into...*
- *I will exalt...*
- *I will sit also...*
- *I will ascend above...*
- *I will be like...*

What do we then have? We have power in the fourth dimension. We have vision and direction in the first dimension. We have harmony between the aspects of the self; mind and spirit in the second dimension. What we do *not* have is a reference point (zero dimension) and thereby no manifestation or level of success (third dimension). Here are a few reasons why Satan's plan could never have worked.

- Faith or no faith, the will of God is paramount to the manifestation of anything within creation and this compels and includes everything. The will of the **creation**, being in line with the will of the **Creator**, is a prerequisite to any manner of manifestation in any realm.
- Satan's knowledge of fourth dimensional law was corrupted by reason of his brightness (Ezekiel 28:17). Easier said, he had delusions of grandeur that caused him to neglect reality. He became so caught up in his own beauty that he disregarded the fact that in order to make what is not reality manifest he must speak the word of God. Speaking the word of God brings us into harmony with God's perfect will which is always complimentary to God and can never be the reverse.
- The vision of the created thing can never go beyond the vision of the Creator. Science can build upon science for we have a basis from which to build. The design of the space shuttle is based on the law of gravity. There, however, can be no expansion in that regard, concerning God, the creator of the laws that govern every dimension, who has neither beginning or ending. Satan could never have achieved his vision because it took him outside of his created purpose.

There is unity in the fourth dimension and cooperation between the Godhead. They act in harmony and as one. God's thoughts, words, and deeds are all beautifully synchronized and balanced within the trinity. Likewise, God insists that there be unity and balance with those that are in His will and act according to His purpose. In other words, there is a protocol whether you are a soldier or a general. Satan tried to break this protocol in much the same manner as men try to defy the physical laws of the third dimension.

I believe that God has given us the bible so that we would not only know His will and love, but to understand what we are up against. I believe that the bible is a book of WAR! I believe that it is overflowing from cover to cover with information on how to wage war and do battle victoriously. I believe that Adam was trained in spiritual warfare, but never having a paradigm to follow or ever having engaged in it, he lost his first battle. Here's a question, "Do you think Adam knew of Satan's existence and fall from grace?" Of course he did. It is as simple as God has created man for a purpose and Satan is attempting to stop that plan. This is the bottom line of any war as I have stated in the beginning. Two opposing sides of thought and purpose. We have in scripture, example after example of innumerable methods of waging war against every form of enemy attack. Every book of the bible is the story of mankind's triumph over the enemy no matter what face the enemy wears; no matter what battlefield he draws us onto to fight. It has all been given as instruction on how to conquer any situation that arises. In fact, Numbers 21:14 calls the bible *"...the Book of the Wars of the Lord..."*

The Spirit of God "...divides to every man severally as He will..." (1 Corinthians 12:11) so that everyone receives as God's Holy Spirit wills it from His word. Some people have been given ministries of healing, ministries of faith, ministries of prosperity, but as for me, I have been given spiritual warfare. I have no particular love for fighting and actually am termed a non-confrontational personality. I will, however, wage war when it is necessary and I suppose that I got tired of getting attacked by Satan and never fighting back. Given the choice between peace of mind and prosperity I would surely choose peace of mind. I never intended to spend any of my time delving into the battle tactics of Satan, but God has given me this lot in life and I do it willingly. I see spiritual warfare as plainly as others see God's love or His grace and mercy, or His manifold blessings. The magnificent thing about spiritual warfare is that all we have to do is be obedient and stand. It is Jesus Christ who, in the final battle, will deliver the death blow to the enemy. In Paul's letter to the church at Ephesus, he writes in chapter six verse thirteen (Ephesians 6:13) ***"Wherefore take unto you the whole armor of God, that ye may be able to withstand in the evil day, and having done all, to stand..."***

Take the whole armor of God... in order to stand. This is a very famous spiritual warfare scripture and usually most teachings stop right here. Spiritual warfare can never be summed up by Ephesians chapter six alone. If America had ended this present war upon the capture of Saddam Hussein or any other dictator, then we would have missed the opportunity to thwart and defeat terrorist cells globally. Iraq would have simply been laid waste by the terrorist cells seeking to fill the vacancy left by that dictator and re-established a stronger base of operations from which to carry out Jihad (Holy War). The outcome of our spiritual war is pre-determined and has been written in the Book of Revelation to help us keep and maintain our focus and courage during the course of the war. Prior knowledge of victory should give us all the incentive we need to make it through the skirmishes of this life.

Perhaps all of the years that Paul spent in prison and all of the suffering that he endured at the hands of the enemy, forced him to view his Christian walk as a daily struggle against Satan. He understood that he was in a battle and he knew what was at stake. He charges his young apprentice Timothy to remember that:

- Christ came into the world to save sinners of which he (Paul) called himself the chief...
- ...Christ's trial would be the first to all who should thereafter believe in the finished work unto eternal life, and...
- ...that he, (Timothy), [by example of Paul and the prophecy on his life] *"...may be able to war a good warfare!"*

I too charge all who continue in the pages hereafter, to recognize that you are never ever alone. Even when you think that there is no one around; when you think that you are by yourself; realize that there is a whole other dimension; another world that is moving all around you. There are things in the fourth dimension that affect our third dimensional lives from day to day. This book is FYI (For Your Information) and is intended to increase your awareness and to make the reader more alert. Let's face it Dear Readers – *Knowing is half the battle!*

Notes And Reflections For The Reader:

Notes And Reflections For The Reader:

The Legality of It All

4th Dimensional Principles & Laws

"We live in a world of laws, rules, precedence, committees, sub-committees, policy, regulations, red tape, and legal systems run amok. This is not conjecture; this is pure and simple fact. Nowhere on earth can a man go where he is not subject to the laws of God, man, other people's way of thinking, someone's alternate perception of reality, time, chance, and/or nature. That particular wonderland place ('no law land') simply does not exist. I am writing this chapter to inform you Dear Reader, that when you depart this earth for the great beyond, there shall also be laws, rules, and regulations set into place. These have been established by the 'Word of God', since the foundation of the universe and are as unmoving and unshakeable as heaven itself. We see it in God's word to man, *"...but the heavens and the earth which are now, by the same 'word' are <u>kept</u> in store..."*

(2 Peter 3:7)

The object of this chapter is to set your feet on the path of conscious progressive thought. It is intended to be as informative as possible and to assist you in how you perceive the 'allowable' as opposed to the forbidden. Time and space are the constant confinement of temporal man; so, with due respect to each of them, every possible example of subject matter that I have gathered may not be covered in these pages. I can not motivate your thoughts on such matters as these; only stimulate you to ponder the reality that there is more! I intend to reveal that there exist 'other' constants in our present reality and in the next; besides death and taxes..."

People do not jump off of buildings because we respect the Laws of Gravity. We do not drive our vehicles at an excessive rate of speed because we respect the Laws of Motion. We may stay away from potentially harmful situations because we value the Laws of Action/ Reaction. These are physical laws that we have all come to know and heed. Few of us tempt these laws in the course of day to day life. We may not even know how they work, but we regard, revere, and even fear them as unwavering constants not to be taken lightly.

Physical laws establish a basis or foundation for daily thought and action. If we understand that these laws govern the universe in which we exist, then we can base our ideas, plans, inventions, and future actions on the ones that we recognize and/or understand. Without these laws, there would be chaos! Imagine if these laws were random? Imagine not knowing what day we would have gravity or what day we would not?

There is 'divine order' in each realm: the spiritual, the mental, and the physical. Zero dimension must remain fixed and immovable, while there must be a movement from point to point in the first dimension and so forth. We will learn how our compliance to or defiance of these laws benefits or incapacitates us. We will also learn how these laws can and do interact from realm to realm.

Breaking a law in one realm can create an imbalance in another and vice versa. In knowing what we know about physical laws in our own dimension, I ask only that you remain optimistic and open minded Dear Reader. It could mean the difference between living victoriously in every realm or remaining defeated, simply because we make repetitive mistakes.

{Since I have personally not yet read a book that specifically covers true spiritual principles, forgive me Dear Reader for any artistic license I have taken in giving certain ones a name.}

Law #1: "The Law of Divine Existence"

"I AM…" the phraseology and divine terminology of recognition and acknowledgment. It is how God describes himself; as simply *being or existing*. God is self-cognizant or self-existent. This is very difficult to imagine because we are given no grounds or basis for which to explore this point other than the fact that God *is!* What was the first thing that God said? Our physical minds find it an impossible concept to grasp; that anything that exists or that *we* can conceive of or believe in, has no beginning; goes beyond our ability to fathom. So there is no standard approach to what God's first expression may have been. Was it to create heaven, or the angels, or His throne? We may never know the first articulation of God if ever there was one, or it is even *reasonable* to imagine one, but what we do know is that it was indeed His Word; His *Logos* and His Word is none other than Jesus Christ. This is why Revelation 3:14 calls Christ, *"…the beginning of the creation of God."* Colossians 1:15 calls Christ, *"…the image of the invisible God, the first born of every creature."* Does this mean that Christ is one of God's creations? Religious cults have tried to reduce Jesus to a created being, but this is simply not the case. The fact is that God has always existed and that the Holy Spirit has always existed, and Jesus (The Word) has *always* existed. This is the Trinity; the divine, triune Godhead. I do not presume to explain God's existence, merely to reveal the power of the spoken word; a gift that God has given us and us alone as far as His 'material' creation.

Having an ability to do something and doing it for the first time does not constitute creation. This denotes dormant power. Since God's ability to speak was always within Him, Christ becomes the first born of creation as God utters His first articulation that we can even conceptualize and that latent power causes phenomenon to occur. Not to degrade God to ever having been a child, but to parallel the comparisons of ability and drive home the point, we shall use that scenario.

A newborn has what we may term potential. It has a mind, with which it can think, the potential to walk, the ability to learn, and the power to speak. When that child speaks its first words, it is at the same time that child's creation and an expression of that child and who it is at the same time. The potential for speech always existed within the child; as a part of the child. It lay dormant and simply had not been made manifest. Was this something that the child created? Perhaps a better way to rationalize it is that it is something that the child brought forth from within itself.

This is how *I* picture at least this aspect of God. I would not be surprised if that was the first task of the Logos or Word of God (Jesus); to declare His/God's divine existence – "I AM". This is only a finite beings rationalization and attempt to explain the unexplainable. We are a reflection of our creator and mirror him in all facets of our own existence (Genesis 1:27). We, however, have limited knowledge, but God's goal is that we reflect Him our creator. Therefore certain things are denied us for the time being, but all things will be made known to us according to Romans 1:17; 8:18, 29. Paul also says in his first letter to the church at Corinth that, *"For now we see through a glass darkly; but then face to face: now I know in part, but then shall I know (even as I am known)."*

1 Corinthians 13:12

This is an awesome revelation, for by this law we see the tri-unity of the Godhead as well as why Christ was the only member of the trinity who could have effected salvation. The spoken word is the only thing that can bridge the plane between every dimension. The word can define our reference point, articulate thought, illustrate vision, inspire success and convey power.

In addition to the divine expression of existence, it must be understood that God exists *by* Himself. When I say "by Himself" I mean that He is self-sustaining. There is nothing that God requires in order to exist. There is nothing that perpetuates His existence or continues His existence. He exists outside of *and* within everything that we know and all that we know nothing of, at the same time. The fact that He has been ascribed the titles of all knowing (omniscient), all-powerful (omnipotent), all-present (omnipresent) and immutable (absolute and unchanging) are the summation of God in our finite terminology. *"...*

God is a spirit..." (John 4:24), and resides on a plane of existence that is outside of our ability to comprehend in any other way than to acknowledge its reality. We must compare the differences between our dimension and a dimension greater than our own in order to understand what it might possibly be to be *all-in-all* and exist in the fourth dimension (spiritual realm). Without God, there is no imaginative way to envision complete and absolute nothingness. This is why He must be our reference point. The beginning of everything that we know and can know.

The 'Blank' Theory

The blank theory is an exercise that I used as a teaching tool for youth.

It states, "What is 'Blank' or complete nothing?" "What color is it?" When I got the initial responses they were black, white, invisible, etc...and I stated that 'white' exemplifies the absence of *all* color while black is a representation of, and is inclusive of the presence of *all* colors, while invisibility means that there must first be something to be able to see through, but God hasn't created color yet... How would you even see these imaginary colors because color, at its most basic definition requires light!" God has not said, at this point in 'blank', "Let there be Light!" "So what does blank or nothingness look like?" Again they tried to explain 'blank' from the standpoint of emptiness that would be an echoing space, darkness; themselves standing in the middle of nothingness/darkness, etc... Then I asked what would be carrying the sound waves, because air is necessary to carry sound, which then leads me to ask, "What would you be breathing?" because God has not yet created oxygen, nitrogen, carbon dioxide or the elements?." "That leads to the question, "What would you be standing on in the middle of this 'nothingness/darkness'?" "God has not yet created or separated the day from the night so how could there be 'darkness'?" "Is there anything there?" and if so, "What would it be made of?" "How would you move around in 'Blank'?"

I tell them to dig so that they can come up with the most rational conclusion of what 'blank' may be…I point out to them, "There is no sun, no moon, no stars, no galaxies; there is no whiteness or blackness, nothing has been created in 'blank' so there can be no sound; no air or elements or possibility of *them* even existing there!"

Then and only then do they begin to come to the realization that God is a LOT bigger; a LOT more powerful and a LOT greater than they had ever dared imagine or think!

This is what we must wrap our finite minds around in order to imagine an Omniscient, Omnipresent. Omnipotent God – if that is possible?

So ask yourself, "What is 'Blank'?"

Law #2: "The Law of Expression"

The power of the word, both spoken and unspoken is unimaginable. We may think that we have some idea, but I am positive that when its full revelation is given, it will be beyond our imagining. John 1:1,2 reads, *"In the beginning was the Word, and the Word was with God and the Word was God. The same was in the beginning with God."* This speaks of the second person in the trinity. The verse is describing the *living* 'Word', Jesus as we will see. John chapter 1: 3 and 4 states, *"All things were made by Him; and without Him was not any thing made that was made. In Him was life; and the life was the light of men."*

Since God spoke everything into existence, the Word of God must have been what He spoke or rather the 'Voice of God'. When God says anything, action takes place.

My children (all six of them) not only know the sound of my voice, but they know the *manner* in which I speak; that's distinction identifies me to them. Likewise when I speak, action takes place (or at least the delusion that I maintain. John 1:14 says, *"…and the Word was made flesh, and dwelt among us, and we beheld His glory, the*

glory as of the only begotten of the Father, full of grace and truth."
God's spoken Word became flesh in the form of the man Jesus the
Christ. His Word moved from the divine 4th dimension to the finite
3rd dimension to become sublime.

Think of our own words. Think of the things that we so nonchalantly
throw out into the air: the jokes, the empty thoughts and vain thoughts.
Those angry unintentional words; and then picture them taking shape
taking form and then coming to life. This is what the enemy moves
on; what can trigger an attack. It is like giving him insight into our
battle plan and when he's heard our words and assessed our condition,
he moves his forces.

*(On that note; I will apologize in this book to everyone that I have
offended with my words. To my wife Tammy first as God is ministering
the words on these pages to me first!)*

To further emphasize the power of expression through words,
Revelation 19:12 says, *"...His eyes were a flame of fire, and on His
head were many crowns; and He had a name written, that no man
knew, but He himself..."*

Verse thirteen of this same chapter says, *"...and His name is called
the 'Word of God'..."* and verse sixteen says, *"And He has on His
vesture and on His thigh a name written, King of Kings and Lord of
Lords."* What is that name? King of Kings and Lord of Lords. If it is
anymore than that only The Godhead knows that name, but whatever
the denotation on His clothing at His return, that name is full of pure
power! It will be a name that says: truth, salvation, confirmation,
authority, justice and judgment. *His* words will be like a two-edged
sword that will cut down the forces of the enemy's kingdom both
spiritual and physical.

The only human being who may have ever known the *full* power of
the spoken word would probably have been Adam. Without getting
too far off track, Adam was the only man (other than Christ) that
ever had the honor to be in direct fellowship with God without being
'born' with a sin nature. His task was to name the animals, perhaps

even the plants, and eventually his wife. These names not only label and identify objects that form the basis for the languages of antiquity and today's modern languages and dialects, but in tracing them back to their root meanings we find that they depict characteristics and function. I believe that much of what God may have disclosed to Adam has dissipated and been lost over the different dispensations of mankind since man's fall in the Garden of Eden. It is possible that we are able to have this knowledge restored to us through our fellowship with God in Christ, but I have personally never read anything that goes beyond the idea of simply the power of 'positive thought' accept in scripture where the word tells us to "think on these things". This is to say think on God's word. No one has put into practice the power of *'positive manifestation.'* There are some that utilize the power of prayer in healing; which is bible based, and definitely those who use the *'name it, claim it'* scenario, but this remains hit or miss for the most part. People who worship Satan and bow themselves before false Gods (actually demons) have more success in their practice than Christians do. Why? They are completely sold out and committed to what they believe! Most Christians simply are too bound by doubt and worldly things to achieve a complete revelation about speaking spiritual things into the physical dimension.

A pastor may pray and lay hands on the sick and speak a prayer to end all prayers, so why then is not everyone he touches brought to complete and total healing? Why do the people that are supposedly raised from the dead *or* have their missing body parts grow back, supposedly, as a result of God's *'word'* in action, never documented in a manner that is conclusive? For the most part we are asked to accept that documentation by faith and this simply is *not* Gods way. With technology today, there are cameras everywhere, ways to get information from the jungles of Africa to the most remote parts of the North Pole, and even transmit and receive pictures from space. People in scripture were healed by the disciples when their shadows passed by them or from articles of clothing that had touched them. So if Jesus said that *we* would do the things that *He* had done and *greater*, then I do not want to be forced to guess if what I am seeing on a video tape from some other church in some foreign country is real.

On the other hand, the Satanists are sold out. When you see magicians floating across buildings or walking on water, it is not always an illusion. They have sold out to Satan to receive spiritual supernatural power. Although there is always an alternative show where another magician will reveal how a trick was done, but that is also a product of misdirection. It is a back and forth which opens the door to confusion. Even on the smallest level we must remember that God is not the author of confusion. God is a God of truth! These people pray, they speak incantations (yes, the word 'abracadabra' is an actual demonic incantation), they meditate and then they *do*. Satan gives them spiritual power in order to trick and lure people into the darkness. How much more then should we be speaking the things of God, the Holy Word of God and seeing life altering manifestations of His power that will lead multitudes to the light?

In Christ we are given an example of how powerful the gift of speech actually is. If God's own Word can become living flesh and blood, then our own words can produce fruit for the kingdom of God to the changing of the world. The book of James says that if we can control our **words**, we can control our whole bodies. James 3:8 also says that no man can completely tame the tongue, but I believe that it can be moderated. Our words themselves actually come from our soul (2nd dimension), but they are manifest in the physical realm (3rd dimension) by our tongue. If we truly give thought to what needs to happen, then we will begin to understand that this all ties back to our reference point. When our thoughts and actions are in line with God's will, then we can bring the things of God into our reality with our words.

Read James chapter three for a clear understanding of the power and potential of the tongue from which our words are formed. Then begin to meditate on how Jesus actually operated through His own words (*in line with God's will*) while here on earth.

The unspoken word (power contained) as well as the spoken word (power released) exists and moves in all realms. ***That*** is its power.

- ▪ In zero dimension it exists as <u>faith</u> (unspoken)

- In the first dimension it exists as <u>vision</u> (unspoken)
- In the second dimension it exists as <u>hope</u> (spoken/unspoken)
- In the third dimension it exists as <u>substance</u> (spoken)
- In the fourth it exists as <u>power</u> (spoken)

Words have the power to move between dimensions and effect change in each one. A third dimensional man can speak into the fourth dimension and produce change as in the model of prayer. This is why when we pray we purpose in our hearts to align *our* will with the will of God. The goal is to get a response from God as in Daniel's case (Daniel 10:11, 12). We seek answers from God through His Holy Spirit that now resides here on earth and await answers from both the Spirit of God and through the angels that still minister to us according to God's purpose for our lives. I must point out that while the angels are called 'ministering spirits' (Hebrews 1:14), we are ministered to directly by God's Spirit in *this* present dispensation. So why do we need angels? The Holy Spirit is another personage of the Trinity so He is also omnipresent, but that doesn't make angels obsolete. They also know the word of God and minister to us in different ways as well as being in place to defend us on behalf of God against the enemy. Remember the time has not yet come for God to completely do away with Satan and so until then, the angels have this task. Conversely, a fourth dimensional being can speak into the third dimension by speaking to the minds and spirits of man and cause change to occur. This is how God, angels, Satan and demons communicate with us. This is why our minds have to be tuned to the Word and will of God and renewed.

As far as the other dimensions are concerned, I do not know if we should or can consider such ideas alive as we label life. We can however look at the fact that thoughts, ideas, visions, dreams, and such like things do have a *manner* of life. They exist within our minds. They move from inactivity to activity. They grow and change and develop. So the transformation of words from thought or vision to articulation and then manifestation is in itself miraculous.

God Himself envisioned a three dimensional universe filled with beings with whom He could fellowship. His mind and His Spirit were in union concerning the matter and He spoke it into existence by using His 'Word'. It was Jesus Himself who walked in the Garden of Eden with Adam and Eve, but previous to His human state. Genesis 3:8 says, *"And they heard the voice of the LORD God walking in the garden in the cool of the day."* God's voice can walk – Hallelujah!!!

Everything that is manifest here in our realm was created in some part through this Law of Expression. However, there are other laws that must be utilized with it, but this law frames whatever it is that is intended to be formed. The Bible says that, *"In the beginning God created..."* The how is in Colossians 1:15-17, *"(Jesus) Who is the image of the invisible God, the firstborn of every creature: for by Him were all things created, that are in heaven, and that are in earth, visible and invisible, whether they be thrones, or principalities, or powers: all things were created by Him and for Him: and He is before all things and by Him all things consist."* 2 Peter 3:5-7 says, *"...by the Word of God the heavens were of old, and the earth standing out of the water and in the water...but the heavens and the earth which are now, by the same Word are kept in store..."* This 'Word' always has and always will be Jesus the Logos (Living Word). This is the power of the second spiritual law.

Law #3: "The Law of Faith"

> *"Now faith is the substance of things hoped for the evidence of things not seen."*

Hebrews 11:1

The power of faith, in accordance with the Word of God, *is* the power of creation. Think about that statement for a moment. This is not a physical or temporal blueprint, but rather a spiritual one. Everything that exists or that we can imagine that can exist must come from something else in the third dimension. Everything that is manifest by man comes from some component found within the environment in which we exist. Scientists are continually finding more and more components of matter in our universe, but they already exist within our universe. So, if man wishes to create an automobile or a skyscraper, he must first take raw materials and refine them for use. This is not the case in the spiritual realm. In Genesis 1:1 the Hebrew word for **created** is *BÂRÂ' baw-raw'*; a primary root; (absolutely) to create *"In the beginning God created the heavens and the earth."* This includes not only the earth and the sky or first heaven, but outer space, the second heaven and the Holy City or third heaven where we find the Throne of God. There was nothing else in existence prior to God before He created these things (Go back to the 'Blank Theory). So the idea is that God made the things that make up every other thing with no raw materials whatsoever – no 'Big Bang', no primordial soup, no atoms, no electrons, nothing! *How*? Faith! God knew that He could not speak into nothingness and not expect results. He fully expects that what He ordains will be made manifest. Would it be ridiculous to assume that God uses the same spiritual principles; the same Law of faith that He asks us to use? Again, Hebrews 11:1 shows us two words that describe what faith is and its capabilities. The first word is Substance and the second is Evidence.

Substance: **Gk. Hupostasis (hoop-os'-tasis)** – meaning: a setting under, essence, assurance, and confidence. It is from a compound of *Hupo*: which means under, underneath, below…and *Histemi*: meaning to stand, set, establish. So we see here a word that explains that *faith* is the under-standing, the essence, of what makes up all that is manifest and what can be made manifest. Webster's Dictionary defines substance as: a) the essential nature; essence b) fundamental or characteristic part or quality c) the ultimate reality that underlies all outward manifestation and change d) physical material from which something is made or which has discrete existence.

Evidence: **Gk Elengchos (el'-eng-khos)** – meaning: proof, conviction, convince. We see that *faith* is also the proof that what we cannot see is real or can be made real. Webster's Dictionary defines evidence: a) an outward sign; indication b) something that furnishes proof c) testimony d) manifest, distinct, obvious, apparent, plain, clear, e) readily perceived or apprehended f) implies presence of visible signs that lead one to a definite conclusion g) such sharpness of outline or definition that no unusual effort to see or hear or comprehend is required h) the quality of being unmistakable i) the absence of anything that confuses the mind.

No one explains faith better than Paul in his letter to the Hebrews. Faith is the basis of *what* we hope for; what our hope is *made* of. Faith is also the proof of what we cannot see at this present time. In Hebrews chapter 11, Paul writes that:

- *v.2 "For by it the elders <u>obtained</u> a good report..."* – received a blessing from God
- *v.3 "Through faith <u>we understand</u> that the worlds were framed..."* – gained knowledge of spiritual things
- *v.4 "By faith Abel <u>offered</u> unto God a more excellent sacrifice than Cain, by which <u>he obtained witness that he was righteous</u>, God testifying of his gifts: and by it he <u>being dead yet speaketh</u>..."* – we are made righteous or worthy and gain favor with God. We also leave a testimony in the physical realm that can carry over into the spiritual realm.
- *v.5 "By faith, Enoch <u>was translated</u> that he should not see death..."* – are able to move from the physical to the spiritual, according to the will of God.
- *v.7 "By faith Noah...<u>prepared</u> an ark..."* – we obtain salvation if we hear and obey.
- *v.8 "By faith Abraham...<u>obeyed</u>..."* – we are able to trust God so that He can fulfill His purpose in our lives.
- *v.11 "Through faith also Sara herself <u>received strength</u> to conceive seed..."* – have our physical existence blessed so that God can work through us. [Abram had his name changed to Abraham after God added the Hebrew 'H' and Sarai to Sarah. This is essentially breath and it being from God is life. God breathed life into Adam and he became a living soul.]* - **Genesis 2:7 - And the LORD God formed man of the dust of the ground, and <u>breathed</u> into his nostrils the <u>breath</u> of life; and man became a living soul.**
- *V.17 "By faith Abraham...<u>offered</u> Isaac...accounting that God was able to raise him up, even from the dead..." [God told him to offer Isaac, not sacrifice him. That is why the angel*

had to prevent Abram from killing Isaac.] – we are able to envision the impossible.

- *v.20 "By faith Isaac blessed..."* – we are able to prophecy, seeing God's vision for our future.
- *v.21 "By faith Jacob blessed...and worshiped..."* – are able to believe in things that are not yet manifest in the realm in which we live.
- v.22 *"By faith Joseph made mention (prophesied)...gave command..."* – we are able to speak into the lives of and also plan for our progeny.
- *v.23 "By faith Moses when he was born, was hid three months of his parents (Jochebed and Amram), because they saw he was a proper child..."* – we can stand against fear and are seen differently by the world and covered by God.
- *v.24-28 "By faith Moses when he was come to years...refused his Egyptian heritage...chose to suffer affliction...forsook Egypt...kept the Passover and the sprinkling of blood..."* – forgo the trappings of this world, resist the wiles of Satan and stand against our enemies. We will recognize the laws and ordinances of God and their importance.

*[Bara *fr*. Strong's Exhaustive Concordance Heb. Dic. #1254]
*[Hupostasis *fr*. Strong's Exhaustive Concordance Grk. Dic. #5287]
*[Elegchos *fr*. Strong's Exhaustive Concordance Grk. Dic. #1650]

- *v.29 "By faith they (the Israelites and a vast multitude) passed through the Red Sea..."* – are able to achieve the impossible and defeat our enemies.
- v.30 *"By faith the walls of Jericho fell down..."* – we are able to pull down the strongholds of the enemy.
- *v.31 "By faith the harlot Rahab perished not..."* – are protected in our sinful state as God gives us the opportunity to realize His love for us.

v.13 "These all died in faith, not having received the promises, but having seen them afar off, and persuaded of them and confessed that they were strangers and pilgrims on the earth..."

All of those people and countless others died believing that they were strangers here on earth and that they would become something more than flesh and blood after they died. So the Law of Faith is nothing more than belief, while also being the power to effectuate action and create change. It is the knowledge that our minds have the power to bring our ideas to materialization. Scripture tells us that every man is given a measure of faith (Romans 12:3) and from that measure, even as the servants who were given different talents (Matthew 25:14-30), we are to increase that faith. How do we increase it? Romans 10:17 says, "So then faith cometh by hearing and hearing by the 'Word' of God." This principle is something that can ultimately determine how we regulate our lives, deal with situations, settle on solutions, resolve issues and establish our view of reality. As Christians we have (we are supposed to have) total faith in God and His 'Word'; our reference point. Any outside stimuli, circumstance, standpoint or perspective that deviates from that reference point should send up a red flag in our spirits. Why? Those who seek after the one true God, seek for a relationship based on faith and trust in a creator who gave everything out of unconditional love for His creation. Faith is what we rely on until what God has promised us is within our grasp.

In Matthew 17:20 Jesus tells us that if we have faith, as small as a grain of mustard seed (the smallest of all seeds, we would be able to move mountains.

Law #4: "The Law of Reproduction"

The Law of Reproduction is this, *"...Everything after its own kind..."* as we see in Genesis during the creation and restoration. This law is the basis for the continuance of life as God has intended. Any deviation from this law has extreme and disastrous effects.

In Genesis, God ordained that everything would produce after its own kind and thereby maintain the pattern that God set forth. Since the enemy's goal in war is to undo or distort what God has created, he breaks these fourth dimensional rules realizing that they will have adverse effects on the third dimension.

In Genesis 6:2 we see, ***"That the sons of God (angels) saw the daughters of men that they were fair; and they took them <u>wives</u> of all which they chose."*** This was in direct opposition to what the Father had pre-ordained as far as reproduction was concerned. Verse 4, of this same chapter, states, ***"There were giants in the earth in those days; and also after that, when the sons of God <u>came in</u> unto the daughters of men and they bare children to them..."***

Sidenote: Ponder this, why did they take themselves wives? I believe that this was part of the deception. They had to pass themselves off as humans so that the women would not suspect that they were angels. Think about it.

Many theological professors have explained the presence of giants away by calling the Sons of God *men* instead of angels. The scripture is very clear however, concerning a definite distinction between the two and does not refer to, the producers of the giants as the sons of mortal men, but of God. Man is qualified as a Son of God only after Christ's completed work on the cross whereby we are sons as Christ is a son and we are joint heirs to a heavenly inheritance through His shed blood. The book of Jude 1:6, 7 also confirms this breaking of the Law of Reproduction saying, ***"And the angels which kept not their first estate, but left their own habitation, He hath reserved in everlasting chains under darkness unto judgment of the great day. <u>Even as</u> Sodom and Gomorrah, and the cities about them <u>in like manner</u>, giving themselves over to fornication..."*** The similarity in the nature of the sin is clear. It is sexual sin. Their first estate refers to their breaking of this law and losing their place in heaven as a result. Heavenly angels left their estates or their respective heavenly places and had sexual intercourse with human females. The word **estate** or ŏikētēriŏn (oy-kay-tay'-ree-on) translated from the Greek, means habitation or house. This word, interestingly enough, is derived from the root word ŏikŏs (oy'-kos) meaning family, relations, home, household and temple. The idea and implication is that these angels have gone outside of their respective purpose or function to defile themselves and the women that they lusted after. The word ŏikŏs is conclusive in describing the fact they left their relatives; the other angels, and their designated and anointed places in heaven; a place that they called home, and the holiness and glory of God that they shared while enjoying His presence. I have often wondered why they are bound in chains in darkness. It occurs to me that sexual sins bind us and prevents us from maintaining a Godly perspective. The drive to procreate is one of the strongest desires of man and in most instances it is above every other kind of lust.

*[Ŏikētēriŏn *fr.* Strong's Exhaustive Concordance Grk. Dic. #3613]
*[Ŏikŏs *fr.* Strong's Exhaustive Concordance Grk. Dic. #3624]

To be bound where one cannot move is very symbolic of what this sin does to the individual that indulges in it. To be in darkness is to cut off the means by which this sin enters into the mind for truly there can hardly be sexual sin without there first being the lust of the eyes; hence the punishment is for that being to be bound in darkness where they cannot see.

1 Corinthians 6:18-20 tell us to, *"Flee fornication. Every sin that a man committeth is without the body; but he that committeth fornication sinneth against his own body. What? Know ye not that your body is the temple of the Holy Ghost which is in you, which ye have of God, and ye are not your own? For ye are bought with a price: therefore glorify God in your body, and in your spirit, which are God's."*

These Sons of God broke the Law of Reproduction by descending from the fourth dimension and into the third dimension to commit sins that God has stated are sins against your own body. Keep in mind that the angels, before committing this act, are holy and mankind exists in a sinful state. What this produced (*See: Law of Reciprocity*) was the abomination that the scriptures refer to as giants. These were especially offensive to God because it was an act of direct disobedience by His 'Sons'. It was also a direct attack upon God's authority. A discourse on the giants and how they were created would take far more pages than I am personally willing to commit to in this study. Suffice it to say, perhaps mark it as a side note, I have attempted to have discussions with pastors, ministers, deacons, and other astute persons of intellectual prominence on this subject, only to find that they are unwilling at best to engage in any such speculation. Why? Of that answer I am uncertain, but if it is in scripture then I am willing to go to every possible source in order to obtain the truth. If is a part of Satan's plan to cause harm to the body of Christ, then I am willing to fight against it or be prepared to recognize it when it appears. The bible says that God wiped out the giants in the flood, but also says that there were giants that had to be dealt with after the flood as well. The logistics of this particular battle plan seems to suggest that Satan is not beyond continuing his efforts on this particular front. One source from the internet suggests that Satan will use this tactic to breed the anti-Christ. True or not, the attack that often proves to be the most devastating is usually the one that we are ill prepared to counter.

The flip side of the sexual coin implies that if Satan cannot deceive us into *producing* things that are offensive to God in our lives, then he will deceive us into producing nothing! What he hopes to gain from this is found in Matthew 21:18-20; the incident of the fig tree. When the fig tree did not produce fruit, then it was good for nothing. As the story goes, Jesus curses the fig tree which dries up and withers away. This was also the case in Sodom and Gomorrah, and in the neighboring cities. The Sodomites, from which we get our modern word 'sodomy', were performing unseemly sexual acts with members of the same sex and/or with animals, neither of which can produce anything. Sex, for the sake of having sex alone can take on an aspect that can become very ugly, very fast. Something that has been created by God to be pleasurable and productive can be warped into an obsession that can destroy a person from the inside out. Desire can turn to lust, lust to infatuation, infatuation to action, and action to greed. Greed is what the pornography industry is all about. The human body can only contort or engage in so many different positions and so we see *group* sex acts, *same* sex acts and *same sex group* acts, acts of *bestiality, fetish* sex and finally *snuff* sex (where someone is murdered during the act of sex). What we do not realize is that there is emptiness in the pursuit of continuous self-gratification that drains our minds, bodies, and spirits. Once a soldier is drained; dries up and withers away, he is simply ineffective and good for nothing. The enemy has not changed his agenda. His plan always includes very simple tactics that cause us to do most of the work in destroying and sending ourselves to hell. The homosexual movement has exploded in the last decade and now the push for acceptance into mainstream of society is claiming countless young lives! When I see adolescent girls holding hands with other girls and attempting to portray the male role in a relationship, it strikes me as the height of foolishness. To think that the enemy can blind the human mind so completely is astounding to me. Men who have abandoned all traces of masculinity and embrace and indulge in an overly 'flamboyant' version of the female disposition border on the insane. What would we say to a cat who was barking or an elephant who was trying to fly? We would call it insanity. These people have missed the shear beauty and individuality of their creation. Man is designed to procreate and woman is designed to procreate yet in completely different and equally beautiful ways. I notice that the desire remains in each of them no matter their choice. It is always to have offspring of their own. To move against the design of the creator is at best a very dangerous indication of a serious problem. At the very least, it is strained and uncomfortable. God created Adam and Eve and ordained sexual intercourse within the confines of the institution of marriage to be between one man and one woman. What is the problem? Satan is again deceiving them into being unproductive and destroying the 'purpose' of millions.

What we fail to realize is that sexual intercourse begets intimacy and this is a form of power. It is the power that God has given to none of His other creation. Flowers reproduce, but their form of life is static and intrinsic. Animals reproduce, but their reproduction is basic and naturalistic; they operate on instinct. Angels were not given the divine permission to reproduce, but rather used their powers to usurp the authority of God and the free will of human beings. Only mankind was given the directive to be fruitful, multiply and replenish the earth. Included in this directive was the ability to reproduce; the authority to reproduce; the mechanisms with which to do so and the fruit that reflected the image and character of the initial creator. There is no emotional or spiritual connection between pollinating plants, procreating animals or angels that convert to human form. When a human man and woman have sexual intercourse, it is at that time that God can allow a doorway into the fourth dimensional realm to be opened. Through intercourse, an immortal soul can be brought into the third dimension in the form of a child. Think about this; many forms of life on the planet reproduce, but only humanity has the ability after conception to grow into a thinking adult that can choose to fellowship with its creator and accept salvation.

We have the ability to create life; to recreate in *our* own image the same way that God created us. Genesis is very specific in pointing out this very fact especially in light of the new sin nature that is found in mankind after the fall of man in Eden.

> *"And Adam lived an hundred and thirty years, and begat a son in his own likeness, after his image; and called his name Seth..."*

Genesis 5:3

This is, at the same time, <u>in accordance</u> to how God intended for man to reproduce *and* <u>in direct opposition</u> to the intent and ultimate function of what was produced. The sin nature caused Adam to produce sinful offspring. Adam knew that all those that would be born after him would be born into sin; hence the name change for Eve in Genesis 3:20 from 'Woman' to 'Eve' – *'mother of all living'* because at first they were both called Adam. Genesis 1:27 tells us that God intended or knew that He would form woman, but did not until after no helpmeet was found for the man. Paul tells us in 1Timothy 2:14 that, **"...Adam was <u>not</u> deceived, but the woman..."** So the essence of what the scripture is conveying is that Adam understood what he was doing; perhaps out of love; perhaps to show us a type of Christ in sacrificing himself and taking on a sinful nature. It appears however that scripture, in adding the fact that Adam calls Eve a different name, suggests it to be a reminder of her being deceived. Conversely, a portion of the woman's punishment deemed that she would forever remind the man of his failure to act against the serpent/Satan in Eden.

Genesis 3:16 - *Unto the woman he said, I will greatly multiply thy sorrow and thy conception; in sorrow thou shalt bring forth children; and thy <u>desire</u> shall be to thy husband, and he shall rule over thee.*

Desire is not a good thing. It is consistent controversy between man and woman. Desire is the word used to denote that the woman would always be in opposition as far as her thinking as a constant reminder of the differences between the sexes and the fact that the man should have taken the leadership role, since he walked with God before Eve was formed. Adam got called first after he sinned and he hid himself from God's voice (Jesus) because he was naked and knew that he was disobedient.

So I mention these truisms to point out that the very first attack of the enemy was in part to prevent mankind from fulfilling God's initial command to be fruitful, to multiply, to replenish the earth, and to subdue it and have dominion over it.

We should view this as God's perfect will for mankind. We see Satan attack mankind in the Garden of Eden and then again through intercourse with angels which indicates that the Law of Reproduction is of great importance with regards to both sides. Nothing produced, in either case, was a product of what God had ordained. Even as we look at Genesis chapter six, what was produced of this union between angels and women was an abomination to God. I do not believe that Satan knew exactly what would be produced, but he must have had some plan. A portion of the plan was that he would stop the Messianic bloodline through which the savior would be born. The problem was that the act of sex requires all three parts of our triune beings: mind, body and spirit to be involved and *with our own kind*, in order for the production of 'fruit'. Remember, God sees us, in certain instances, as trees. We are compared throughout scripture to grass bearing flowers, trees producing fruit, and branches connected to the vine. The 'fruit' may be of low quality or high quality; good or bad, but always recognizable as the 'fruit' of the same tree. When we cross breed different trees, we engage through sexual intercourse with beings not of our own kind, (hybrids), or if *we* go against God's designated procedure for being 'fruitful', the result is mutated fruit or no fruit at all. The consequences are:

- *The wrong doors are opened.*
- *The wrong fruit is produced.*
- *Nothing at all is produced.*
- *The part of us that is closest to God, our spirit man is compromised.*

In the case of the angels, the wrong doors are opened and the power of the fourth dimension is given to beings that had no fellowship with God. Not only did they lack fellowship with God but they were also absent of the **"...breath of life..."** (Genesis 2:7). Angels were created differently; they are spirits and a flame of fire (Hebrews 1:7). God breathed the *breath of life* into man and he (man) became a living soul and that breath was intended to be perpetuated in the union between a man and a woman. We are made in God's image (outward appearance) and in his likeness (internal appearance). These are the things that connect us to God. In many instances, we find in scripture that the giants had physical characteristics that clearly showed that they were abominations to God's plan for mankind. The wrong fruit was also produced in this case because they were created by beings that had lost their fellowship and association with God through sin. These giants would never have an opportunity to become children of God. The bible tells us, **"Be ye not unequally yoked...for what fellowship hath righteousness with unrighteousness? And what communion hath light with darkness?"**

2 Corinthians 6:14

The Sodomites, on the other hand, were producing nothing! I wonder if that is in fact the very problem that plagues the homosexual community. The rate of suicides and violent crimes of passion are higher in the gay and lesbian community than in any other social group. A lack of productivity is, in a way, worse than producing the wrong thing. Being ineffectual can harm the mind and cause it to fracture. Failure can lead to depression and this in turn can lead to deviant behavior having expressions both inwardly and outwardly.

People who turn to the *same* sex, seeking the intimacy that was designed to be given by the *opposite* sex, always have deep rooted issues that may or may not be able to be identified. Improper role models, lack of a parent, early exposure to sex, coercion, molestation, traumatic experiences and inability to cope with adversity and the people that introduce them to this lifestyle are often called 'fathers' and 'mothers'. All can play a part in turning to a wrong sexual viewpoint or to the same sex to fill certain needs.

The parable of the talents speaks of three servants. Two of these servants were productive with what their master had given them before he left for his journey. The third servant hid his talent in the ground and upon his masters return had nothing to show save the one talent that he had been given initially. The unproductive servant was then severely punished and his single talent taken away (Matthew 25:14-30). The story is an allegory of Jesus entrusting certain things to us here on earth until His return. The servant was admonished that he could at the very least have put the money in the bank to gain interest. This would have been productivity at the simplest level; being productive by being smart. This story represents a lot more than monetary thrift. It represents having knowledge of what God's expectations are, based on our relationship with Him and our ability to be obedient. This is how God views homosexuality, bestiality, and sexual perversion. People who commit these sins could very well have chosen to remain single rather than pursue behavior that would sink them further into sin and perpetuate the gulf between them and freedom from sin. God will let mankind have his way when it comes to fleshly idolatry until the stench of sin becomes more than what God is willing to tolerate (Romans 1:21-32). Homosexuality steals more from the psyche than is ever realized until it is too late. Feelings of inadequacy, exile, confusion, depression, and futility pervade the gay and lesbian community. Why? God allows them to have their way. Romans 1:25-28 says, ***"...who changed the truth of God into a lie, and worshiped and served the creature more than the Creator, ...for this cause <u>God gave them up</u> to vile affections: for even their women did change the natural use into that which is against nature: and likewise also the men, leaving the natural use of the woman, burned <u>in their lust</u> one toward another; doing that***

57

which is unseemly, and <u>receiving in themselves that recompense</u> of their error which was meet. And even as they did not like to retain God in their knowledge, <u>God gave them over</u> to a reprobate mind, to do those things which are not convenient." The very act is the height of self indulgence and selfishness and always leads to a progressive moral and psychological deterioration. Pay attention to what the gay community has to say. They claim that they are 'born' that way which would then mean that God created them to be unproductive. Then compare it too what God says in His word and draw your own conclusions. Matthew 25:30 states, *"...and cast ye the unprofitable servant into outer darkness: there shall be weeping and gnashing of teeth."* Again we see sexual sin punished by darkness and likewise in Sodom the men who wanted to sleep with the angels that came into Lot's house were blinded.

When the part of us that is closest to God is compromised during illicit sexual activity, it becomes more difficult to draw that person to the kingdom. They sit on the throne of their own heart and have been allowed by God to be blinded. If our bodies are the temple of God (1 Corinthians 3:16, 17) and sin is considered the only sin that is against ones own body (1 Corinthians 6:18), then this type of behavior is a lot like burning down your own house. Who suffers?

Finally, since mankind is separated from God by sin, God cannot sanction intimacy with anything that is unlike Him. Intercourse is ordained by God within the institution of marriage. It is the earthly representation of the relationship that God will have with His people in eternity. It represents the oneness of mind, body and spirit and the culmination and completion of us being in perfect harmony, as He is in perfect harmony. It represents the peace of two parties coming together in mutual agreement or, with regard to our study, the *opposite* of war. Sexual intercourse with several different partners or with a partner with which we have not been ordained or obligated to through covenant is not recognized by God. When a couple is united in marriage before God, there becomes a trinity. God, man and woman become one in covenant. *"Marriage is honorable in all, and the bed undefiled: but whoremongers and adulterers God will judge..."*

Hebrews 13:4

This holy union was ordained by God in Genesis 2:18-25. The command is everything after its own kind in unity and in harmony within the will of God. Today, mankind has defiled himself with every possibility of sexual sin. One would think that we would run out of ideas. That is not the case. We have become a generation of thrill seekers searching for the next sexual adventure or fetish. We believe that once we accomplished the outrageous, then we should seek the outlandish and even try the impossible.

God is ever looking to see what type of fruit we will bear or to see *if* we will bear any fruit at all. Jesus says, "Every tree that bringeth not forth good fruit is hewn down and cast into the fire (Matthew 7:19)." Likewise in Mark 11:12-21, Jesus curses the fig tree that bears *no* fruit, proclaiming that it would bear nothing again forever. It then becomes fairly plain to see how God feels about what we produce. It does not matter in which realm we produce the fruit, The Law of Reproduction is one by which we are measured in all. If we are not producing the type of fruit that God can enjoy then He has no use for it or us. Our goal should be to produce a crop that the Father can enjoy and be proud of. Think of the fact that God refers to us in His word as trees. Even the plan of salvation states that: one plants, one waters and God brings the increase. Shouldn't we strive, press forward, and grow 'in' Christ the true vine so that our fruit is good to God?

Law #5: "The Law of Obedience"

You cannot be a soldier in God's army without real life application concerning this rule. It is not possible! Soldiers take orders; it's as simple as that. The problem is that oftentimes soldiers want to concede to their own personal version of a given command rather than simply being obedient. I too am guilty of this in many ways and find I must constantly war against my own flesh to do what I know to be right.

The reason for this is that man is no longer a harmonious being. God created man to be led by his spirit; a spirit that ultimately is led by and fellowships with God's Holy Spirit. The spirit would then dictate to the emotions and the emotions, or soul if you will, would direct the body. When sin entered into the equation, so did death. When God cautioned Adam not to eat from the Tree of the Knowledge of Good and Evil for, *"...in the day that thou eatest thereof thou shalt surely die..."* Remember that a day is with the Lord as a thousand years and a thousand years is but a day. Man has not lived yet past a day. Methuselah came close, but he still died the same day according to God's word. *But of the tree of the knowledge of good and evil, thou shalt not eat of it: for in the day that thou eatest thereof thou shalt surely die.*

Genesis 2:17

He was speaking of spiritual as well as physical death. Man's physical death is a result of not being able to eat from the Tree of Life, but spiritual death came instantaneously to humanity because true death means separation from the presence of God. This is what *eternal death* will mean, **separation** from ones creator, without my inclusion of the eternal punishment that will accompany it. Unregenerate mankind is now ruled by the appetites of the soul. The soul now directs the body and the spirit of man has none of the fourth dimensional power and authority that God intended. For the most part, the part of God that He breathed into us remains in the backseat while the soul and the body drive.

Paul tells us that the sin nature inherited from Adam's disobedience in the Garden of Eden causes him (us) to sin even when he (we) know(s) right from wrong and desire(s) to be do right.

> *"For that which I do I allow not: for what I would, that do I not; but what I hate, that do I. If then I do that which I would not, I consent unto the law that it is good. Now then it is no more I that do it, but sin that dwelleth in me."*

Romans 7:15-17

Paraphrase: *"I do not want to allow what I am doing into my life because I already know right from wrong. What I want to do is what is right, but I am having a hard time and don't do it. I am doing exactly what I hate! I am telling the law that it is good (not taking into consideration that I am no longer under the law, but under 'grace' because of Christ!) So I recognize that the reason for this is because of the sin nature that is in me."*

There is obviously an inherent difficulty with being obedient. Eve was incited to disobedience through trickery and Adam by way of Eve. The struggle for us comes because of the fact that disobedience is now a *spiritual* trait of unregenerate man inherited from our predecessors. It is also progressive because it is a symptom of what is initially wrong with the whole of humanity. Death is degenerative and so the indication of the disease manifests in a multitude of ways. So while one generation's child may say "No!" the next generation's child may add a roll of the eyes, some body language, some expletives and so forth.

In a world that is slowly descending toward chaos, the struggle to maintain the gift that God has given us has become increasingly difficult. Never let anyone tell you that Christianity is an 'easy' road to walk. It's the straightest path and the greatest imaginable reward awaits those who stand and do not fall, but easy is not the word that I would choose to use with 'Christianity' in the same sentence. If your walk is easy then the enemy is not being effected by it. Many Christians will not see things this way, but the story of Job will set them straight. The first verse of Job states that, ***"There was a man in the land of Uz, whose name was Job; and that man was perfect and upright, and one that feared God and eschewed evil."*** (Job 1:1) Job's walk should have been easy according to what is preached across the pulpit today and yet in God's permissive will, Job was allowed to be assaulted by enemy forces. I used to think that this story in the bible was an isolated incident that was meant to teach us humility, patience, and even trust in the Lord. I thought all of these things until I read about a humble, patient, man who trusted in God with his life and family had God brag on *him*. The point is that our walk can be as perfect as Job's. We can be as obedient and trusting and faithful as Job and still be allowed to come under fire. It may not seem fair, but I have researched scripture forward and backward and never in scripture is God described as fair. God is described as just and righteous which categorically holds a different concept. Fair implies that righteousness may be imputed, but that the possibility of partiality exists based on making all parties equal regardless of their present standing. Remember God is NO respecter of any person. Righteousness implies that obedience has motivated the reward or punishment depending on any given situation. So while God is fair in the sense of being just, He is again, no respecter of people (Acts 10:34). So what is obedience? Why is it so important to mankind's success in life?

Obedient: \ö-bed-e-en(t) a) submissive to the restraint or command of authority: *willing* to obey **b)** submissive to the will of another **c)** compliance with the demands or requests of one in authority **d)** implies the predisposition to submit readily to control or guidance **e)** having a character that permits easy handling or managing **f)** suggests a willingness to yield or to cooperate either because of a desire or because of natural open mindedness.

It is easy to see why the natural predilection to be obedient has been corrupted by sin. Since the spirit of man is no longer innately born into fellowship with God, the appetites of the soul tend to be selfish, as opposed to selfless, thereby stripping man of the intrinsic desire to be led by his creator. The Law of Obedience is the most painful to our flesh. When the spirit of man is regenerated, the war with one's self ensues. The soul struggles to maintain its appetites while the spirit struggles to stay in the presence of God. This is why scripture tells us that, *"... no flesh should glory in His (God's) presence..."* (1 Corinthians 1:29) and *"...there shall no flesh be justified in His sight."* (Romans 3:20). The flesh is caught in the middle because after salvation it has a new master and resists spiritual direction.

Another problem arises when we understand that as third dimensional beings that everything in our environment is designed to stimulate and cater to the flesh; food, beauty, sex, sights and sounds, and even interaction with other people. It will do anything that indulges the five senses: Touch, Taste, Smell, Sight, and Hearing. The instinct of the soul is to fight to win back control of the flesh and the flesh initially fights *with* the soul because it craves what it has become accustomed too. The spirit of man seeks to fill that hole that God has created within us that can only be filled with His presence. Our minds become divided because it is an entity that exists in the third dimension, but has the capacity to dwell in the realm of the spirit. This is why Romans 12:2 says, *"And be not conformed to this world: but be ye transformed by the <u>renewing</u> of your minds, that ye may prove what is that good, and acceptable, and perfect will of God."* That perfect will is that we re-train our minds so that our souls; our will, our emotions, and our intellect; allow His spirit to direct our bodies and simultaneously come under subjection to God's will.

What type of Christian are you? Does your soul still direct your flesh or have you instilled enough of the Word of God internally that you are able to take your hands off of the steering wheel of your life? Do you have faith that He knows what is best for your life or do you still cater to what feels good?

Isn't this the problem that parents run into with their children? At some point in life every child wants to find his/her own way regardless of their parent's instructions. Obedience shows knowledge of protocol and respect for authority. It shows that the submissive party recognizes the authoritative party. It is only through obedience that progress is made and through a lack of it hat transgression comes.

Let's look at the word *progress*. Before I give the dictionary definition. May I point out that without progress there can be no success. It should be a regular practice for Christians to analyze their *spiritual* progress, or lack thereof, on a consistent basis. It becomes increasingly difficult, with time, as I am sure that some of my readers no doubt know. It is a *daily* struggle to maintain momentum even concerning 'kingdom' business. This is why we must always, *"... press toward the mark of the prize of the high calling of God in Christ Jesus"* (Philippians 3:14). This is why we are not to get, *"...weary in well doing"* (Galatians 6:9). The enemy is looking for those Christians that are stagnant and unproductive because these are characteristics are indicative of a weak point in our relationship with God. A better way to put it is that without movement, we are sitting ducks!

Progress: \präg-gres\ - **a)** a gradual betterment (as an objective goal): ADVANCE **b)** steady development **c)** forward or onward movement **d)** a royal journey marked by pomp and pageant.

The Law of Obedience doesn't lend itself simply to the strict compliance with the commandments of God, but also to those implied requirements that will ultimately lead to improvement in our Christian walk. A sure way to come as close to obedience as possible concerning God's word, is to mentally note scriptures that outline patterns for success. *"If you fulfill this on your end..."* then, *"...I, God, will guarantee that on my end."*

By paying close attention to detail in the written word, we find innumerable patterns and combinations of patterns that work for our personal good and the good of the 'kingdom'. We are to, ***"Study to show (ourselves) approved unto God, a workman that needeth not be ashamed, rightly dividing the word of truth"*** (2 Timothy 2:15). When we study, we gain progress in being obedient because we are internalizing God's will for our lives. It is not the studying that necessarily instigates the forward momentum in our Christian walk, but rather the real application of what we know about our master that wins His approval. It cultivates experience The word 'study' is actually only found three times in the entire bible and the word 'studieth' twice. Our progress in every area of life comes through application and functionality. 'Spiritual Warfare' is perhaps the scariest and most difficult for us to embrace. We must grapple with the concept that we can be harmed in any number of ways by an enemy that we cannot see. If we do not fully capture the 'prosperity' concept, then our excuse is...*"God will make a way"*. If we do not move in faith in every area of our lives, then our excuse is...*"God knows my heart"*. If we don't receive instantaneous healing, then *"It must not be in God's will"*.

1. God has already made the way.
2. God does know our hearts and the Word says that they are continually black.
3. It is NEVER and has NEVER been in God's will for us to have any kind of dis-ease.

A spiritual battle, however, *will* scare the HELL out of Christians – and it should! It will bring you close to death or begging for it like Job. Everything that we strive for in Christianity is a part of *the* grand battle. And while the ultimate battle is not our own, but the Lord's, we fight to show those that remain captive that they can be set free, but as the Lord fights for us we must stand! Watch your local bible study in any church and see for yourself how the subject is diluted by limiting it to Ephesians chapter six or by downplaying its importance altogether. Poor health is most often a neglect of the body (God's Holy Temple) and prompted by the enemy. So are poverty, lack of faith, fear, and lack of the joy of Christ. All these and more are battles that the Christian must wage while carrying out the prime directive of winning the lost.

During the course of our progression we must try not to slip or fall backward. This is one of the enemy's goals. Remember that no one is born with a regenerate spirit, but rather with an unregenerate spirit. We must all be led by the Spirit of God into the glorious light of salvation. We must also stay within that light once we get there. Let's look at another definition.

Transgress: \ tran(t)s-'gres\ - a) to step beyond or across **b)** to go beyond the limits set or prescribed by: Violate <~divine law~> **c)** to pass beyond or go over a set boundary **d)** to violate a command, duty, or law **e)** sin

I like to think of transgression as moving *backward* over a line that you have already crossed over while going *forward*. Each step forward should be accompanied by a learning process and then by applying what we've learned to multiple situations to assure, and insure, its practical use in our individual lives. This is what makes the word of God so rich; while it is all encompassing, it is also individualized according to the student's revelation of the truth from God. The definition of transgression as sin is rightly included when we consider the great lengths to which God went to institute salvation. God has given us too much for us to carelessly lose ground in our spiritual battles. While there is forgiveness for transgression, a loss in any event can mean severe damages and even casualties.

When a person is moving backward, they are not in perfect balance. Moving backward to achieve, to gain or to fortify position in battle necessitates extensive practice and requires great skill. Boxers cannot easily maintain their center of gravity while going backward and only a select few are effective offensively while moving in the reverse. A boxer that is moving or being moved backward by his opponent will always 'cover up', secure their defense, and search for openings in their opponent's offense. The problem is that they amass abuse during the period of time that they are forced to maintain the defensive position and may never have the opportunity to return fire. Many a prize fight has ended when someone has been backed into a corner and is never afforded the opportunity to regain their momentum. If the enemy ever has ample opportunity to force you backward; force you to stay in the defensive position as opposed to the offensive position, then he will attempt to finish you off once your back is against the ropes. It's not impossible to fight off of the ropes, but it is uncomfortable, risky, unpredictable, and by no means the way that a trainer prepares his fighter.

By the previous definitions, we see that if we do not remain teachable then the enemy has an opportunity to inject sin into our lives. He will impede our forward motion and either drive us backward or cause us to become stagnant. Let me say that again, *"Satan will drive us backward! If allowed"* Think of how far you've come in your Christian walk. If we were boxers, then we would plant our feet, hold our defense while maintaining our offense and consistently go forward. In the spiritual realm, this represents ground that we've conquered, occupied, and prevented the enemy from recapturing. Disobedience allows the enemy to harm you spiritually and push you backward essentially retaking ground that you have been charged to stand on and occupy until Christ's return. Disobedience is the number one cause of God's displeasure with His children. As a father of six I can say with some degree of assurance that nothing irritates me more than disobedience. When I have given my children instructions and they are disobedient it shows a lack of respect of the position in which God has placed me and an arrogance that could cause them to suffer at the hands of the enemy. A parent's instruction may be for the child's protection, their betterment, or to communicate God's will and life's lessons. On the other hand, the child cannot readily see that everything is not always what it appears. Experience is *not* always the best teacher; it is however, always the harshest and cruelest. The book of proverbs is the book most frequently read by Jewish parents to their children to point out life's lessons. Honey is placed on their tongue before the reading of scripture to emphasize that the word and wisdom of God is sweet. I strongly suggest it as a teaching tool and method to all of my readers with children. What I used to do was buy candy or sweets for them when I was doing bible study with them. As they responded or participated, in the teaching, they were rewarded. This made them look forward to bible study every night after dinner. As that went on, their friends began to desire to be included as they spent the night with the children. They began to accompany the children to the house of God on Sunday. They wanted to participate in church events and many of them came to Christ. The Word of God is attractive; but far more so when it is presented correctly!

In the realm of the spirit, obedience brings us in line with the will of our Father and under His umbrella of protection. It brings us into fellowship with Him and allows us to see things from a point of view that we cannot see while we are *out* of His will. There is also a safety in being obedient; an invisible shield that the enemy cannot easily penetrate. We become pliable to what our Father in heaven wants to shape us into. The more obedient, the quicker and easier we are able to meet our calling and fulfill our individual anointing. Romans 8:29 states, ***"For whom He did foreknow, He also did predestinate to be <u>conformed</u> to the image of His Son, that He might be the firstborn among many brethren."*** Our job is to make it *convenient* for God to make us like Jesus. The enemy begins to view us as a problem and finds it difficult to distinguish us from Jesus. We are hidden in Christ!!! ***"For ye are dead, and your life is hid with Christ in God".***

Colossians 3:3

Disobedience moves us out of God's will and prevents God from protecting us. The further from His will we are, the more dangerous our situation. Satan and his fallen angels immediately know when we are out of the will of the Father. After all, they know the rules much better than we do and recognize when we are out of line with the rules set in place by God for our protection. Disobedience is the enemy's 'hole-in-the-fence' and the way by which they invade our territory. In the spiritual realm, our rebelliousness allows the enemy to get close enough to us to blind our eyes and whisper in our ears. In the physical realm, we then find ourselves tempted by the trappings of this world. Keep in mind that each trap set by the enemy is designed to lure you in; further and further until the way back to the Father is obscured. Obedience is the key to our success in both the third and fourth dimensions. When we obey our Father, this gives Him the ability to trust us, to bless us, exalt us and elevate us to the position of Son-ship.

One last note about the Law of Obedience; there are advantages as well as disadvantages concerning this law. Deuteronomy chapter 28 paints a very vivid picture of both and offers us extensive insight concerning our choices with regard to each. Chapter 28 paints a picture of how we will be blessed and rewarded for being obedient and staying in our Father's will. In my opinion however, the most profound of all the scriptures concerning obedience is Jeremiah 7:23, ***"Obey my voice and I will be your God."***

Law #6: "The Law of Responsibility"

God has not designed us to stumble through the vast intricacies and complex workings of His vast creation. We were created for a great many things; many lost through the fall of Adam and yet the potential for fellowship has been restored. With that fellowship, comes relationship and with that relationship, comes responsibility. God Himself is responsible for all that He has created because He has relationship *to* and *with* His creation. God created the earth and mankind from it. Man's responsibility was to take care of and have dominion over everything on earth. God's responsibility was to take care of man. When God created Eve, it was out of an act of responsibility and further, it became man's responsibility to care for that gift from God. Eve was not given the same responsibility as Adam, but rather her charge was to help Adam to *be responsible*. So we have here an outline for each person's *level* of responsibility.

Should all things have gone as planned; time and eternity would be a much different place.

Response – ability; the word lends itself to the idea that there should be a favorable/unfavorable reaction to one's ability/inability to respond correctly within the bounds of relationship. Each part of God's creation has a purpose and a part to play in the grand scheme of things. The moon has as great a part to play as the tides that it effects on the earth. The spider is equally as valuable as its prey and the virus as instrumental as its host. Each has been specifically designed by 'The Creator' and all have their own individual function. Some things enjoy greater levels of position in God's plan than do others, but all are necessary.

"Hath not the potter power over the clay; of the same lump to make one vessel unto honor and another unto dishonor?"

Romans 9:21

Adam's position or level of responsibility was relinquished in the Garden of Eden. He was not released from his responsibility, but rather lost his dominance; one aspect of that responsibility. In other words he was demoted in rank. Think of it in the military terms of a general losing his stripes, but still serving in the armed forces. He no longer commands or retains the authority that he once possessed, but is still serving in the military yet in a lesser capacity. It is easy to speculate on what Adam *should* have done and on what his potential reaction *should* have been, but we are merely outsiders looking backward in time. The essence of the matter is that Adam had authority over Satan who had formerly lost his position and his responsibility. Adam was given authority over the serpent by God and also over the woman; to protect and instruct her. So what happened? A large portion of Satan's plan was to nullify Adam's *response*-ability and he used something that Adam *loved* as a way to do it. It was also Satan's plan to attack God by using something that He (God) loves and by turning it against Him. Fortunately God is never surprised or caught with His guard down. The plan of salvation was in place long before Satan's attack on the human race was formulated.

> *"...she took of the fruit thereof, and did eat, and gave also unto her husband with her; and he did eat."*

Genesis 3:6

Before we dissect this scripture, let's think outside of the box and use our imaginations for a moment. Science implies that mankind only uses 10% of their brain capacity. That means that we have or *had* 90% that we may potentially use but is currently dormant. Adam had to have been the most knowledgeable man to have ever lived. He walked with, was taught by and trained by the One True and Living God. He had a special relationship with the Father and walked with Him in Eden for an undisclosed amount of time. What did Adam have time to talk to God about? Did Adam ask God about how to cook and prepare food; what the sun stars and the moon were created to do; how his own body was created and what was it capable of doing? The answers that man has had handed down through the centuries and the discoveries we are now making in today's information age must pale in comparison to having such questions answered by God himself. What must Adam have taught his children and grand children? What did Adam know about the realm of the spirit and the laws that we are discussing presently? These are questions that should stimulate our minds to cause us to ask even more questions.

So here is how this works at least in theory. Adam's initial understanding of his charge and duty were perfect. Adam's initial understanding of Eve was perfect as were his charge and duty concerning her. Now scripture tells us that Eve was deceived and not Adam (1Timothy 2:14), but it does not say that Satan was with them when they ate. So the seed of doubt and mistrust was planted by Satan, probably at a time when Adam was not around. I often explain that being in the garden together can be like being in the same neighborhood together. It doesn't necessarily mean that they were standing next to one another. We do not know how large Eden was. Once the seed had taken root in Eve's heart it began to dictate the thoughts of her mind and eventually the actions of her body. All she had to do then was see the Tree of the Knowledge of Good and Evil and actually confirm the enemy's words. You must realize that

Satan planted the potential for lust in her heart as well; a seed needing only to be watered by the eyes in order to spring to life. So she takes the fruit from the tree… Scripture says that Adam was with her, but the implication is not necessarily that he was *with* her. Perhaps he was several meters away performing his duties or perhaps his back was turned. I've been to the supermarket *with* my wife and been in one isle while she was in another. Does this mean that I was not at the store *with* my wife? Did Adam see Eve pick the fruit and then consume it and not stop her? If this is the case then we would be suggesting that he was perhaps convinced before he actually partook of it. Did Adam have a partially consumed piece of fruit handed to him? In the first case, Adam becomes co-conspirator with Eve to free themselves from God's authority by becoming, ***"…as gods knowing good and evil** (Genesis 3:5)."* Even the false hope of being *'as gods'* was not presented to Adam, but rather to Eve, and this leads me to rest my theories on scenario number two. I believe that Eve presented Adam with a piece of fruit that had already been partially eaten. This scenario allows us to better understand why Adam's ability to respond correctly in this situation blossomed into a spiritual battle. In scenario one, as most people believe, Adam would have been just as deceived as Eve to have been there when the serpent was seducing her and then watching her retrieve the fruit and eat it in front of him. The test came when Adam was forced to choose how he would respond to the fruit that was then offered partially eaten.

The Law of Responsibility was challenged, at the point when Adam was forced to choose between the woman he had grown to love and God whom he had: known, trusted and with whom he had or should have had a stronger relationship.

Does Adam reject the fruit and allow Eve to suffer the consequences alone? Genesis 2:22 says that God brought the woman to Adam and Genesis 2:23 says that Adam named her 'Woman, or *taken out of man'* She was *his* responsibility as were the communicating of *his* (which became *their* instructions) duties to her as his helpmeet. Instead, Adam eats the fruit and suffers the consequences that should have been hers alone since the Word of God tells us that he was not deceived. Adam was not deceived by Satan's promises of being equal to God or by the forthcoming consequences of disobedience to God. He was *clearly* told what would be the consequences of eating the fruit.

We should never forget that Jesus and Adam are compared to one another (1 Corinthians 15:22, 45) in the sense that they both carried the potential for redemption concerning mankind. What Adam could not do in that he was weak through the flesh, Jesus could do in that He was strong through the spirit. Adam was a type of Christ in that he sacrificed himself for the sins of his wife as is Jesus, in that he sacrificed himself for the sins of His wife; those who would become the church or the 'bride of Christ'.

What Adam perhaps did not know was that in breaking the Law of Obedience, the hedge of protection was removed from them both. In addition, they were no longer covered by the glory of God and their third dimensional authority and their access to the blessings of God were lost. Not to mention that every aspect of man would die; the spirit was separated and died immediately. The body dies as the payment of time is paid and spent and the mind enters into a progressive degenerative state that worsens with each passing generation. Adam and Eve's transgression leaves a vacancy of position and authority that must be filled and who should step into that position but Satan. Jesus tells the seventy evangelists in Luke 10:18, *"I beheld Satan as lightning fall from heaven."*

There is no mention of Satan being given any position whatsoever over the earth or in the Garden of Eden, however, it also does not say that he was denied access to anything or any place on earth, hence his presence in Genesis. [Read the book of Job where God asks Satan, "Where have you been?"] Ephesians 2:2 calls Satan, *"...the prince of the power of the air..."*, and John 12:31 calls him, *"... the prince of this world..."* Where did he come by these titles and authority? The positions were vacant! So like the thief that scripture calls him, he stole them. In Luke 10:19, however, Jesus follows up His previous statement by revealing to the seventy that mankind's authority is partially restored and soon to be fully restored upon his finished work on the cross.

Even though scripture tells us that Adam was not deceived, our politically correct society will not allow a solid teaching from that standpoint. Adam is clearly a type of Christ and must be treated as such or we fall into the same trap that is laid by evolution that we are merely random pawns in the game of life. The outcome was not random, but rather a consideration of man's choice; of freewill; a choice that God in His omniscience had prepared for either way.

Did Adam neglect his responsibility? No, he made the wrong choice as men of responsibility often do. Wrong, only from the standpoint of not trusting God and maybe putting his love for his wife before God. This is where Abraham succeeded; he trusted God with what he loved most. There are always consequences for our decisions. When we make the correct choices the consequences are favorable; when we make the wrong choices we are made uncomfortable by our decisions. The consequences for this particular decision had repercussions in every realm and for every party.

- The first consequence was outlined in Genesis 2:17 – **DEATH.** This was, as I have already stated, spiritual, physical and mental death to mankind. Death was also brought to God's creation as God made clothing for man from an obviously innocent animal. (I'm thinking it was a sheep?)
- The second was that Adam and Eve would be removed from the Garden of Eden never to return. The punishment prevented them from being caretakers of the things of God (the priestly aspect has been removed) and from eating from the Tree of Life (eternal fellowship with God displaced). [The angels were set into place after God removed them from the Garden Eden so that the angels would *keep* the way. That was to prevent them from eating from the Tree of Life and living in a sinful state for eternity. This simply set up God's plan for Christ to come on the seen and point the direction back toward the Tree of Life through His Son.]

> **So he drove out the man; and he placed at the east of the garden of Eden Cherubims, and a flaming sword <u>which turned every way</u>, to keep the way of the tree of life.**

> **Genesis 3:24**

- **The Serpent** – was cursed to eat dust and go upon his belly all the days of his life. Not only was this a symbol of humility, but also a curse that will last into eternity according to Isaiah 65:25.
- **Satan** – was sentenced to be forever defeated at Calvary by Christ, by the seed of the woman. The punishment is eternity in the lake of Fire. He was initially successful in removing Adam from his position, but he did not succeed in regaining his own. At best, he is allowed to plague mankind at present.
- **Adam** – man's responsibility is still the same, but the authority to maintain his position and fellowship has been severed. Responsibility without recognized authority is always a struggle. His duties as the man that God created are the same. He must still instruct and protect his wife and inherently their children. He longs to take care of the things of God and to fellowship with his creator, but the way is obscured. He does these things under extreme adversity; what was once simple has become abnormally difficult. Man is now at odds with his creator, his wife, the world and Satan.
- **Creation** - is now under a curse and therefore will not yield to man the way that it had formerly. It awaits destruction on the final day when God will destroy it by fire and create a new heaven and earth.
- **Eve** – the vessel by which man would glimpse the intimacy of God in marriage and preview God's creative facet by reproducing offspring would now do so in extreme sorrow. It is, for the most part, in intense pain that women bare children even to this day. Whereas men and women were created equal in spirit (Genesis 1:27) and formed equally (Adam from the dust of the ground and Eve from an aspect of Adam), the married woman would now be made subject to her husband. Her *desire* would be to her husband or rather to continually

force him move in the position for which God created him. [The Hebrew word for DESIRE is **shûwq** – *shook*: meaning to run after or over, to overflow] The double meaning is appropriate for she *runs after him* because God has created her for him, but *over him* because man is to never forget his role as husband, so he is ever forced to maintain his Godly role in the life of his wife or be usurped by her.

- **Mankind** – is cursed to be born into a sinful state with a sinful nature. The consequences of sin and death are constantly warring to keep him separated from God.

The Law of responsibility is never to be taken lightly. God has placed us in our respective positions as husbands, wives, mothers, fathers, pastors, prophets, ministers, teachers, etc… and with those positions come responsibilities. In many instances we are responsible for not only ourselves, but others as well. We are responsible for making sure our children are raised in the care and admonition of God. Obeying this law is a demonstration of our desire to remain in God's will and acknowledgment that we respect what He has placed in our care.

Another way to look at Genesis 3:24, is that God placed cherubim in the East of Eden, with a flaming sword that turned every way, to '**keep**' the way to the Tree of Life. (God always wanted mankind to eat from the Tree of Life. That is why the angels were charged with ***keeping the way***! Scripture does not say that their intention was to keep Adam and Eve out of God's garden forever, only to stop them from eating of that particular tree. To keep the way gives us the impression that the cherubim are '*on guard*' and man *can* re-enter and partake of the Tree of Life with the right credentials; those credentials being the acceptance of the free gift of God through His Son 'Christ Jesus' sacrifice. The cherubim's are, however and were keeping the way in preparation for the day when 'every way' could return and eat. The intention of expelling Adam and Eve from the garden, at that time, was to prevent them from eating from the Tree of Life while, now, in their sinful flesh. In scripture, the sword of the spirit is the Word of God [Ephesians 6:17] and the swords that the cherubim's are holding are flaming swords turning *everyone's* way to keep and bring mankind back to the Tree of Life! [I can imagine that one of those cherubim got leave of his duties to actually roll back the stone from Christ's grave saying to himself, *"I have been waiting and guarding for a very long time, for __this__ day, when the way to the Tree of Life would be reopened!"*] Place what I have just written along side this scripture: **"I am the WAY, the TRUTH, and the LIFE!"**

> *Jesus saith unto him, I am the __way__, the __truth__, and the __life__: no man cometh unto the Father, but by me.*

John 14:6

The way that the cherubim were keeping was *__the__* way through Christ Jesus. Remember that God knows the end and has, since the beginning; that's why He is the Alpha and Omega. The *__truth__* is in direct opposition to what Satan the 'Father of Lies' told Eve in Eden. We do not get to go through any other way than the truth. For this reason, God stipulates that the *__way__* back to the 'tree' of life is through truth; the flaming swords!

> *For the word of God [is] quick, and powerful, and sharper than any two-edged sword, piercing even to the dividing asunder of soul and spirit, and of the joints and marrow, and [is] a discerner of the thoughts and intents of the heart.*

Hebrews 4:12

Finally, God always sees man as a tree; bearing fruit, not bearing fruit; bearing good fruit or bearing bad fruit. This is why Jesus is:

John 15:1 *I am the __true vine__, and my Father is the husbandman.*

*[Other scriptures that refer or elude to men as trees are: Matthew 3:10, Mark 8:24, Luke 3:9, and Jude 1:12]

Law #7: "The Law of Reciprocity"

The Law of Reciprocity is simply this, "You shall reap what you sow". How many of us think we know this law? In Genesis 2:16-17, God did not request that man not eat of the tree; He did not ask him not to eat of the tree; it was a command! God was not only instructing the man of His perfect will, but He was also teaching Adam a basic law, that in retrospect effects every aspect of our three dimensional beings. The disobedience perpetrated by Adam and Eve in Eden allowed sin and death to enter into a perfect world. The impact of disobedience as we have stated, reverberates through all dimensions and creates a chain reaction that will effect all future generations. Again we see some of the same consequences:

- The physical repercussion of breaking this law is *physical* death.
- The mental repercussion of breaking this law is a constant deterioration of God's value system within the heart of man.
- The spiritual repercussion of breaking this law is separation from God and *eternal* death.

This spiritual law has a physical counterpart: "***for every action there is an equal and opposite reaction.***" This is a statement of NEWTON'S LAW OF ACTION VS. REACTION. The things we envision, think of, and pray for cause movement in the spiritual realm. In turn, the answers are *manifest* in the physical realm. Things that take place in the physical realm can also have effects in other realms. We must take care in everything that we do, think or speak. A person that consistently complains of physical infirmity is actually speaking into the spiritual realm and tearing down their hedge of protection in the physical realm. They may be destroying or giving Satan a license to destroy their immune system. They give the enemy legal right to attack their bodies by misusing the power of their words. Remember, God has given man alone the power of speech along with the ability to manifest those words and thoughts. A person that pursues a life of seeking after wealth will eventually become a slave to that pursuit. They will begin to work longer hours, take on responsibilities that revolve around their quest, sacrifice relationships and eventually forsake all that they once held important in order to achieve an unobtainable goal. Someone who continually engages in viewing pornography will invite spirits that preside over that area of sin to plague him or her. They can become obsessed with *all* forms of sexual sins. They may begin with the seemingly innocent masturbation (and I have heard many Christian pastors okay this activity for young men. Aside from photographs and movies this will lead them to graduate to orgies, same sex or multiple sexual relationships, sodomy, fetish sex, sado-masochism, and even bestiality, simply because a little is never enough. Satan will see to that!

Look at every aspect of life this way; from children, relationships, money and so on; we work in all areas of life for *seeds* to plant. We must then wait to see what grows and brings forth an increase. With children, we work to train them in hopes that they will bring forth Godly children. My mother trained me and now she has an increase of a Godly daughter-in-law and six godly grandchildren from me alone. When my children have children, they will bring me an increase, but that increase can also be attributed back to my mother. Think about the one person who ministered to Billy Graham.

In our relationships we live Godly before our friends and those who know us and watch as God blesses and prospers us. We minister to our friends and our associates at various times of necessity and are ministered to by those friends who share our faith in the gospel. As mature Christians, we look for the Holy Spirit of God to minister to us by watching the defeats and victories of those around us. These interactions cause us to tailor our behavior and actions to aid us in our walk.

With our money, we tithe 10% and are blessed by the 90%. God uses the 10% to test our faith, spread the gospel, feed the hungry, shelter the poor, and we in turn are continually blessed with the ability to give. It's amazing what God can do with 10% and a good steward. We should strive to make as much use of our 90% as God does of the 10% that we give in tithes.

Let's also look at our words and actions in the sense of sowing and reaping. How much of what we *say* is profitable for the kingdom? How much of what we *do* is profitable for the kingdom? Not much on average. Why? Because our mind set is not continually <u>focused</u> on the kingdom. We are generally not continuously in evangelistic mode, or doctrinal mode, or service mode, or ministry mode, or exhortation mode. Much of this has to do with the times that we live in as well as society. Think about the early church; it appears that they were able to *accomplish* daily living without becoming *ruled* by daily living. Therefore we see in Acts 2 that worldly possessions and circumstances were not a hindrance for the saints. All throughout the book of Acts, because of their continual kingdom speech and kingdom actions; signs, wonders and miracles were ever present. We also see that God added to the body of believers by the thousands daily! Prosperity preaching should not dwell on how to make the believer earthly rich, but rather on how to bring increase in the areas of life that will ultimately benefit the kingdom of God. We should be hearing prosperous speech, dedicated service to God and to our fellow-servants in Christ, ministering the gospel, exhortation, admonition toward the end of holiness and sanctification, blessings, and helps to the needy. This will bring the type of prosperity and increase that will be mutually beneficial to us and our God.

If we look at life in the sense of farming, we understand that what we plant will grow. If we plant seeds of destruction, then we shall reap destruction. If we plant God's word in our hearts, then we will harvest the blessings that the Father has promised. The older generation understood that when they taught us that, *"What goes around comes around!"*

Law #8: "The Law of Debt"

In principle, the Law of Debts is the same in every realm. It goes hand in hand with the Law of Reciprocity. It is what we accrue and what is owed to us; after what we produce because of our works. Whether we submit to this law or even understand this particular theory, we *will* 'pay up', so to speak, in one way or another.

79

The Christian view is that *God* created man. Every opposing view seeks to escape the very essence of this law - accountability! Evolution, Reincarnation, Scientology, New Age Doctrine, and so forth all seek to remove accountability from the human psyche. So if we adhere to the latter viewpoints then eventually morality has been done away with. Once morality is erased then each person is allowed to live as they see fit whether it inadvertently is counterproductive to society or not. Think about what is beginning to become the standard belief as far as 'truth; is concerned? The enemy has injected the idea into society that each person's truth is acceptable to them and so we should accept that person's truth out of our love for humanity and with two simple words 'politically correct'; morality is **gone**! Satan has spun his same web the same way yet again. God's Word says that we are to speak the truth in love [Ephesians 4:15]; that truth being God's truth so that we grow in Christ; not each *man's* truth. The point is that the idea of society or being social (nowadays we even have 'social networks), which is a human necessity, requires that we interact with one another in a capacity that compliments the needs of the whole rather than the desires of the few or the one - God. The enemy has elevated this to a point that mankind can no longer function without this. When accountability is removed then the ability to interact socially is negated and eventually lends itself to chaos. Exactly what we are seeing in today's world. If we choose to believe the former, that we are accountable to our creator, then what is it that we owe God? My initial response would be the reverse of that or, *"what don't we owe Him?"* Man was created to fellowship with God, hence the propensity to be *social* creatures or rather we have a commonality in our creator. We were created to exemplify God's will and sovereignty in the third dimension while being created with free will and the ability to experience the totality of His glory. Initially this is a wonderful concept, but there are extenuating circumstances. Satan has perverted God's creation by introducing sin into this perfect equation, thereby necessitating a savior to redeem us and make possible reconciliation with our creator. We **owe,** *in this,* a debt that we can never repay nor could have ever paid in the first place. What could we offer God for eternal life when we have an indwelling nature of sin separating us from His presence? What could we ever *do* to gain access to heaven? Nothing! That is why salvation is a **gift** from God to us.

> *"For by grace are ye saved through faith; and that not of yourselves: it is a gift of God: <u>not of works</u> lest any man should boast."*

Ephesians 2:8, 9

Christ has borne the burden of our sins and for this we are bonded to Him by this debt. Our eternal lives are indebted to Him and so as Christians (followers of Jesus the Messiah) we serve Him gladly and set an example for others. Paul says,

> *"But I would that ye should understand brethren, that the things which happen unto me have fallen out rather unto the furtherance of the gospel: so that my bonds in Christ are manifest in all the palace, and in all other places; And many of the brethren in the Lord waxing confident by my bonds, are much more bold to speak the Word without fear".*

Philippians 1:12-14

In the physical realm, a man pays what he owes for integrity sake and/or for fear of the ensuing consequences. There is a burden that one must bear until the debt is relieved or has been paid. It is also this way in the spiritual realm. While it is true that salvation is a gift, the debt of *gratitude* should be the common response. Showing gratitude means that we will not purposely place ourselves again in the situation of being willfully sinful thereby creating a barrier between ourselves and God. We follow Christ because He leads the way concerning the application of that gratitude being that He is and was without sin.

As I have already discounted any belief system that ultimately excuses us from accountability, I place my faith in the grandiose idea that we all must hold within us some factor of accountability; some knowledge of our own sin nature. It is intrinsic to our nature and thus the application of operating within the moral guidelines of society lights our very souls whether we choose to ignore it or dumb it down or not. When we return a lost item or give back to our community or correct a child, we are lifted internally. That is an inward clue of our spiritual connection with a righteous creator. A popular concept today is that, *"There is no right or wrong, good or evil; only decisions and consequences".* This is even the theme of a popular video game, but there *is* right and there *is* wrong; both good and evil. To deny these is to attempt to deny our very programming as is also the idea that we have no divine creator. It is a perplexing concept that man tries to deny what is hardwired into every part of his being. The new modern way is to question *all* that says or points to God especially His children. Paul describes it in this way in Romans 1 he writes, **"For the invisible things of Him from the creation of the world are <u>clearly</u> seen, being understood by the things that are made, even His eternal power and Godhead; so that they are <u>without</u> excuse...who changed the truth of God into a lie, and worshiped and served the creature more than the creator..."**

Here is our mortal requirement and should be our moral standard for accountability to God. Paul is explaining to us that the things that we can physically see are an undeniable indication of what we cannot physically see. God's creation speaks for itself, but man has denied God in hopes of removing his own accountability *to* God. Paul says that the truth has been changed into a lie and that we bow down to and are servants to the created <u>things</u> as opposed to the one who had the power to create those things.

Evolution is a 'faith' that removes all purpose and accountability from the young minds to whom it is taught. Mankind is reduced to nothing more special or exalted than an animal. Random probability and natural selection hold man answerable to no one. Reincarnation offers innumerable chances to achieve enlightenment through the idea of repetitious *works* and, in this, bypasses the sovereignty of God. Man is in a continuous cycle of achieving perfection and in so doing need not rely on the finished work of Christ. Scientology boasts a strict morality, yet makes man accountable to *man* rather than holding him accountable to his creator; and so it is with other belief systems.

If Paul is correct about man being, *"...without excuse..."* in not believing in God, then that very knowledge causes us to be indebted. Does not every man who realizes that he is not an act of random chance first feel the desire to know his creator and second have a longing to know what his creator desires of him? We then thank Paul that we are able to recognize that we are not the ultimate authority, but rather we were under authority. In Matthew 8:9 we see that a Roman soldier, who was not a follower of Christ, understood this concept better than Christ's followers. He had enough rank to command, but he still recognized the hierarchy of authority and the need for submission to that authority.

The Law of Debt obligates us to *render* or to be *rendered too* what it is that we are due according to the Law of Reciprocity. These two laws are very closely related, but are by no means the same. The Law of Reciprocity says that we shall reap according to what we have sown while The Law of Debt states that not only shall we reap or receive, but that we are often obligated to give or be given to. We are compelled by The Law of Debt to give something back to show that we respect the source of our blessing.

In agricultural terms we may look at this requirement as: sowing the seeds that we have been given, planting a different seed according to what we've been given, taking care of and nurturing the soil, or just simply pulling out the weeds so that the plant can grow unhindered. A true farmer knows that there is more to farming than just the harvest or, in other words, living under The Law of Reciprocity only. Reaping is often the easy part; if not easy, then at least always filled with hope and expectation. Paying back (planting), whether obligated or implored, is not always easy and often takes discipline and practice.

Let us use this law to our advantage. Let us give as we have been given and return in kind so that we will understand how fulfilling it is from a 'God' perspective and create opportunity for ourselves whereby we can be trusted to receive.

Law #9: "The Law of The Mind"

When dealing with the mind, we are treading upon unfamiliar territory. The mind is virtually unmapped, uncharted territory. It seems to exist in all four realms or at least have the capacity to transcend the bounds between them. It most assuredly interacts on each one of these levels and therefore is subject to stimuli from each. The decisive factor for victory is determined by the mind's harmony with either the *spirit* or the *flesh*. If we strive toward and are able to align our mind and spirit, then we can rest assured that we will obtain spiritual recompense. If we have aligned our mind with our flesh then we have formed an alliance whereby we will insure compensation according to that flesh. If we spend all of our time catering to the flesh, then the physical man is the part of our being that is exalted and becomes dominant. As Christians, we seek to align our minds with our spirits and hence reap spiritual things. tells us, concerning the mind,

"Let this mind be in you, which is also in Christ Jesus..."

Philippians 2:5

Without expounding on this particular scripture, we can only conclude that in order to obtain spiritual prominence we must determine to have the mind of Christ in us. With His mind and spirit in unison, Jesus was able to bring His whole body under subjection and thus obtain a reward beyond measure. Philippians 2:9 states that God has highly exalted Jesus for His own glory and that God has given Him a name that is above every name.

God understands that the largest portion of the battle takes place in the mind of man. That is why Satan attacks the mind first. It is why he attacked the weaker vessel, Eve, as opposed to Adam. Eve's instruction and the knowledge of her duties and responsibilities came from Adam and not from God. Satan attacked her mind, and as I have previously stated, the changing of one simple word in the truth, makes it a lie.

And be not conformed to <u>this </u>world: but be ye transformed by the <u>renewing </u>of your <u>mind</u>, that ye may <u>prove </u>what [is] that good, and acceptable, and perfect, will of God.

Romans 12:2

When talking about warfare, we all know that when a target is located it must line up with the sights of the instruments that we are using. Once we have our objective in our sights, then all of our instrumentation will line up those weapons in the direction of our target. It is what sets or aligns our path. Once we order our path, we can then prescribe some form of action to it and remain reasonably sure; without factoring in outside interference; that the objective will be met.

Another truth about the mind is that it is the field of battle. [Read Joyce Meyer's book: 'Battlefield of the Mind'] It is within our minds that the fighting is taking place, where the bullets are flying, and where missiles are being launched. The focus of the mind can be derailed by the enemy thereby throwing our physical and spiritual man into turmoil. People who are depressed lose weight or can become obese, their hair can fall out and they can become physically sick. They can become suicidal or homicidal. Depression is only one form of the enemies attack on our minds. The enemy can skew a man's reality and cause his view of the world to be inconsistent with true facts that ultimately blur that person's view of reality. A person that does not have a true grasp on reality is harmful to both himself and society. Even the unsaved man or woman has been mentally blinded by the enemy to never mentally focus on sin with regard to eternity. Remember, what transpires within our mind determines our decisions. If we lose the battle there, then we can essentially be manipulated by the enemy for *his* purposes. Imagine a computers hard drive. It is designed to function in a certain way and to respond to certain stimuli like the mouse, keyboard, printer, software and hardware. If we introduce software or the internet to our hardware, then we must take specific precautions to make sure that the hard drive is not compromised. It takes only a few seconds for a virus, a worm, or a hacker to corrupt our computer's brain. It is the same with the mind. It does not take the enemy long to hack into our minds and find out where to download software that will cause our minds to crash! The software that Satan introduces to our physical hard drives appears to be user friendly and feigns as if it is compatible with our systems. It in fact carries a very dangerous virus called 'sin-sation' that can destroy the mental program of the unsaved and saved alike. The unsaved are born with this virus which continues to corrupt their systems from birth until death. The saved have had there systems restored and rebooted and now have anti-virus protection, but they must run a 'systems check' on a regular basis as highlighted by,

> **"Study to show thyself approved unto God, a workman that needeth not to be ashamed, rightly dividing the word of truth."**

> **2 Timothy 2:15**

We sincerely cannot go any further with this particular discussion of the mind, for to do so would ultimately lead us down rabbit holes that would prevent us from finishing this our study. A final note is in order however. Our minds are designed to be an asset to whatever we are aligning it with. God the Father, God the Son, and The Spirit of God are constantly and consistently of one mind. So too were the minds of men created in this fashion or rather for this purpose. It is very important that we note that when our minds are in line with our spirits and our spirits are in line with the will of God then the next step is to align our minds with those persons who are like-minded. In other words, if we take the example of Pentecost, the disciples were all in one place, on one day (Sabbath) and on one accord. This is the reason that the Holy Spirit was able to in-fill every person there to the extent that their language was transformed so that they could communicate the gospel message of Christ to those who may not have otherwise listened or even understood. It was to the glory of God the Father through Jesus Christ and His teachings that allowed the disciples to align their minds and come together on one accord, in the same place; at the same time. What keeps us from having that collective power corporately today is the fact that we are *not* on one accord and do *not* have *all* things in common.

Sidenote: *Remember that God's word gives us the outline for how man is to speak in other tongues. Today what we hear come across pulpits and in prayers is the enemy taking us backward to the tower of Babel. The language is at best babel and there is no understanding whatsoever. No man can understand the other mans speech, yet it is being portrayed as 'holiness' and accepted without two or three witnesses as God commands that should accompany the speaking in tongues. This is the criteria for the speaking in other tongues. The fact is that the disciples were 'understood' and the word of God gives us the specific languages minus the different dialects that have since come from those languages. Seventeen to be exact.*

Acts chapter 2 v.9 Parthians, and Medes, and Elamites, and the dwellers in Mesopotamia, and in Judæa, and Cappadocia, in Pontus, and Asia, v.10 Phrygia, and Pamphylia, in Egypt, and in the parts of Libya about Cyrene, and strangers of Rome, Jews and proselytes, v.11 Cretes and Arabians, <u>we do hear them speak in our tongues the wonderful works of God.</u>

That was the purpose of the gift of tongues; so that the gospel would be spread throughout the world. Note that every man heard in their own language the wonderful works of God. Does anyone ever tell you nowadays that they heard any of the works of God or do they simply fall backwards under another spirit and wake up claiming that they have a new revelation? Further let me add that this is often accompanied by these people being slain in the spirit or 'killed in their spirit'. This is what the word *slain* means! This was a movement started on Asuza Street in Los Angeles, California by former slaves who were holding onto their heritage from Africa. There is no place in God's word where falling backwards is ever a good thing. In fact, just the opposite.

Law #10: "The Law of Pre-Destiny"

"For those whom He foreknew, He also predestined to be conformed to the image of Christ"

Pre-Destiny does not imply Pre-Determination. This must be cleared up first and foremost or our discussion will be extinguished before it has had a chance to begin. The question often posed is that, *"If God knows the future, then mankind can never exist as an agent of 'free will!'* This statement appears to be initially true, but when we dissect it the opposite becomes clear. The way that this topic should be taught is that pre-destiny does not frustrate God's grace. The fact that God has foreknowledge of the future does not deem Him responsible for the actions of mankind. Mankind has been created with a free will. This can be illustrated in the following scenario.

"I have been invited to a banquet in a mansion set high atop a hill. The mansion overlooks the highway that leads up to the estate. As I am speeding along the highway in my car, with the music turned up full blast, I am unaware of an accident that has occurred further up ahead. My host is able to see both my car on the highway and the accident ahead simultaneously from his vantage point. He decides to call me on my cell phone to warn me to slow down and be cautious of the accident. I, however am unable to hear my phone because of the music and the fact that I am preoccupied with thoughts of the banquet as well as taking in the scenery. At some point, along the path that I am taking, I will either notice the phone ringing or I will continue forward to impending doom..."

If the road behind me represents my past; the portion of the road that I am on, in my car, represents my present; and the road ahead with all of its twists, turns and impending doom represents my future, I cannot rationalize that an onlooker would determine *my* actions within *my* car. I did not say that an onlooker *could not* determine my actions, I stated that I cannot *assume* that he will. The car that I drive is my own. The road on which I choose to travel is a result of my own decision. The volume of the music and the admiration of the scenery is a product of my own personal desires. The fact that my host has foreknowledge does not obligate him to action. Now if the host is God (of course this is the point) then, the degree to which He may go to get my attention may depend on a number of factors; the most urgent being **grace**, the second being **mercy**. No matter what the case; whether I notice that God is calling me on my cell, or whether I choose to play my radio at a descent level, or choose to watch the road rather than the scenery, or whether or not I choose to drive at a safe speed; this is the 'free will' that God has created in me and for me.

I can further use this example to illustrate the fact that God is not bound by or confined to time, but rather exists outside of it. Ecclesiastes 9:11 tells us that: *"… time and chance happen to everyone."* As the onlooker is not confined to the stretch of highway on which I travel in the scenario, He is also not subject to what may happen along that time line or stretch of road at any given point. Scripture says that we can see that God's viewpoint is so far above and different from our own that it would be an exercise in futility to try to understand things outside of time, beyond what we find in scripture, because we *are* confined to time.

Isaiah 55:8,9 tells us that God's answer to our thinking is this: *"For my thoughts [are] not your thoughts, neither [are] your ways my ways, saith the LORD. For [as] the heavens are higher than the earth, so are my ways higher than your ways, and my thoughts than your thoughts."*

God is the host in this scenario and we are *all* invited to the banquet. The only thing that is pre-destined (as scripture plainly states) is our place setting at the banquet table. Revelation 19:9 says, *"Blessed are they which are called to the marriage supper of the lamb…"* Who will attend?; only those that exercise their 'free will' to accept Christ's invitation and attend the banquet. All they need do is RSVP the invitation, [that has been written in blood], to come as Christ Jesus' guest.

There is a commonly held theory concerning predestination and election that removes man's 'free will' from the equation. This is a very dangerous standpoint. To assume that God has not relinquished

His sovereignty over man's will is to reduce us to automatons or robots. It is a narrow minded view that essentially flies in the face of what God is able to accomplish either by using His divine omnipotence or by choosing not to use it. God *could* have elected certain ones to go to heaven and certain persons to go to hell, but what then would we have to 'choose' concerning Christ and salvation? The standpoint that upholds that God receives glory, whether a man is preordained for eternal life or eternal death, is that God recognizes that some vessels will choose to be vessels of for honor and some will choose to be for dishonor.

> *"But in a great house there are not only vessels of gold and of silver, but also of wood and of earth; and some to honor and some to dishonor."*

> **2 Timothy 2:20**

The great house in this case is the house of humanity. We must remember who we are; we are not the creator! Yet we still have free will to choose the right road or the one that leads to destruction.

> *"Surely your turning of things upside down shall be esteemed as the potter's clay: for shall the work say of him that made it, He made me not? or shall the thing framed say of him that framed it, He had no understanding?*

> Isaiah 29:16

This is exactly what mankind is saying today.

To use this scripture to say that God has chosen some persons to go to hell for His glory is wrong. The first part of this passage states that, "…in a great house…" that is to say that those vessels of dishonor are already *within* the great house, that house being humanity. Remember the bible is written to the elect; the saved! For the unsaved it is for them to be able to receive Christ. This scripture only speaks of the level of blessing and hierarchy of position that will exist in heaven for the vessels that shall be honored. How can we know that we are elect if God has already determined that some are slated for hell? The terminology dishonor let's us know where certain vessels will appear in this 'great house.' Why would we bother with accepting Christ as a demonstration of our free will if, in the end, we have *no* choice; no ultimate 'free will' to choose? The bottom line is that The Doctrine of Election or The Doctrine of Predestination does not frustrate grace. Who God preordained or predestined or elected was "whosoever will. The word say let him come!" Read Revelation 22:17 and ask yourself whether or not every man has the opportunity set before him to come!

The question will also arise, "what about those that never have the opportunity to hear the gospel?" Two things, the first being that if we serve the kind of God that the bible describes then we may factor in what I call 'Divine Providence'. God is not described as fair in scripture, but rather as just. It would not be just, at least according to our finite intellect, to deny any man some form of opportunity, whether it is spelled out for us in scripture or not. So we should assume, of what we know about God, that there is some form of provision made for that person who cannot hear the gospel. We can safely say that God is not pouring mentally challenged or autistic people into hell. They have gifts and talents and were created for a purpose and thereby have a function in God's plan. The second answer to this question is Romans 1:16-20. In v.16 we read about the power of God to save everyone that believeth. The scripture also tells us, as I have already mentioned, that the fact that there is a God in heaven is made apparent to all whether they have heard the gospel or not. [Romans 1:20] It is built into us! Surely God is not purposely shielding the eyes of some that they may go to hell, but rather every man has the opportunity to believe and accept. The verse says that it is for God's chosen people first Israelites] and then to those outside of those covenant people [Gentiles] so that we see opportunity for every man. Verse 18 shows us that there is a penalty to pay for all who hear and then reject the truth. Again we see the preeminence of choice. In verses 19 and in verse 20 we see that even the person in the Amazon or African jungle that never hears the gospel has no excuse because the creation of God speaks of His existence and omnipotence. These verses even go as far as to say that no man has an excuse, with the exception of those that are physically or mentally incapable of receiving the gospel message. They must at the very least have the ability to reason logically and know that they did not create themselves.

>*"Come now, and <u>let us reason together</u>, saith the LORD: though your sins be as scarlet, they shall be as white as snow; though they be red like crimson, they shall be as wool."*

Isaiah 1:18

If we are born into sinful flesh and yet do not have the ability to reason with God, then we cannot accept the gift of salvation that require our reasoning skills. This requires us to think abut God's offer an then make a decision and choose. If we are not able to do that, then an eternity in hell would simply be unjust.

I point this out to show that God is a righteous and just God. Our system of justice and internal conscience are a reflection of God creating us in His likeness and in His image.

Why is pre-destiny a spiritual law? Simply put, Since God can see and has foreknowledge of future events, then pre-destiny becomes a law simply because the consequences of certain actions are pre-determined. Certain consequences that have been set into place to deter us from *actions* that will hinder us from being able to make the correct decisions; decisions that are beneficial to eternal life. We see yet again, the presupposition of choice and 'free will.' Pre-destiny exists as a spiritual law simply because law exists. We should not think that as Christians we are excluded from this law or that because we are under grace that the law does not apply. Christ Himself has stated that He did not come to destroy the law, but rather that the law through Him might be fulfilled. states,

>*"Think not that I am come to destroy the law or the prophets: I am come not to destroy, but to fulfill. For verily I say unto*

you, till heaven and earth pass, one jot or one tittle shall in no wise pass from the law, till all be fulfilled."

Matthew 5:17

The entire point is that the Law of Reciprocity is always present within the Law of Pre-Destination. They are a part of one another in the regard that pre-destiny is only God's knowledge of what we have planted.

Law #10: "The Law of Creation"

"In the beginning God created..."

Genesis 1:1

Being made in the image and likeness of God, we have similar yet limited capabilities. We are finite while God is infinite. Some people understand this, but become have been deceived by Satan and afford too much authority to man, ignoring the limitations associated with being created beings and that man can make himself immortal. A prime example of this is the New Age Movement. New Age activists understand that mankind has untapped promise and that we do not fully utilize our mental and spiritual potential. Their fatal flaw is that they attempt to abound in these areas without permission and/ or guidance from God. They ultimately leave themselves open to spiritual attack by the enemy because they lack the protection that we receive by being in God's will. I recently read a book called 'God's Debris' that seemed to have all the answers to man's questions concerning God or to such things it alludes. While the author takes no responsibility for the ramifications that believing such ideas can have detrimental effects on an individual, he includes no disclaimer to the extent that these are simply *his* ideas and thoughts. At the end of the book, the narrator claims to have been having a discussion with an Avatar. In Hinduism, this is the belief of the human incarnation of a Hindu God. [Research will show that the word Avatar has crept into the English language and many cartoons and video games as well as Facebook who allows people to create their own Avatars. There is also a very popular movie by the same name in which humans are technologically linked to grown bodies that by comparison to the human body would seem like Giants or God's. The strange or perhaps scary part of this movie is that at the end the human spirit is translated into one of these bodies.]

In essence, what the book, 'God's Debris' was proclaiming was that it was up to mankind to determine his own fate, as it were, because he himself had not only God like qualities, but because of God in him (as a portion of God's Debris), he himself was God. The book spoke of God destroying Himself and about God's inability to see His own future and other such things that only a finite mind could conceive. The point is that this is all completely New Age doctrine that misleads mankind into believing that he can be his own God. The odd thing about it is that knowledge of the One True God and His Word would quickly allow us to recognize this as the very first deception of Satan used against Eve in the Garden of Eden.

> *"For God doth know that in the day ye eat thereof, then your eyes shall be opened, and ye shall be as God's knowing good and evil."*

Genesis 3:1-5

My intention is not to pick on the book God's Debris, but rather I use it because the argument is the opposite of God's Law of Creation. It poses the point that God, with His 'finite' imagination, can challenge Himself with nothing more than destroying Himself and reforming Himself through mankind. It occurs to me that the very word 'God' suggests something beyond our understanding and for us to speculate on His plans and motives, beyond what we have been given in scripture, is an exercise in sheer foolishness without considering to ask Him is an exercise in foolishness. God's character is, and never has been, nor ever will be that of destruction for destruction sake or out of boredom. It is true that God destroys, but only with the intent to purge and to cleanse or protect. Never has it been for lack of imagination or out of shear cruelty.

As God has seen fit to create and has derived personal pleasure in the act thereof, so He has placed within us the ability; to be creative and to create shows our connection to our creator. The ability to be creative is a product of being self aware. I am not necessarily speaking of the ability to reproduce; that is a blessing as well as the resourceful ability to recreate in our image the way that God has created us. Creativity is an inward desire to produce, for the most part, something that is pleasing to oneself; and in most instances, for that end alone. As we think, we desire to fill a need to be productive, to be useful, and to give value to our existence from our own perspective. Morality should never be sacrificed or anything that places us in opposition to God's will. God has placed within us this ability and desire for His glory and His alone. The painter is fulfilled in the masterpiece created by his own hands, but never as much as the painter who has captured the vision and idea of his creator. In other words, the Renaissance, arguably the greatest period creation, in terms of art, in man's existence, is fraught with man's attempt to capture and put into expression his ideas about God and the fourth dimension. *"A proud man is the man who builds a house with his own hands and envisions himself raising a family there."* He, however, is no prouder than the man used of God to witness salvation to a sinner knowing that this man will have a *home* with God and an eternal family. No man has ever been more proud than of his own child and their *success* in life except the man whose child has found their *purpose* in life according to God's plan.

In the mental and spiritual realms, we have the same potential to create as does the Father. It no doubt takes an act of faith to make manifest something that was merely a thought within time. I believe that God has shown us a small portion of His own greatness in giving us this ability. We think; we act in faith; we manifest... Is this not how God created us? (Genesis) The Law of Creation is that if we act in faith and are not hindered by outside forces, then our thoughts become manifest within our reality. This could be compared to **Newton's Law of Motion** in physics – *"An object will continue in a straight line and at a constant speed unless acted upon by an outside force..."* We have the ability to create as long as we are not hindered by doubt, fear, Satan, low self esteem, etc... What we create is an indication that we are like our creator, but ultimately better and more fulfilling to us when it glorifies God. God produced all that is in the earth, the plants, the animals, the fish, the creeping things, etc. These and man in like manner produce after their own kind to the glory of God. Since God has created man in His own image and likeness, this gives man authority to do certain things that God's other creation does not have. David says in psalms 139:14, ***"...for I am fearfully (with great care) and wonderfully (unsurpassable and perfectly) made..."*** or created. Since we are self-aware, we can contemplate not only our existence, but also what we bring into existence. This is applicable to the mental, physical, and spiritual realms. Scripture tells us that we are to think about our thoughts and take every one captive making them subject to the authority of Christ.

> ***"Casting down imaginations and every high thing that exalteth itself against the knowledge of God, and bringing into captivity every thought to the obedience of Christ; and having in a readiness to revenge all disobedience, when your obedience is full."***

> **2 Corinthians 10:5**

This means, in the mental realm, we are to take control of the thoughts that we think and create a pattern of thinking that lines up with the will of God. God creates the vision and we create the thought processes that will help to fulfill that vision. We are also to be led by God in our creative processes so that we are assured that the things that we create will glorify Him. In the physical realm, we have been given the institution of marriage within which we create. God has established this divine edict so that we can create an intense bond with our husbands or wives; one man and one woman; who reflect a portion of us that can only be found in them. This edict allows us to create children and a family which is the earthly portrait of the heavenly relationship between God and His people. Two become one flesh not only in their thinking and actions, as is also the case, but one flesh in the form of the child. Each child has something from each parents flesh, hence two become one. It is a truth that this institution can *and* is being perverted, but the true sense of why it was established is being lost in civil unions (homosexual unions being disguised under **_God's_** institution of marriage) and the constant practice of bringing illegitimate children into that bond. God's way proves to be profoundly more healthy for man, woman, and child. This is the best illustration of the Law of Responsibility in association with The Law of Creation.

When we create, it is a reflection of ourselves and in effect a reflection of our creator. That is why we are to raise our children in the fear and admonition of God. We are to help create fertile ground for God to have a relationship with our children and with future generations. We are to nurture the inherent need within our children and a desire for them to seek that relationship and their ultimate purpose in life according to God's will. God did not create us so that we alone could come to the knowledge and way of salvation, but rather so that through Christ Jesus, the first born of many that might be saved; the example through faith and belief in His resurrection from the dead. This should always begin with our families. It is interesting to note that in scripture, that once a man is saved, his immediate family often follows and then his neighbors and then the gospel is exponentially spread in this way. In Acts 1:8 we find Jesus telling His disciples that they shall be witnesses unto him, *"...both in Jerusalem (immediate family), and in all Judea (friends and neighbors), and in Samaria (those in their community and where they travel) and unto the uttermost parts of the earth (the entire world)."*

Finally, in the spiritual realm, we have been given the ability to create what is not normally manifest in the natural or physical realm. Most people don't think of it this way, but when a child is born, something is taking place in the spiritual realm by which a new spirit is being created and is being given a physical body. Contrary to what is or has been written or preached, there is no 'well of souls'. The human spirit of a child is not present in either parent until the moment of conception. This is what we loosely refer to as the 'miracle of birth'. It is in fact one of God's greatest miracles.

We also create situations and opportunities in the spiritual realm both positive and negative. It is possible to create the very situations that effect our lives by the seeds that we plant and that are planted throughout the years of our lives; especially the early years. Our decisions, friendships, habits, and so on all play a roll in what is produced during the course of our lifetimes. This coincides with the spiritual Law of Reciprocity. Our parents can create spiritual opportunities for us by teaching us to know God through His word at an early age, by praying for us and blessing us daily. The Law of Creation is one that is not only a spiritual law, but one that is linked together with other spiritual laws. The Law of Creation causes the *inner* being of a person; their thoughts; their ideas; and their emotions to be expressed outwardly; *outside* of that person. The ability to create is a direct reflection of our creator. In giving us this ability, God is expressing to us the joy and pleasure that He gains by expressing *His* inward self. It is synonymous with what we read in Genesis 1:31, *"And God saw everything that He had made, and, behold it was very good…"*

Law #11: "The Law of Inheritance"

"…by the spirit of adoption…"

Webster's Dictionary: a) The act of inheriting property, b) the reception of genetic qualities by transmission from parent to offspring, c) The acquisition of a possession, condition, or trait from past generations, d) something that is or may be inherited. TRADITION, e) a valuable possession that is a common heritage from nature, POSSESSION.

The Law of Inheritance is that we are made beneficiaries of spiritual traits and property or properties, in the same manner that physical characteristics and property are passed from generation to generation, in the natural realm. We inherit physically, mentally, and in some instances, spiritually certain traits from our earthly parents but are inheritors of spiritual: life, gifts, blessings, talents, and rewards from our heavenly Father through our Savior Jesus Christ.

We know or at least understand that an inheritance is something that has been intended for us to possess, as a result of the will or intention of another party or parties. Usually it is contingent with regard to that party or party's absence whether temporary or permanent and leaves one with the responsibility of: caretaker, steward, or custodian of said possession(s). There are positive inheritances and there are negative inheritances, depending on the standpoint of the inheritor. A person who inherits a great amount of wealth as a result of a family member's death may be viewed as extremely fortunate from an outside standpoint, but if the inheriting party has no concept of stewardship or of the value of their newly acquired wealth, then it can never be a positive asset to that individual. It is as the scripture says,

"Give not that which is Holy unto dogs, neither cast your pearls before swine, lest they trample them under their feet, and turn again and rend you."

Matthew 7:6

Be careful that you assess to whom you are presenting Holy things. If the spirit of God is not moving you, then you may be placed in danger of confrontation or worse because the inference is that dogs and swine represent those people who are not willing to receive, appreciate or inherit Holy things. They are thereby offended to the point of rejection and may turn on you. The word 'rend' carries the meaning of ripping or slashing, so here Matthew is utilizing two animals that are known for being able to brutally harm and/or kill a man when offended. We understand that when we inherit the gift of salvation, this saves us from the *wrath* of God, through the gift of Jesus Christ, and that we are commanded to share it with all who would accept and partake. Our duty then is to make sure that we are led by the Spirit of God as to: when, where, how, and in what forum we present these Holy things.

The executor of a will has a set place and time for reading the contents of the will and is in a controlled environment when he carries forth the deceased's wishes to the benefactor. I cannot walk into a mosque or up to a group of drug dealers and begin to share my spiritual inheritance unless I am *sure* I am being led by the Spirit of God. I may get hurt, and then I would certainly be of no use to anyone. I cannot walk into a bar or a night club and use the deejay's microphone to start preaching. I would probably not be received and therefore, I have made the gospel ineffectual to those people. I must be a good steward over my inheritance the same as if it were a worldly inheritance and even *more* so.

As referencing the way that an inheritance is managed, the inheritor must be especially wary of their specific situation. We must be intelligent enough to understand under what circumstances we inherit certain things *and* be wise in how we deal with these facts.

Concerning the negative and from the standpoint of sin, we see in Romans

> *"Wherefore <u>as by one man</u> sin entered into the world, and death by sin; and so death passed upon all men, for that all have sinned...(For until the law, sin was in the world: but sin is not imputed when there is no law. Nevertheless death reigned from Adam to Moses, even over them that had not sinned after the similitude of Adam's transgression, who is the figure of Him that was to come."*

> *Romans 5:12-14*

Through one man (Adam) everyone has *inherited* a sinful nature and the curse of death. Even though those who did not sin from Adam to Moses were not charged with sin, death was still sovereign meaning that the penalty of eternal separation from God had to remain. It was not until Christ paid the ultimate price to free mankind from the grasp of death that those who died, without the law, could have fellowship with God in eternity. We see this separation in Luke 16:22-23 concerning the beggar and Lazarus and also where scripture speaks of 'Abraham's Bosom,' in the Old Testament; where men die and are gathered together to be with their fathers and to their people's.

As a result of Adam's disobedience to God, sin and death are passed down to every man, woman and child as well as the fact that the curse of that sin still effects all of creation. It is interesting to note that sin is not passed down from the woman, but rather the man. Woman is however the vessel that bears and reproduces that sin. This is how Christ could be born into the world without having a sin nature. While God took on the *form* of sinful man in the form of Jesus, He did *not* take on the nature of man. He was able to resist sin even while being tempted *by* and *with* sin. Romans 8:3 says, *"...God sending His own Son in the likeness of sinful flesh..."* not in the image. Jesus was like us in all ways, and yet He was not inherent in nature or character. Why he had to be born of a virgin. In other words, Jesus' predisposition was not sinful or inherent, as it is with man. He was of a different spirit or makeup, which are alternative definitions for character and means He did not inherit what man inherits. So while we may see that Jesus can chronologically be traced back to Adam (Luke 3:23-38), it is through Mary His mother that it is recounted and not through Joseph. Matthews letter to the Jews was merely to prove Jesus' royal lineage, hence the recounting from Joseph back to Abraham only. Joseph did not pass down the sin nature inherited by mankind through Adam because he had nothing to do with Jesus' birth. Was Mary a sinner? Yes, she was accountable for her own sin, but she was undefiled as a virgin. Her innocence was still intact and so she could become a vessel of honor when the Spirit of God came upon her.

My intention is not to spend precious words on verifying that the transmission of the sin nature comes from the father, but some discussion and clarification is necessary. In short, it is a matter of scientific fact that the father contributes half of the genetic material to the fetus and the mother contributes the other half; twenty three (23) chromosomes from each to make a complete strand of DNA with forty six (46) chromosomes. Jesus did not have genetic material donated from a human father. Therefore there is no sin nature from Joseph or any other human man. The bible clearly states in Leviticus 17:11 that, *"...the life of the flesh is in the blood..."* and *"...for it is the blood that maketh an atonement for the soul."* Now, it is also scientific fact that the blood of the fetus does not mix with the blood of the mother. The fetus produces its own blood and excretes waste through the umbilical chord which also allows nutrients and oxygen to reach the child. Therefore there is no sin nature from Mary because there is no sinful taint on the *flesh* that is forming within her womb.

This is a brief (very brief) synopsis of the scientific standpoint of how sin is passed down from the parents and how it is transmitted through the father.

The religious standpoint on the transmission of the sin nature is simpler. First we must deal with the object of *'Original Sin.'* 'Original Sin' represents the first sin from which all other sin emanates and that is reproduced in man. The concept of the transmission of sin is called 'Federal Headship' which means that, *"a person's father represents his descendants."* Therefore each of us is created in the image of our common father Adam in whom initiated 'Original Sin.' While Adam was created perfect by God and was considered God's son (Luke 3:38), he became the son of Satan when he sinned. The bible says in John 8:42-44, *"If God was **your** Father, ye would love me: for I proceed forth and I came from God; neither came I of myself, but He sent me.... Ye are of **your** father, the devil, and the lusts of **your** father ye will do..."* We see here that until we can love Christ Jesus and His finished work, that we are not all children of God (as sinners often mistake and profess as an excuse to not have accountability), but are *creations* of God. We do **not** become God's children again until we accept the blood sacrifice of Jesus, because His blood has made atonement or compensation for our sins. According to 'Federal Headship', we represent our ancestor Adam in his sinful state as the son of Satan, not God. The bible also states that sin came into the world through Adam and not through Eve who was first to sin.

> *"Wherefore as by **'one'** **man** sin entered into the world, and death by sin; and so death passed upon all men..."*

> **Romans 5:12**

While we know that Eve sinned first and Adam following after her example sinned likewise, the bible tells us that it was not the man that was deceived, but rather the woman. Most men look at this from the male standpoint of course, supposing that it is a cause for shame on the part of the woman for having been deceived. In actuality, the ax falls both ways and heavier on the male side. It is rather to the shame of the man for being knowledgeable of a situation, over which he **had** control, and for taking no action *or* the improper action. Since Adam was the only one given a direct mandate from God, it remains to be seen as to whether or not he rationalized his actions before executing them. How many of us have wondered what may have happened if Adam had never eaten the fruit? It is my opinion that is far less, if anything at all, comparable to what did happen. As I have mentioned, the instruction concerning God's command went solely to Adam. This is how sin entered in through Adam and not Eve. Remember, *"...sin is not imputed where there is no law..."* (Romans 5:13) God's command is as good as or the same as the Law! There is no mention of God having told Eve anything concerning the Garden of Eden, since she was created to be a helpmeet for Adam. The responsibility for instructing the wife, in the things of God, were the husband's. So, *in my opinion*, Adam could have potentially not eaten the fruit and been held accountable only for not instructing Eve properly. Adam would not have been sinful and the choice of how to reprimand the woman would have rested on the shoulders of God or delegated to Adam as God saw fit. As it is, the bible clearly states that sin entered in as *by one man*. The bible does not look at Adam and Eve in the sense of being one flesh because this was a spiritual sin and therefore the dissertation in Romans holds Adam solely accountable for what mankind inherits as sin. Romans 5 reads this way, *"Wherefore as by **one** man sin entered into the world, and death by sin; and so death passed upon all men, for that all have sinned... For if through the offense of **one** many be dead, much more the grace of God, and the gift by grace, which is by **one** man, Jesus Christ hath abounded unto many. And not as it was by **one** that sinned, so is the gift: for the judgment was by **one** unto condemnation...For if by **one** man's offense death reigned by **one**; much more they which received abundance of grace and of the gift of righteousness shall reign in life by **one**..., Jesus Christ. Therefore as by the offense of **one** judgment came upon all men to condemnation; even so by the righteousness of **one** the free gift came upon all men...For as by **one** man's disobedience all became sinners, so by the obedience of **one** shall many be made righteous."* This is now the inheritance of all children born of women?

Some things are immediately recognizable and undeniable concerning this spiritual law. From birth, children are disobedient, they lie, they steal, they get jealous, they are envious, and so forth. These are the traits that are deposited into children at the time of conception and are an indisputable example that these spiritual laws are in effect even as we ponder and dissect the subject. These are the things that we would choose not to have as a part of our character, if given the choice, but it has been bequeathed too us by Adam and passed down to us through Eve. Paul propagates a whole exposition on sin, in his letter to the Romans. We will look at the Law of Sin and Death momentarily, but he clearly explains, in this letter, that sin is inherent in our members and that as we are born into it, it is born into us.

Thank God almighty that there is also a positive inheritance for mankind through Jesus Christ! We have the New Testament or God's New (Will) and Testament to mankind, whereby we are no longer under the law of sin and death, but rather under the law of grace. Grace imputes to us: gifts, blessings, and an inheritance from God that we would otherwise not be worthy to receive. Nor could we under our own aspirations to be good or do right. Isaiah 64:6 tells us that, *"...we are as an unclean thing, and all our righteousness is as filthy rags; and we do fade like a leaf; and our iniquities, like the wind have taken us away."* Romans 3:23 states, *"For all have sinned, and come short of the glory of God."* The patriarch Abraham was considered to be a friend to God. With that friendship, as with any other, there was trust. We often see the biblical principle of man trusting God with the path of his existence, the desires of the heart, and the disappointments of his life. With Abraham, we see that intimacy with God can also solicit trust and blessings from the Father, as expressed in Genesis 13:14, 15:7, 17:5, 18:19 and so on. God's promise to Abraham included not only God's will and blessings for His chosen people Israel, but an outline for those generations that would receive an *inheritance* with Israel as a result of the 'spirit of adoption.'

> ***"For as many as are led by the spirit of God, they are the Sons of God. For ye have not received the spirit of bondage again to fear; but have received the spirit of adoption, whereby we cry Abba Father...not only they, but ourselves***

Born on the Battlefield Too

also, which have the first-fruits of the Spirit, even we ourselves groan within ourselves, waiting for the <u>adoption</u>, to wit, the redemption of the body."

Romans 8:13, 8:23

In ancient Rome, adopted sons shared the same privileges and were entitled to every right as sons born into the family. There was no differentiation in the home or in public between the adopted son and the true son. So within God's New (Will) and Testament, not only are God's chosen people promised an inheritance, but we (gentiles) who have been grafted in (Romans 11:17-24). Everyone who accepts Jesus Christ as their Lord and Savior has right to the 'Tree of Life' and the inheritance which is the Kingdom of Heaven! The bible tells us that we can never imagine the promises and blessed things that God has in store for those who will accept this gift and are born by His grace into His family. Jesus is the firstborn of all who believe, meaning that He, by conquering death and coming back to life, has shown us what lies ahead for believers. We, like Christ, shall also be raised from death unto eternal life and are now joint heirs with Jesus in *all* that God has in heaven.

The funny thing about mankind is that Satan keeps us so involved and preoccupied, with the ways of this world, that we fail to recognize that we also have an inheritance here on earth! We have an inheritance in the blessings of this world while we are in it. God does not intend for the unsaved to own the blessings and wealth of this world, but rather His own children. Too often we feel that as Christians, we should remain humble and meek never enjoying what life has to offer. Why? This entire planet has been created for man to enjoy; the entire universe for that matter. Who better to inherit these wondrous blessings than God's own children? As an heir of God and joint heir with Christ I claim all that God has for me here and in the world hereafter.

"I claim that through the spirit of adoption I will receive spiritual, mental and physical gifts. I will receive all that I

105

am entitled too and train myself to be a good steward over the things that God has left to my charge."

Law #12: "The Law of Thought"

This law is tricky. No one knows quite how the human mind operates and only a smart someone would recognize the human mind as one of God's great mysteries. The mind of man is what makes that person who they are and it is also something that is eternal. That is or should be, I think, the scariest part for anyone that is separated from God and going to hell. The fact that a person will think about, know and understand why they are in hell is enough to make us wonder about how God has created the human mind.

Scientists will never know as much as they aspire to know about the operation of the human mind until they consider asking God a thing or two about what His plans were in its design. The bible says in Proverbs 23:7 that, *"For as he thinker in his heart, so is he..."* So what does that mean? As a rule, at least for the majority of the population, our thoughts precede our actions. Our thought life ultimately precedes what we actually *do* as well as helps us in the things that transpire in our daily lives. Most children are the happiest people on the planet because their thought life is not constrained or been tainted by the cares of this world. Their freedom from responsibility gives them a liberty in life that we often find ourselves longing for, once we reach a certain level of maturity. The next happiest people are those that enjoy what they do in life; enjoy their jobs, their surroundings, their spouses, etc... This also gives those people a certain level of liberty. As Christians, we are to have the freedom in Christ Jesus that dominates every aspect of our life and causes our thought patterns to be transformed. We are told that we are not to be **conformed** to this world, but rather **transformed** by the renewing of our minds through the reading of God's word (Romans 12:2). This means that we can be transformed here on earth; changed by having our thought life changed.

If we are the type of person that is accustomed to being negative and looking at life from the "glass is half empty" standpoint, then no matter what the circumstance, we will always find despair in it. This thought process has a depressing effect on our spirit, on our minds, and eventually on our physical bodies. Our faces would draw down, our shoulders would slump, our feet would drag and a whole host of other physical attributes that portray our mindset can emerge outwardly. A person that has a positive attitude in life exhibits positive qualities. Their faces beam happiness, they are smiling, they have a spring in their step, and a very good posture. Body language is a result of what is on our minds being manifested *in*, executed *by*, and/or projected *from* our bodies. Think about it. How often can we tell what a person is thinking by their body language? God knows how important our thoughts are and He also realizes that He has designed our minds to be eternal; to be bonded to our spirit man. Our bodies are the only part of us that will return to the dust that it came from. It then stands to reason that God does not want an abundance of melancholy, sad-sack, "woe is me" Christians in heaven. This is why our minds are to be renewed **now** with the Word that God gave us. Did we ever stop to think that the time for us to prepare for heaven is **now**, while we are here on earth? Not just at the time of our salvation, because salvation is the ticket to get us through the *'pearly gates'*, as it were. What about getting in shape, putting on our best clothes, getting our hair done, learning how to speak the language, learning about the country, the natives and the indigenous foods and so for starters. We would do all of these things and quite a bit more if we were preparing for a trip to another country, so why not the same and more for God? It is so very important that we begin to ask God to remove those things from our minds that prevent us from becoming like Christ. Things that soil our new spirits and hold us back in life – those things that are character flaws and vices and issues. My pastor would say *isms* and *schisms*.

In the previous chapter, I have claimed, that the mind and the spirit are linked together in the second dimension, that they are two sides of the same coin or a two dimensional plane. We cannot derive our thought patterns from following the world's blueprint; just as the world will never conform to our thought patterns, belief system, or ideology. Each seems foreign to the other. The world's way is revenge, while our way is forgiveness. The world's way is dog-eat-dog, while our way is love thy neighbor. The world's way is kill or be killed, while our way is life and peace…

> *"For to be carnally minded is death; but to be spiritually minded is life and peace. Because the carnal mind is enmity against God: for it is not subject to the law of God, <u>neither can be</u>."*

Romans 8:6,7

The renewing of the mind and certain thought processes; the way we look at things, think about things and process information, will not take place over night. It will not necessarily take place at the time of salvation, how could it? A born again Christian is considered to be a babe in Christ. Like a baby, he must begin slowly to crawl, and then to walk; to drink milk and then to eat meat. Along with this comes a gradual change in that persons thought life. Their worldly view begins to wane and fade becoming their Godly view. Their earthly needs begin to change into spiritual needs. The Law of Thought is like a person who thinks about eating all the time and gains weight eventually becoming obese. What happens when the time spent on thinking about food is replaced by something else? Their thoughts are focused elsewhere and their concentration turns from obtaining the next meal to, let's say, putting the next presentation together for the boss. It is possible to become so caught up and involved in what you are doing that one forgets to eat. I often forget that it has been hours between meals when my mind is focused on one thing or another. If I choose to ignore my cravings then my mind has won out over my body, but if I succumb to it then the reverse is true. I only use food as an example, but with any unhealthy vice or habit when renewing your mind you must consider balance. We must take out the bad and replace it with the good and balance our lives accordingly so that we do not form new bad habits and vices. This is also true in the spiritual realm. If my mind is focused on the things of God, then I do not worry about natural things that may keep me out of the perfect will of God.

Why is this a spiritual law? Because God says, "I Am that I Am," the start and conclusion of a conscious thinking mind. Perhaps William Shakespeare said it best in human terminology, *"I think, therefore I am."* The Law of Thought is an indication of identity and an identifier of ones character. We often judge people; place them into categories and even measure our own self worth by how others think and how well we match up to their thinking or what is perceived to be the normal way of thinking by the majority.

Law #13: "The Law of Grace"

"...For by grace are ye saved through faith and that not of yourselves, it is the gift of God not of works lest any man should boast..."

Ephesians 2:8,9

We now live in what is known as the 'Dispensation of Grace.' This simply means that we are now able to accept a gift from God that we do not deserve. That gift is the gift of the sacrifice of Jesus the Savior and our salvation from God's wrath against sin. Grace is a precious thing indeed and actually has nothing to do with our abilities, talents or independent qualities. It consists of love, compassion, caring, mercy and the desire of well being and best interests of someone other than oneself. I often state it this way, "As Christians we should strive to be ***self-less*** as opposed to ***self-fish***!" It is not restricted or set aside for our children, or to the homeless person on the street, or even to those whom we forgive, but a divine trait placed within us by our creator. It is not the same as God's grace, but rather the emotion of empathy that we feel when we are moved to act in some capacity of kindness toward our fellow man. On the flip side of that coin, God can exercise His grace toward people through other people. He may move someone to an act of grace through us or someone that may or may not be a member of the Kingdom. We only need to learn to recognize the hand of God when He moves it. We may understand it in part, but we do not have the ability to bestow the same *type* of grace as God. Jesus said that, *"...greater love hath no man than this, that a man lay down his life for his friends* (John 15:13). Speaking with regard to

109

Himself, Christ speaks here of the grace of God toward every man. However, God's grace is much more in depth than any idea that we may perceive or understand it to be to it is fullest by simply stating that it is: "God giving us something that we do not deserve." Yes, that *'bottom lines* it, for simplicity sake, but by no means provides a total picture of God's plan for grace toward mankind.

Paul's letter to the church in Rome is an exposition on the gifts that we receive, through the grace given to us by God. With that *grace*, we are freed from the penalties of certain laws that otherwise would have insured our eternity in hell. With that *grace* we receive rights in the Kingdom of Heaven and privileges according to our son-ship through salvation (Romans 8:14-17). Grace is liberation and freedom. It is an expression of love that humbles us and touches our hearts. Grace is the quality of God that allows us to understand the extent of His love toward His creation. God left His throne in heaven, in the *form* of sinful man, to rescue us from the penalties that we would have incurred for breaking any of the previously listed spiritual law's or any that will be listed. Satan ultimately seeks to impose those penalties wherever possible, but grace stands as a partition between us and the ***death*** sentence, when we believe the word of God.

To personally experience the grace of God, during the course of life here on earth, is mind numbing. When we fully expect to pay a penalty for our actions, no matter what they may be, and no penalty is incurred; grace has abounded! When I have been delivered from situations where the outcome should have undeniably been disastrous, then I recognize the grace of God at work in my life. Even when we feel that we are not being afforded grace, trust me, we are! It is at those very times, when we are most aware that the enemy is seeking to destroy us, that God's grace is in action. Won't it be amazing when we get to heaven and will see and have everything revealed to us? Jesus told Peter that the enemy desired to sift him like wheat; because Jesus knew. We will know about all of the accidents that were avoided; all of the times that people desired to do us harm, and could not; all of the times that God's grace stood between us and sudden doom. All of those times we chose to take a different road to work for no reason or to walk to the store a different way. When we chose to say one thing instead of another or to pray before taking any course of action; God's grace was in operation. The Law of Grace is an allowance from God. It is not to be misused or abused, although we almost always do it in one form or another. That resides within the permissive will of God and is afforded to us because we have yet to be conformed to the image of Christ which is God's *perfect* will.

"For now we see through a glass, darkly; but then <u>face to face</u>: now <u>I know in part</u>; but <u>then shall I know</u> even as also I am known."

1 Corinthians 13:12

<u>Law #14: "The Law of Impartation"</u>

This law indicates that something, whether it be physical, mental or spiritual, can be passed from one entity, persona, or object to the next via some method of transference be that method mental, physical, or spiritual. Husband and wife do it mentally and physically all of the time. God imparts His love to us spiritually when we believe His word. Let's use faith as our first example. *"...Now faith cometh by hearing and hearing by the word of God"* (Romans 10:17). Scripture tells us that each one of us is given a measure of faith [Romans 12:3] and that this measure of faith can be increased by hearing the word of God, practicing the word of God, and by believing on the word of God. Scripture also tells us that we move from faith to faith (Romans 1:17), because this is how the righteousness of God is revealed to us and that the just; how those justified by God through Christ, should live according to this. So we see that measures of faith are imparted to us through our experiences and more specifically through our study or intake of the word of God. Our faith is also increased as we draw closer to God in times of trial and tribulation. This is how Job was able to persevere when tested by God and why he was allowed to be tortured by Satan. We will question our circumstances and cry out for God to deliver us, but we cannot give in or turn back! This faith comes through our eyes in the case of reading and through, our ears in the case of hearing and through our memory in the case of putting God's internalized word into practice. God's word in our memory resonates with itself and connects with itself to accomplish its purpose and will not return to Him void. Faith is imparted to us through our understanding of what God says to us through His word.

Healing is imparted to us much differently. It is imparted to us through our *faith* level. Sometimes we can pray for healing and receive it simply because we know what God says concerning healing and sometimes it is imparted to us through the laying on of hands or through the speaking of God's word into our spirit. This is representative of how the spiritual realm can change and alter what is in the physical and mental realms. I have often wondered how this works. I have even called my pastor wondering which party must have the greater faith; the party who is imparting (conductor) the healing or the party that is to receive (receiver) that healing. In some regard, it may be both and I have gone back and forth between the two. The idea is essentially very simple and we'll compare it to electricity. On the one hand, the conduit or conductor must be in place. This seems simple enough unless the vehicle, through which the importation is to flow, is not faithful enough to be in place. Then you have a problem! The receiver has to be in place and operational so to speak. If we use the example of a car battery or an electrical switch; then each receptacle must be operational; the battery must be able to receive a charge or the receptacle/outlet must be in working order. If this is not the case then it doesn't matter if the conduit (jumper cables or electrical line) is in place or not; the transfer will not take place. This is the example of the faith that is required with respect to either role. In the case of the person 'laying' on hands (conductor) there must be ample faith to actually move in action according to what God says must happen. In the case of the person that is in need (receiver), their must be faith enough to receive and accept what is about to be imparted. Therefore, when the current comes, the lines between the current and what is to receive the charge, are in place and the receiver is also in place and ready to function upon receiving the charge. It is the same with our salvation; we must have the faith to receive what God has already spoken in His word. We can receive what God says in His word and have all of God's promises imparted to us, be it healing or blessings, knowledge or even peace.

Through the sacrifice of Christ, salvation is imparted to us whereby we have eternal life. Jesus has created a dwelling place in heaven for all who believe in His finished work on the cross. He died a physical death so that the sins of mankind could be removed. Remember, Jesus took on the sins of the world and in so doing had the sentence of hell (spiritual death) as a consequence (Hebrews 9:27). As a man, He died taking on the sins of the whole world, but yet with no sin of His own and so hell could not hold Him. He spent three days in hell defeating Satan; taking back the keys to hell and the sting out of death, as well as emptying 'Abraham's Bosom'. These victories on the battlefield of hell, brought the importation of salvation to all who believe.

Satan also imparts, conveys or transfers certain things to us in much the same fashion as God except the things of Satan are however meant to destroy us rather than edify us. He imparts sickness, disease, stress, anxiety, disobedience, rebellion, hatred and lust to name only a few. He achieves this through television, radio, the internet, chaos in our lives, wrong perceptions and perspectives of reality, and through using what he knows about the sinful nature of man. The enemy takes advantage of doorways that have been left open in each of us, something we will discuss in a later chapter, in order to accomplish his goals. I believe and write by permission that his most effective tool is familiar spirits. Why? They are intimate with us in ways that we take for granted. They are familiar with our dispositions, our habits, our desires, our quirks, our pet-peeves, our past decisions in life and most likely future decisions or he way will most likely decide, our way of handling situations, our families, our aspirations, our strengths, our weaknesses and how close or far away we've grown in our walk with God. A familiar spirit preys on what it knows about its subject or assignment. The best con men in the world are experts at reading people very quickly, spotting their weaknesses and then exploiting them to their benefit. Read *"The Screw tape Letters"* by C.S. Lewis or *"This Present Darkness and Piercing the Darkness"* by Frank Operetta. These books will give you a very insightful look into what is going on in the spiritual realm with regard to the battle that is being waged in the spiritual realm.

Importation is essentially a give and take. One object/entity gives to or provides something for another object/entity. When we deal with God, the importation is generally something that is needed or desired. When Satan deals with us, the importation is undesirable or unwanted initially. We safeguard against or openly welcome certain importations by guarding or leaving unguarded the doorways that allow them to enter our minds, bodies, and spirits.

When something knocks on the door of your senses, try and test the spirits. Think about what opening the door could mean, and proceed with caution unless you know it to be your friend and Savior.

Law #15: "The Law of Time, Space and Eternity"

The wise man recognizes that there is more to life than the end result of death and oblivion. Ninety-five percent of the world's population believes that there is something more for each one of us after death; that there is a higher power and *that* is why Ninety-five percent of the world is searching for a path that will lead them to the truth. Unfortunately, in terms of eternity, not all roads lead to Rome.

Time can be looked at in several different ways. It can be a liberating concept or a confining reality. Webster defines time as: **a)** the measured or measurable period during which an action, process, or condition exists or continues **b)** a continuum which lacks special dimensions and in which events succeed one another from past, through present, to future **c)** the point or period when something occurs **d)** an appointed, fixed or customary moment or hour for something to happen, begin, or end.

Another way to look at time is like currency. Each individual has a certain amount of it to use as he/she will and, simultaneously we co-exist with *physical* objects that share this same complexity. I use the word 'complexity' because the idea of time is very complex and perplexing, in and of itself. Science still has certain difficulties when it comes to the 'understanding and application of time. In some scientific circles it 'is' referred to as the *next dimension*.

We exist within time and God exists outside of time and apart from it. It is both a measurement and a conclusive defining point for all things temporal. The best way that I have of defining time is '*the journey*' or the '*non-existence, life, and transition*' of all physical things. Time defines the moment between an object that is *not* in existence and the point at which that object comes *into* existence. It is the duration with which that 'something' remains tangible in the third dimension, and the point at which it transitions from one state of existence to another.

Since, mankind exists within time he has a starting point and an ending point. While we live in the third dimension, we also have what may be determined as a three dimensional existence. We are born (point A) and move along a given path (known as time) and we move along this path toward our destination (point C). Me move along point B toward death and from there we transition to eternity (point C). Point A represents our non-existence and sudden existence. This is, in and of itself, a type of transition. Any point along the journey toward point C can be termed our *present* as well as any point along that journey. The point beyond point B, being point C, may be termed our *future*. The journey itself is considered *time*. What we do during the course of the journey is what is most important. This is what shall ultimately be *measured* upon our transition upon arriving at point C.

God expects for us to be good stewards in everything that He has entrusted to us. If we take Matthew 25:14-30 and replace the word talent with time then we get a good understanding of what we should be doing with the time that God has allotted to every man; whether it be a short period of time or a long amount of time. The servant with five talents used his time wisely and the servant with two talents spent it in a way in which his master could approve. The servant with one talent wasted his time and upon his master's return had no excuse other than the fact that he had the same amount of time (regardless of his number of talents) and did nothing with it. The idea is, *"What are you going to do with the time that you are given?"* As each of us moves along on our own individual journey's, let's make absolutely certain that we make the right decisions, the right choices and spend the currency of time wisely.

To use Webster's first definition of time (the measured or measurable period during which an action, process, or condition exists or continues), we may better understand biblical dispensation or the order of events under God's divine authority. Generally, there are considered to be seven (7) dispensations between the creation of man and the restoration of man; Genesis – Revelation. They are listed as follows:

1. The dispensation of Innocence – from the creation of Adam and Eve to the fall of man
2. The dispensation of Conscience – from the fall of man until the flood
3. The dispensation of Human Government – from the flood until the call of Abraham
4. The dispensation of Promise – from the call of Abraham until the Exodus (Moses)
5. The dispensation of Law – from Moses until the 1st advent of Christ
6. The dispensation of Grace – from the 1st coming of Christ until the 2nd coming of Christ
7. The dispensation of Divine Government – from the 2nd coming of Christ until the last rebellion of Satan

It is amazing to witness and mind numbing to try to fathom how exactly God has woven such things together. Events occur in eternity and in the physical realm simultaneously and yet are so far removed from one another that it seems implausible that they could ever work together. This is what I refer to as the different dimensions or levels of God!

Yet, we know that Romans 8:28 says that, ***"All things work together for good to them that love God, to them who are the called according to His purpose."*** So to look at the big picture, we can see that from the creation of Adam, until now and looking forward to what God has promised, that He has called man (men) according to His purpose and the events that God has placed into motion both inside and outside of time have always worked together for the benefit of man and for God's ultimate glory.

If we look at time as the *'continuum that lacks specified dimensions,'* then we can see how the spiritual realm interacts with the physical realm and vice versa. There are no parameters that prevent the intermingling of the these two realms save Gods' word and even *that* He leaves to the choice of His created beings in certain instances and under certain circumstances. Take the story of Job for instance and the events that led up to and ensued as God proved His servant. Satan was allowed to interfere with Job's journey; with Job's movement along point B. Take also Genesis chapter 6 when the angels chose human wives or remember Elijah and Enoch who crossed the threshold between time and eternity without having to pass through death. Methuselah could not die until the flood came for that is indeed what his name means. Sampson bargained with the time that he had by asking God for strength to defeat his enemies one last time, which resulted in his death. Hezekiah petitioned for fifteen more years by asking God to remember his obedience. Jesus the Christ could not die until certain events in time had taken place. Time can be spent, bought, bargained, traded or sold according to how it glorifies God. There is still a conundrum, even with all of today's technology and advancements, with the calendar and actual global time. There is a day *missing* and science cannot explain it. God can! The day that is missing is the day that God made the sun to stand still for Joshua so that he could win the battle. Time exists for us to use for the duration of certain events and then it will be gone or spent. I specifically like the word **continuum** because it indicates that time is a part of eternity or that they at least exist side by side. The concept of time is, in and of itself, self-defining according to scripture because at some point it will cease to be and only eternity shall remain. It is at that point that we will step outside of the constraints of time and into the absence thereof. We will move from what is now a figure of existence and into the fullness of existence. Again we will utilize this scripture because it drives home a lot of different points on a lot of different levels.

> *"For now I see through a glass, darkly; but then face to face: now I <u>know in part</u>; <u>but then</u> shall I know even as also I am known."*

> **1 Corinthians 13:12**

117

This scripture speaks to the change that will take place when time ends. It speaks to what we can experience within time and what *more* we will experience outside of time.

Paul's reference here is interesting in that he is stating that what is happening now is a mere reflection of things to come and what darkens our viewpoint now is *time*. The word 'glass' (esophagi/ e'-sop-tron) used by Paul in the Greek refers to a mirror while the word darkly, a combination of two words (en enigma/ en e'·neg-mä) the word *en* denoting a fixed place in time and *enigma* from which we get our English 'enigma' meaning mystery or secret. He is telling us that what we are now seeing within time is a reflection of the great mystery that God will reveal in eternity at the end of time. The only boundaries that exist to mankind are those set by God for His plans and purposes so that His ultimate goal is carried out through to the end.

Time is not absolute and is subject to modification. That is a strange concept all by itself, but God has changed things within time and even altered time itself in His wisdom and divine judgment. In Joshua 10:13, the sun and moon stood still so that Joshua and the children of Israel could finish their battle. God actually stopped the rotation of the earth which is in part how man measures time. In 2 Kings 20:10 God causes the shadow of the clock to move backward 10^0. Also, in 2 Kings 20:6 and in Isaiah 38:5 God adds 15 years to Hezekiah's life beyond the appointed time for Hezekiah to die according to Hebrews 9:27.

****NOTE:

[In the late sixties and early seventies there was a story published that said that NASA had found a lost day while calculating rocket trajectory for future missions. "Has NASA discovered Joshua's **Lost Day**?" Their computers supposedly stopped until the computers were reprogrammed with the missing day from Joshua 10:13 which only calculated 23 hours and 20 minutes. This still leaves 40 missing minutes until we factor in 2 Kings 20:10 where Hezekiah asks Isaiah for a sign from God in which He makes the sun move backward 10^0 or exactly 40 minutes.]

To date all accounts of the story have been reduced to a hoax or inaccurate at best (Apologetics Press: Reason and Revelation 1991 – Bert Thompson PH.D.); no one is willing to verify or admit to the supposed NASA account. Since then a retraction of the original article has been printed and the story modified. This is all fine and well with the exception of the fact that the book of Joshua says that it was **about** a whole day and Isaiah says that the sun went backward 10^0 or rather that there are 40 missing minutes according to 2 Kings. Most of the account has been disproved or explained away, but the origin of the story has never been verified. Harold Hill, the originator of the original magazine article, with the claim about NASA, mysteriously retracted his statement and NASA denies that he was ever a consultant. This seems a bit far fetched for someone to fabricate, but hey, stranger lies have been told. Whether NASA found the missing day or not, there are only two accounts in scripture where God has tampered with the normal rotation of the earth and these are them. The math works on God's end and so the Law of Time and Eternity works. My problem with the various retractions and rebuttals are, that if for some reason NASA is hiding the fact that it found the bible to be true, then why claim that they can calculate the fact that earthquakes have caused the earth to speed up or slow down and that time has been thrown out of kilter?

Jet Propulsion Laboratory/ California Institute of Technology: **NASA Details Earthquake Effects on the Earth *January 10, 2005***

This at least appears to be what we often see in science that, if it has to do with God, and man cannot prove it or explain it then it is ridiculed and/or explained away. Why won't we just believe God?

The last two Webster's definitions are a perfect picture of what we are seeing everyday. *"The appointed time for something to occur, begin or end."* Are we not rapidly speeding toward some conclusion in human history? Technology is growing beyond our control! More people are starving than ever before in history despite our social advances. Natural disasters are on the rise across the globe. Disease runs rampant in every corner of society. Man's inhumanity to man has become so apparent that it boggles the mind and the human cruelty that we perpetrate on one another, in the 21st century, makes biblical war look like bar room brawls. It amazes me when I re-read certain scriptures! When the scripture says that in the last days, people will have certain attributes that are clearly not the products of love; it is speaking about those persons that are considered to be God's people.

> *"This know also, that in the last days perilous times shall come. For men shall be lovers of their own selves, covetous, boasters, proud, blasphemers, disobedient to parents, unthankful, unholy, <u>without natural affection</u>, trucebreakers, false accusers, incontinent, fierce, <u>despisers of those that are good</u>, traitors, heady, high-minded, <u>lovers of pleasures more than lovers of God</u>; having a form of godliness, but denying the power thereof: from such turn away. For of this sort are they which creep into houses, and lead captive silly women laden with sins, led away with divers lusts, <u>Ever learning, and never able to come to the knowledge of the truth</u>. Now as Jannes and Jambres withstood Moses, so do these also resist the truth: men of corrupt minds, reprobate concerning the faith. But they shall proceed no further: for their folly shall be manifest unto all [men], as theirs also was."*

> **2 Timothy 3:1-9**

I read this chapter over and over again for years; heard it preached for years, but it wasn't until God spoke to me and asked this simple question, "You do realize that my Word is written to the supposed followers of Christ; to Christians?"

THAT blew my mind because it was true! It is easy to see that perilous times are here! It is easy to see that when a persons lifestyle is jeopardized, they abandon what was formerly accounted to them as 'generosity'; very easy to see how someone could become covetous in times of lack; easy to become a boaster when positions and titles don't mean what hey used too or require the experience and study to obtain them. Easy when titles are given to any and everyone without **"...*knowing those that labor among you.*".**

Pride is a state that challenges everyone that is above the bottom rung of the ladder; and then I stopped...'blasphemers', 'unholy', and I really had to pray because I was experiencing the being 'without **natural** affection'. Read the rest, but understand that these are "*God's*" people, at least that is what they perpetrate. As I have said earlier; there is a marked difference between being God's child and God's creation. As true believers, we must draw the line at the point where those that say that they are following Christ have no fruit of the Spirit in their lives and don't reflect His nature. When the Word of God becomes too difficult for the church to hear, then we are definitely on the edge of eternity.

Make no mistake about whether I'm right or wrong about this; those that are ever learning and still can't come to the knowledge of the 'truth', are those that hear it every Sunday! God's people; before anyone else, must take '*ownership*' for their actions, but more so for what they hear!

Finally, there has definitely been a falling away from the faith and even the knowledge or compliance to the fact that there even *is* a supreme, divine creator is being swept away by secular humanism, tolerance, and political correctness.

We measure time by movement and change. It is measured by the movement of the earth and the position of other planetary bodies in our solar system. We also measure it by the way atoms move and change in a certain environment. The passage of time, measured by man, has three principle titles: rotational time, dynamic time, and atomic time.

Rotational time has as its basic unit the mean solar day or the twenty–four (24) hour day, which is the average time it takes the Earth to complete one rotation about its axis. *Dynamic time* relies not only on the orbital movements of the Earth, but on the movements of the moon and/or planets as well. *Atomic time* is the measurement of the absorption rate of atoms at a certain radio frequency. So while man has his way of measuring these particular types of movements and changes in his surroundings, it can be said that it is still not fully understood.

Time is the way that *we* measure events; events that have taken place, events that are taking place, and events that will take place. Add to that measurement 'space' and what we have is the reality in which we exist. Let's define space before we go any further.

If we use Isaac Newton's view of space, then we must consider space as absolute in that it exists permanently and independently of whether or not there are objects within it. Natural philosophers such As Gottfried Leibniz contend that space is the relation between the objects that lie within it and their distance and direction from one another. Still other philosophers like Emmanuel Kant, link time and space together labeling them as one entity "spacetime" stating that they are the elements of a system or framework by which man structures his experience. These last two Webster definitions correspond to the direction in which mankind is moving mentally. I tend to consider Isaac Newton's idea of space more biblical, in that God created an absolute permanent structure for which to showcase His creation. If there were no sun, moon, stars, matter, etc…then the idea of space does not become whimsical. It is entirely possible to have an empty box, devoid of matter including air, and still define what is in the box as space. Space is the blank canvas in which one can place material objects and therewith fill the box. I do not believe that time must be linked to space, since space can exist independently of time. Time can be added to objects within space or the objects within a spatial environment. Time does not effect space, for by definition, space is empty; it is simply there. Time effects the matter that does or can exist within space as assigned by God for: purpose, for succession of events, and for His ultimate glory. So, while God is outside of time and we exist within this spatial environment, with time assigned to us, we find our purpose through a succession of events that will ultimately bring glory to God. That is to say, until He removes the confinement of time from us and we move into eternity.

Time, it appears has been assigned to mankind as a result of sin. Not that there is no succession of events in eternity; those events are simply measured in a way that is foreign to us at present. This law seems to have taken effect on the temporal level at the point of sin or at least at judgment in Eden.

Remember. The Tree of Life was intended to counteract the consequence of time on the human form or, it could be, that time was assigned to this spatial environment and that God intended to override those effects by placing the Tree of Life in the Garden of Eden? Whichever the case, mankind was not created to be confined by time or by this measurement and/or succession of events in this realm. Also remember that we are spiritual beings within a material world... as 'strangers'...

> *"Dearly beloved, I beseech you as **strangers** and **pilgrims** abstain from fleshly lusts, which war against the soul..."*

> **1 Peter 2:11**

> *"These all died in faith, not having received the promises, but having seen them afar off, and were persuaded of them, and embraced them, and confessed that they were **strangers** and **pilgrims** on the earth."*

> **Hebrew 11:13**

... First as spiritual beings created to have eternal life and fellowship *with* our creator, in the physical realm as Adam began and secondly as spiritual beings in the spiritual realm because God knew in the beginning what would happen and how. Christ was sent to correct the problem that was created by Satan for man and to show mankind that He loved us just this much. It was to show us that we were created to have eternal fellowship with Him!

> *"For God so loved the world, that he gave his only begotten Son, that whosoever believeth in him should not perish, but have everlasting life."*

John 3:16

Finally, as we look at eternity, it is that which we think of as *timelessness* or that final event that is no longer confined or restrained by time. If we take a point in time and space and label it start, then we move from the confines of that point within time and space toward a last point we will call endpoint. It is at endpoint that we will move from the confines of time and into the endlessness of eternity or *time without measure*. During the journey from start to endpoint we will encounter all that God has placed within time and space in order to bring His final plan to fruition.

Eternity is the dimension of God and Satan, angels, demons,. During the course of our journey we have the rare opportunity that none of God's other creation has. We may accept a special gift from God in Christ Jesus His Son or we may reject it. The former ensures our eternal resting place and will include all of the gifts and promises that God has promised us through His Son. The latter decision promises that we will be eternally separated from our creator. The point is that we *will* live eternally; it is simply a question of where and how. As Christians we must endure and hold our positions on the battlefield until we reach point B. Satan's goal is to incapacitate, cripple, maim, or kill us along the path to point B before we have a chance to accept God's gift.

God exists and operates outside of the confines of time, yet resides in eternity. Satan, while existing in the spiritual realm (4th dimension) does not exist outside of time, in a sense. His time is measured differently than temporal time, but *by* temporal time, for when temporal time ends, Satan's eternity in prison begins. This, to me, is ironic because he (Satan) was not created to be confined to temporal time, but again we see that because of sin he finds himself *bound*, to some degree, *by* temporal time in that his liberty is lost at (temporal time's) finish. In short, Satan is running out of time to use *time*! At some point, God will speak and temporal time will end or convert to **eternal time**. It is in eternal time that God's plan will play out and the scales balanced. Everything created to exist in the third dimension will have the restraint of time removed and then exist within eternity.

Law #16: "The Law of Sin and Death"

"...Wherefore as by one man sin entered into the world, and death by sin; and so death passed upon all men, for that all have sinned..."

Romans 5:12

Romans chapter 5 begins Paul's dissertation on sin, death and the law. It should be strikingly clear that this Law of Sin and Death grows directly out of the Law of Impartation. One man, Adam, sinned in the Garden of Eden and imparted the sin nature to all who would then be made in *Adam's* image. The sin nature comes through the man because it was the man that received the mandate from God. We see a law within that charge, a commandment that requires Adam *not* to sin. Adam's job was to instruct Eve of God's mandate, so the law was that Adam was to first obey the command himself and second to instruct Eve of their creator's command. Adam did not uphold that directive in that, if he could not relay the command, he also made the decision to partake in its consequences. Adam himself was disobedient so then the transgression or sin becomes Adam's twofold. At that moment; the moment when Adam sinned, God's covering for them both was removed. We generally take their nakedness to mean that they realized that they were physically naked, but the implication is that the glory and protection of God was withdrawn from them. I will also infer that it was also a mental and spiritual nakedness. The actual Hebrew word is ârôwm or ârôm (aw-rome) from **6191** in Strong's Hebrew Dictionary meaning nude or naked, but having the greater sense of being completely bare as well as cunning, crafty, or subtle usually in the derogatory sense.

So from this we see that they recognized that they were not only physically unclothed, but that their innocence was gone as well. A child will run around the house naked and unashamed until they eventually grow older and lose that childish innocence. To *cover* nakedness is a symbol of pride and for someone to be uncovered or naked is to show that they have no shame or that they lack pride. What we are seeing is that in gaining knowledge, from this particular tree, the premier manifestation was the recognition of their severed connection with God; the emotion we know as shame. They tried to compensate with what they could immediately recognize which was the fact that the ***glory*** of God was gone. That same glory, that probably shown on Moses' face, (Exodus 34:29-35) after being in the presence of God, was no longer evident in Adam and Eve. The context of the account would lead us to believe that, with that same knowledge of good and evil came the propensity and craftiness which allowed them to lie about what they had done. They received not only the knowledge of the difference between good and evil, but the ability to utilize it, and without the wisdom, of the proper application between the two. In any event, there was a connection that was severed in Eden, one that would ultimately need to be repaired by God himself. The consequences of that rift are not completely nullified until Revelation 20:14 – *"And death and hell were cast into the lake of fire..."*

Sin is a tricky thing! It literally means to transgress against, or to break the law. If Adam and Eve sinned in the Garden of Eden, then there must surely have been some understanding of spiritual laws prior to the Law of Moses. We also see these spiritual laws in the Genesis account of creation when we read the word "Let" or "Let there be..." indicating that God's divine permission is needed. Spiritual laws were given to Adam by God, along with those consequences and penalties and were meant to be understood by Adam and conveyed to Eve. In breaking these laws, Adam caused repercussions that he perhaps had no idea would reverberate down through the bowels of human history.

Man is separated from his creator on every plane of existence.

- In the ***mental realm***, man's thought life is not in line with God's will. **"For to be carnally minded is death; but to be**

spiritually minded is life and peace. Because the carnal mind is enmity against God: for it is not subject to the <u>law of God</u>, neither can be. So then they that are in the flesh cannot please God." (*Romans 8:6-8*) What is disobedience other than the will to please the flesh?

- Man is separated from his creator in the *spiritual realm*, in that sin cannot exist in the presence of God. God exists in harmony with His Spirit and with His Word. God cannot lie or be disobedient to His Himself (Trinity) and so to allow a transgressor of the law to fellowship or be in relationship with Him would mean that He has broken His own Word thereby becoming Himself a transgressor. There is now no alternative except separation. God, however, in His divine mercy, decides to remove Adam and Eve from the Garden of Eden to prevent them from living in their sinful state eternally. In His divine omniscience He also, at the same time, set angels in place awaiting the advent of Christ when every way would be turned back to the Tree of Life (Genesis 3:22-24)

- Lastly, man is separated from God in the *physical realm* with respect to the fact that we were never designed to physically die. That is why the Tree of Life was in the Garden of Eden and why God prevented Adam and Eve from eating from it. Through one act of sin (or two depending on how you look at it), Adam introduced death into the human condition on every level! We also see that the sin nature places all three aspects of man in a constant state of decay and deterioration.

- Over the course of history, man has become technologically advanced while at the same time becoming morally depraved. It has become necessary, through salvation, to have a new spirit placed within us because we are born into sin and tied to Satan. (John 8:44, 1 John 3:8,10) Man also ages and over time begins to physically deteriorate until eventually he dies. The body that was designed to be renewed by the Tree of Life now ages and ultimately fails. We see this aspect of the curse of sin and then death in the genealogy of Adam (Genesis 5) and in the consequent restraint of man's lifespan by God, in that man would not live past one hundred and twenty years. (Genesis 6:3)

Sin and the consequences of death entered into the world at the very moment of disobedience. Romans 5:14 tells us that even those who do not commit the same sin as Adam are subject to the consequences that originate and are associated with sin itself. Romans 5:17 says that death is allowed to reign because of sin and that even today has partial dominion in this realm through physical death in that physical death is still a prerequisite to eternity pending the rapture.

"And it is appointed unto men once to die, but after this the judgment"

(Hebrews 9:27)

Sin is ever present in our physical bodies and in our minds because these are the two aspects of our triune beings that are not renewed at the point of salvation. The bible tells us to present our physical bodies as living sacrifices in Romans 12:1 and to renew our minds in Romans 12: 2. Think about a sacrifice. A sacrifice is killed before it is sacrificed; so it stands to reason that a 'living sacrifice' will endure pain. Trust me when I tell you that it can bring you to the doorstep of death like it did with Jonah and Job. We present these earthly vessels as living sacrifices because in eternity these earthen vessels will be done away with and we will receive glorified bodies as Christ did after His resurrection; bodies that will be more suitable for the fourth dimension. Our soul which consists of our will, our emotions, and our mind must be *renewed* here on earth in preparation for the Kingdom. These are not changed at the point of conversion because it is who we are; it is the workmanship of God in creating us as individuals. One way to present our bodies as a living sacrifice is to read the Old Testament and see what was done to sacrifices. We aren't to take that literally, but rather practice minimizing the strength of the flesh in order to strengthen the new spirit that God has placed in us. Denying the flesh and seeking the things of the spirit is the beginning, along with prayer and fasting. Prayer denies the flesh the ability to misuse time and fasting reduces the fleshes ability to overpower the spirit. We renew our mind by making God's thoughts and His word paramount in our daily life. If we practice familiarizing ourselves with what God has said then we become accustomed to His will and sensitive to His Spirit.

So as sin works in us, it works to bring about spiritual, mental, and physical death. It is always the enemy's objective to exploit your weakness, so make no mistake that he is using this to his advantage. He will take every opportunity to make you spiritually sick, to make you physically debase, and mentally depraved. Not only is the devil fighting against us, but we have the disadvantage of a sin nature which is already working against us to bring about death. Guess what? Satan wants us dead and separated from God for eternity! We also see in Romans 7:7 that the law frames sin. The law was given as a guideline so that we may be able to better understand what God expects us to do decision wise concerning good and evil and to outline the consequences associated with those wrong decisions. For God to say that, "This is sin," or "That is sin;" "Don't do this," or "Don't do that," does not make the law bad or even unnecessary, but rather acts as a mirror in order that we might see ourselves through God's eyes. When we think an impure thought, the law shows us our reflection in our conscience. When we covet our neighbor's possessions, the law shows us our reflection in pointing out that we are greedy, covetous, and lustful. When we hate steal, disobey, murmur, complain, etc... the law of God convicts us through His Holy Spirit thereby allowing us to see that we are being sinful. The enemy would have us become numb and desensitized to this prompting.

God's law actually kills our mind and physical bodies. Is this so hard to believe in light of what happened in the Garden of Eden? Paul tells us that we are alive without the law because, in its absence, we have no knowledge of sin and therefore cannot be held accountable. However, Romans 7:8 and James 1:15 tells us that sin uses the law to achieve death in us, but without the law sin is dead. Sin causes us to do evil in the sight of God, in spite of the fact that the mirror of the law may be in front of us. The Law of the Mind intends for us to do the will of God, when we are saved, but the Law of Sin wars against our minds in order that it may bring us back under subjection to death.

We serve God with the Law of the Mind, but with the flesh we serve the Law of Sin. Keep in mind that scripture tells us that we cannot serve two masters because we will love the one and hate the other. The way to be in right standing with God concerning the Law of Sin, Death and Eternity is to love God first; seek the kingdom of heaven first; reach for God's will first.

[I bought a hat that says, "God First!" As a reminder. Hard to do something contrary in public when your hat reads what you would like for the world to believe that you are representing.] Selah

The law can be bent depending on where we place our focus, but the object is never to bend the law or even come to a point where we practice such dangers. I mention this only to point out that as the enemy uses what we know about the laws of God to attack us and make us guilty, when our focus is correct and our motives line up with the will of God, grace overrides the penalties of the law or lessens the sentence. Take David eating the temple bread that was for the priests, as an example. David should have been punished the way that Uzzah was in 2 Samuel 6:7.

When we do not adhere to fleshly things, then sin cannot work evil in us and the enemy cannot use us. We can actually prolong our physical lives. We only approach physical death because of sin. What is the first commandment with promise? *"Honor thy father and thy mother: that thy days may be long upon the land which the Lord thy God giveth thee."*

This is the polar opposite of disobedience and the consequences brought on by disobedience. Where Adam was disobedient unto physical death; obedience to the command or law of God, in this particular instance, can bring about physical longevity. Again, if we compare this with Hebrews 9:27 we see that this law can be *bent* not broken. Physical death can be stayed off for a time and only for the glory of God, in those specific instances, but the only person to ever completely fulfill the law and be exempt from its judgment is Christ in that He is God incarnate. *We* become exempt to the consequences of sin through the **Law of the Spirit of Life** in Christ Jesus. We, in this way, are relieved of the penalty of sin and eternal death holds no power over us.

Law#17: "The Law of the Spirit of Life"

"For the law of the Spirit of life in Christ Jesus hath made me free from the law of sin and death"

Romans 8:2

When we accept salvation, we escape condemnation because we do not follow after fleshly things, but rather after spiritual. This spiritual law tells us that the *physical or temporal law* itself can only do but so much. The physical law is weak because the fleshly tendency is to sin and not do the things of God. Remember from the previous discussion (Sin, Death & Eternity) that the law is only a mirror that shows us how God views our actions or what is inside of us. The decision to change what we see in that reflection, as moved by the Spirit of God, is ours. We are convicted by the law, but not changed by it; only inspired to change. The Law of The Spirit of Life allows us to fulfill the righteousness or correctness of the temporal law. The law is 100% correct in what it shows us, even as Christ has said that he did not come to do away with the law, but rather to fulfill it.

"Think not that I am come to destroy the law, or the prophets: I am not come to destroy, but to fulfill."

Matthew 5:17

We agree with the law when we seek spiritual things and are led by the spirit of God. Romans 8:9-11 states that the Holy Spirit makes us alive *in* and *through* Jesus Christ. The Spirit of Life is the Holy Spirit or Spirit of God; the *Comforter*; promised to us in the book of John and He bears witness with our renewed spirit after salvation. We are to look to Him to keep us from falling subject to The Law of Sin and

Death. He is the one that keeps us from going back into the world. He is the one that insures that no one or no thing can pluck us out of God's hands. The Holy Spirit of God is our conscience and our guide. He is the one that forces us to look into that mirror that we would otherwise tend to shy away from; the one that shows us how ugly we are and forces us to make a decision about it! Oh, yes we are ugly whether we would admit it or not! (Jeremiah 17:9) When we are out of the will of God, here comes the Spirit of God to convict us and urge us to move back into His glorious will out of love. He will not force us. This is that same Spirit of Life that draws us to the saving grace of Jesus Christ and allows us to become heirs and joint heirs with Christ Jesus. Following after the Holy Spirit and listening to His prompting, causes us pain and suffering in the flesh. It causes our mortal man to cry out in agony, but it is the suffering that we must endure and also a battle that we must fight and win in order to be free from Law #16. We must look at it from Paul's standpoint: ***"For I reckon that the sufferings of this present time are not worthy to be compared to the glory which shall be revealed in us."*** **(Romans 8:18)**

The Law of the Spirit of Life is the Holy Spirit's law. Jesus said in the Gospels, and in Acts, that He must return to heaven so that *we* may be filled with the power of the Holy Spirit. I must point out that in Old Testament times, the Spirit of God '*moved*' people and '*came upon*' people. In the New Testament, the body of believers, known as the church, is filled with the Spirit of God indicating that God is now residing on the inside. This power transforms us into witnesses for the good news of the Kingdom and comforts us as we walk through this life as strangers in a strange land. Read about the stoning of Stephen in Acts chapter seven; he walked after the Spirit knowing that the Pharisees, Sadducee, Scribes and Jews of that day were not inclined to receive the teachings of Christ. He went to his death in Acts 7:59-60 asking God to keep His promise that he (and every believer) would obtain life according to the Word of God and *by* the power of the Holy Spirit was able to ask forgiveness of his murderers. Stephen spoke with the power and conviction of a man committed to his beliefs until death and in the end trusted that the Law of the Spirit of Life would operate on his behalf. This law negates the Law of Sin and Death in the spiritual sense because it overrules the consequences of sin and prevails over mankind's inevitable separation from God in eternity. This law was designed because God loved His creation so much that He had the foreknowledge to provide a plan of salvation so that we could have a choice to spend eternity with Him.

God created a new type of creature in that we are to exist in both the physical and spiritual dimension simultaneously. Angels live in only the spiritual dimension, but can exist in the physical. It is like us holding our breath to go under water. We can, but we cannot exist there indefinitely.

Law#18: "The Law of Love"

"He that loveseat not knoweth not God; for God is love."

1John 4:8

"And we have known and believed the love that God hath to us. God is love; and he that dwelleth in love dwelleth in God, and God in him."

1John 4:16

Quite simply, God **is** LOVE! Almost nothing more needs to be said after that statement, but when you get to a certain point in life; and begin to understand that what used to be thought of as common is not so common anymore; you too would feel as I do. There yet remains a necessity to take ones best shot at an explanation.

With all that is happening in today's world, what was known as compassion and natural affection is being erased by desensitization and selfishness. Mankind has allowed the enemy to create small cracks in the foundation of global society. He has made the things that generally were thought of in society to be the aspirations of the majority into faded glory.

9-11 was not just a turning point for the American populace, but an indication that the enemy was stepping his game up! He not only changed the landscape of one of the most influential cities on the globe, but he changed the 'mentality' of the people on that globe. Satan injected: fear, apprehension, uncertainty, doubt, and faithlessness, to name a few, into the everyday lives of every man, woman, and child on the planet! He pushed Islam; the direct opponent to Christianity; into our very homes through every possible form of media known to man. He has effectively blurred the lines between right and wrong; he has given humanity an idealism of indifference and has plugged the ears of those that would hear God's Word!

A conversation with one of my fraternity brothers really put things into perspective for me and for him as well. We were talking about how many people have lost their lives in the last 10 years. We listed: 911 and the the destruction of the New York Trade Centers [The Twin Towers], The Iranian war, the Iraqi war, the Afghanistan war, The assassination of Benares Bhutto, the Pakistani opposition leader and twice-serving prime minister (this was done almost identically to the JFK assassination, The Iraqi president Saddam Hussein who was assassinated along with both of his sons; the Egyptian president Hosier Mubarak is forced out of office, the assassination of the Libyan president Mammary Gaddafi, Hurricane Katrina, the earthquakes in South America, the earthquake in Haiti, the Tsunami in Indonesia, the Tsunami in Japan, the nuclear reactor meltdown in Japan, the oil spill in the Atlantic Ocean, the earthquake in Virginia felt as far north as New York City, disenfranchised youth in England rioted in the streets for lack of hope and because of England's current economic crisis...and so on! We were blown away, and he decided, not long after that conversation, to rededicate his life to Christ!

What does any of this mean as far as love is concerned? Time is growing short! Satan knows it and we should know it too. With all that is going on, it is very difficult for man to get a firm grasp on the things that he had become accustomed too only 50 short years ago; 20 short years ago; or 10 short years ago. There is undoubtedly *something* coming down the pipes and the only things that we can safely rely on and be sure of are that: God has already told us what would happen, how it would happen, what to watch for and that we cannot prevent them from happening.

"And ye shall hear of wars and rumors of wars: see that ye be not troubled: for all [these things] must come to pass, but the end is not yet. For nation shall rise against nation, and kingdom against kingdom: and there shall be famines, and pestilences, and earthquakes, in divers places. All these [are] the beginning of sorrows. Then shall they deliver you up to be afflicted, and shall kill you: and ye shall be hated of all nations for my name's sake. And then shall many be offended, and shall betray one another, and shall hate one another. And many false prophets shall rise, and shall deceive many. And because iniquity shall abound, <u>the love of many shall wax cold</u>. But he that shall endure unto the end, the same shall be saved."

Matthew 24:6 - **13**

These are those times. There **will be** a loss of love in these times and what people once relied on and thought would get them through the tough times; conquer all; give them hope when hope was not apparent; is no longer a safety net. God may not be doing it all at once, but He is definitely removing the 'Comforter' from the earth.

"Now we beseech you, brethren, by the coming of our Lord Jesus Christ, and [by] our gathering together unto him, That ye be not soon shaken in mind, or be troubled, neither by spirit, nor by word, nor by letter as from us, as that the day of Christ is at hand. Let no man deceive you by any means: for [that day shall not come], except there come a falling away first, and that man of sin be revealed, the son of perdition; Who oppose and exalteth himself above all that is called God, or that is worshiped; so that he as God sitter in the temple of God, shewing himself that he is God."

2 Thessalonians 2:1-4

*For the mystery of iniquity doth already work: only he who now letterer [will let], until he be taken out of the way.

2 Thessalonians 2:7

No love on earth! No Spirit of God on the earth! Perilous times have indeed already begun!

"How that they told you there should be mockers in the last time, who should walk after <u>their own ungodly lusts</u>. These be they who <u>separate themselves</u>, <u>sensual</u>, having <u>not the Spirit</u>. But ye, beloved, building up yourselves on your most holy faith, praying in the Holy Ghost, <u>Keep yourselves in the love of God</u>, looking for the mercy of our Lord Jesus Christ unto eternal life. And of some have compassion, making a difference: And others save with fear, pulling [them] out of the fire; hating even the garment spotted by the flesh. Now unto him that is able to keep you from falling, and to present [you] faultless before the presence of his glory with exceeding joy, To the only wise God our Savior, [be] glory and majesty, dominion and power, both now and ever. Amen."

Jude 1:18-**25**

Remember I have already told you that we will suffer. God knows our common enemy and Satan knows that God knows. That is why this chapter is called the *'Legality of it All'*. Since God is omniscient, He already knew what Satan had up his sleeve; as far as what God had set into place; as far as how things work. In the different realms; from a <u>legalistic</u> standpoint; what is allowed and not allowed and what he Satan can and cannot do. In some instances, like in the book of Job, God will show that He is sovereign; prove His servants right and His enemy wrong; and do it *all* at the same time. God will use these instances to strengthen His servant's resolve, increase their faith, bless them, get His glory, and encourage others to stay the course while showing His enemies weaknesses; and *all* of these things at the same time!

"Beloved, think it not strange concerning the fiery trial which is to try you, as though some strange thing happened unto you: But rejoice, inasmuch as ye are partakers of Christ's sufferings; that, when his glory shall be revealed, ye may be glad also with exceeding joy. If ye be reproached for the name of Christ, happy [are ye]; for the spirit of glory and of God restitch upon you: on their part he is evil spoken of, but on your part he is glorified. But let none of you suffer as a murderer, or [as] a thief, or [as] an evildoer, or as a busybody in other men's matters. Yet if [any man suffer] as a Christian, let him not be ashamed; but let him glorify God on this behalf. For the time [is come] that judgment must begin at the house of God: and if [it] first [begin] at us, what shall the end [be] of them that obey not the gospel of God? And if the righteous scarcely be saved, where shall the ungodly and the sinner appear? Wherefore let them that suffer according to the will of God commit the keeping of their souls [to him] in well doing, as unto a faithful Creator."

1 Peter 4:13-19

We are created in God's image and in His likeness; so we need to hold on to those things during the course of our walk, while we are suffering like Job and Jonah and while we are on our journey. It is an exercise in futility to say that we 'understand' love, or that we 'know' what love is. The best we can do is to express our interpretation of love from the standpoint of what we do know and what the word tells us. I point this out because there are different aspects of love; different levels and different applications and different situations. Many cultures have several words that describe the aspects of love: brotherly, motherly, friendly, intimate, forgiving, compassionate, pitying, sacrificial, etc…

Love is an aspect of God that emanates from our spirits; it is the ***God*** in us. It is something that is directed toward a certain object, person, thing or perceived necessity for someone or something that we have chosen to focus on. This is why there are so many commandments that deter us from misplacing that aspect of our beings. God is a jealous God and He will never share His glory with anyone or anything. Have no other gods before me, do not make any graven images of anything, do not take God's name in vain, thou shalt not covet…, etc…These all speak to the fact that God wants to be our first and only Love!

What is in our focus, however, does not necessarily mean that the object has a requirement to return that love. This is how God feels when He has poured out **_so_** much of Himself toward making sure that His children, His people and His creation are able to be the recipients of the things that He, as <u>GOD</u>, is capable of giving them. It is why Israel has such a hard time and why the church is having such a hard time now. We don't understand love. We have a hard time *giving* it and *receiving* it.

> **"For God so loved the world, that he gave his only begotten Son, that whosoever believeth in him should not perish, but have everlasting life."**

> John 3:16

Can we or should we ever allow the enemy to make this scripture cliche'? When I pose this question to myself about my children, my love simply does not run that deep. When I look at Mel Gibbon's version of the passion, I cannot without crying and recognizing the difficulty that Mary apparently had and then watching the inference of God having to endure what Jesus went through as 'man' or the foreknowledge of the fact that Jesus was headed to hell. He did so in order to free those that were in Abraham's bosom awaiting His advent on earth. Love? We know nothing about it.

When someone is willing to lay down their life and sacrifice *all* that they have; *all* that they will have and *all* that they will be, in order to see that someone else can receive **_their_** blessings; that is still only a small part of love. When we focus on John 3:16, we can draw out of it a myriad of different emotions. He showed the **_compassionate_** form of love through what He understood about the human condition. He showed the **_motherly_** kind of love through the fact that, only on earth, will we see a mother take the penalty of death for her child. He showed ***intimate*** love through the fact that His goal is to be in relationship with us forever. He showed the ***forgiving*** kind of love in that the ones that He loved, enough to do this for, were the ones that were killing Him. He showed the ***sacrificial*** kind of love through not wanting us to suffer eternally for what He knew that only He could endure. He showed ***brotherly*** love through allowing Himself to be set a little lower than the angels; so that we can know that He has an understanding of our condition and what we have to face in the flesh. On top of that, He made us joint heirs to an inheritance that was His alone and the list goes on and on.

When we love someone or something, we *suffer* for it. We endure pain and anguish for what we love in order to protect and care for it. We bear grief and sorrow, in hopes that our expression of love will find a home with the object to which we are directing it. These expressions are apparent in our daily lives with: our spouses, our children, those we have intended to be our spouses, our friends, our families and in many instances; our associates.

In being created in the image and likeness of God, we have the ability to experience and express His greatest attribute. Think about how all encompassing, love is, and what it causes people to do; *both good and bad*. Love causes jealousy, anger, hatred, murder, joy, bliss, passion, elation, and so on. From one end of the spectrum to the other, love, or the desire for it, permeates the very fiber of our beings.

The Law of Love is this; we can be ***identified*** with God, by the love that people see in us, as His children.

> ***"By this shall all [men] know that ye are my disciples, if ye have love one to another."***

> John 13:35

This law has dominion over *everything* because it is the **Word** of God and because it ***is*** God! The Word of God says that God is a 'spirit' and those that worship Him must worship Him in spirit and in truth.

139

Then it is reasonable to assume that love must be a 'spiritual' thing. It is not an emotional, mental, hypothetical or theoretical undertaking. The Law of Love shows itself even in all that are not like Him; it is the 'Creators' mark. The unsaved are struggling to find that 'love' of God. The world says that they are, *"looking for love in all of the wrong places;"* and this is true. I choose to say say that God has designed a void or space within every man that can only be filled with Him.

I personally believe that all of creation; and all that will be created by us, responds to this law. Didn't God create the entire universe out of love? I tell my students to think about all of what scientists find and discover every day. I ask them to 'Google' images of what the 'Hubble' telescope has seen or imagine what might be in the depths of the ocean where we still cannot tread. Doesn't food taste better when it's cooked with love or don't we feel better in our mother's arms than the doctors?

Adam was created out of love and because of His desire to express that emotion to someone that could receive it *differently* than the angels. God created Eve so that Adam could express that same emotion properly and have a deeper comparison of what love actually is; not simply sex, but the companionship and creation aspect.

It was out of love that Jesus lay down His deity; stepped out of eternity and lay His life down so that He could pay the debt that every man, woman and child had, would have or that ever would be born, would have. It amazes me that the only repayment for what we owe is **belief**! Christianity is the only faith where we are not attempting to reach **up** to God. This is the only faith that outlines God reaching **down** to man!

Law#19: "The Law of the Law"

"Know ye not, brethren, (for I speak to them that know the law,) how that the law hath dominion over a man as long as he liverish?"

Roman 7:1

The reason that the law has dominion over everything is because it is the Word of God; and since God cannot go against His own Word; His Word is *law*. This is why the name of Jesus is above *every* name. There is a differentiation between the written (rhyme) word of God and the spoken Word (logos or Jesus) of God. Either way it is the '*Word*' of God. Man places significance on the differentiation; in theological studies; because of our 'finite' wisdom.

The Word of God speaks to our innermost being and knows the thoughts and intents of our hearts. Jeremiah 31:33 states, *"But this [shall be] the covenant that I will make with the house of Israel; After those days, saith the LORD, I will put my law in their inward parts, and write it in their hearts; and will be their God, and they shall be my people."*

Jeremiah 31:33

The Bible is a living thing; isn't it? Don't the words contained therein speak to the innermost parts of our being when we are in the deepest of need? How often do we have a hard time in life and hear those 'words' of scripture resounding in our ears?

The heart is also where we invite Jesus to live and rule. What *we* forget is to make Jesus our **_LORD_** AND <u>**Savior.**</u> We are generally okay with Jesus being our Savior part; it's the *Lord* part that we struggle with. I have to say that I am guilty as well with regards to this. Lordship requires that we not only accept the gift that is offered, but that we become obedient, accountable, and committed to name a few of our responsibilities. So we can see that there is no difference between the written Word of God and the living WORD of God.

141

Now that we have that established, in either case God's 'Word' is law! Everything in existence is subject to God's law even God. He stands on and holds himself accountable to His words.

> **"...For when God made promise to Abraham, because he could swear by no greater, *He sware by himself.*"**

Hebrews 6:13

> **"Remember Abraham, Isaac, and Israel, thy servants, to whom *thou squarest by thine own self*, and sadist unto them, I will multiply your seed as the stars of heaven, and all this land that I have spoken of will I give unto your seed, and they shall inherit [it] for ever."**

Exodus 32:13

God can resend His word like He did with Moses but He will never undo something that pertains to the 'law'. With Moses, what God did was turn His wrath away from the children of Israel.

> *Wherefore should the Egyptians speak, and say, For mischief did he bring them out, to slay them in the mountains, and to consume them from the face of the earth? Turn from thy fierce wrath, and repent of this evil against thy people. Remember Abraham, Isaac, and Israel, thy servants, to whom thou squarest by thine own self, and sadist unto them, I will multiply your seed as the stars of heaven, and all this land that I have spoken of will I give unto your seed, and they shall inherit it for ever. And the LORD repented of the evil which he thought to do unto his people.*

Exodus 32: 12-14

God repented or rather changed His mind and stayed His anger so that He would not need to choose another people or give the enemy cause to ridicule His plan for His chosen people. Moses was reminding God of His *own* words and this is how we are supposed to pray in order to get results. He scripture tells us that God's Word will not return to Him 'void' (**Isaiah 55:11**), but it will accomplish what He sent it to do. He did not have to spare Israel and He did not break any 'spiritual laws'; He merely stayed His wrath. His 'word' let's us know that He is a God of wrath and judgment as well as a God of grace and mercy. I never thought about this until I realized that being in the image and likeness of God, we have the ability to mirror his emotions. Frustration is demonstrated in scriptures; in Genesis 6:6, Exodus 32:9&10, Judges 2:18, Jeremiah 26:19, Amos 7:3 and 7:6 and Jonah 3:10.

- Moses touched God's heart because he exemplified one of God's character traits – love and compassion. Moses used the Law of Grace even before mankind had moved into this particular dispensation.
- God's repentance means only that He sighed in exasperation at having to continuously deal with what He termed a 'stiff-necked' (hard headed) people.
- The evil that He thought to visit upon Israel was not a result of God's being wicked or unrighteous, but only speaks to the consequences that God has already set into place, for disobedience and defiance.

God cannot lie; so His law is binding upon: creation, eternity, Satan, mankind, demons and angels alike. Does it make sense for God to act outside of or to be exempt from His own Word or law? I should think not. God is not confined, restricted, or limited by His Word; He is, in fact, *justified* by it.

As parents we understand that when we make our children subject to rules, regulations, stipulations, directives, consequences, etc…we also understand that for them to act against those components causes confusion in the mind of that child, the entire house and amongst the entire house.

> **And if a house be divided against itself, that house cannot stand.**

Mark 3:25

God operates within the same laws that He has set before us. If God says, *"Thou shalt not steal,"* then it is because He is not a thief. If God says that, *"Thou shalt not covet,"* then it is because His children are taken care of and will not be left in want. If God says that the just shall *'live'* by faith, then we can see that Jesus did it; accomplished things through and by it and we can also assume that this is also how God operates. What we must understand is that He has set those laws before us to make us more like Him and show us the way to be conformed to His *living* 'Word' Christ Jesus. He is pointing the way back to the 'Tree of Life'!

The law seems binding and to some degree that is true in a contractual regard, but has only been set into place for direction and guidance. It makes complete sense that a Father would try to prevent His children from making decisions and/or taking actions that would ultimately cause them harm.

I illustrate this to my children this way; *"As children growing up you will want to escape the confines of your parents and break free of the limitations that you had when you were younger. I have no problem letting you grow up; God designed you to do that no matter what I think. My job as a parent is to show you, not the road to walk, but to show you how to walk the road that you choose. As you are growing up, you will gain certain liberties and freedoms. Those have been earned over time and will not be taken from you unless YOU cause them to be removed. If you desire to break free of the limitations and protection of your parents and begin to run toward an electrified fence, then it is my job to first tell you that the fence is electrified. If I cannot stop you from running toward it, I may have to say it again and if you will not stop going in that direction, I may have to yell! Finally, if you are insistent on having **your** way, I may have to chase you and then tackle you to prevent what **I** already know are the results of handling an electrified fence."*

God does this as well, but His frustration results from the fact that He is spiritual and we are material. The instructions are in His Word, but we are a 'stiff-necked' illiterate (unread) people. All we have to do is read His Word!

Let me put to rest first a commonly misquoted scripture (One thing that I know and am sure of is that people hate to be misquoted and/or have their words misinterpreted. Destroying communication is a trick of the enemy and can be seen in every war movie ever made. If we kill the man that has the radio, then he cannot call for reinforcements.)

- Money is *__not__* the root of all evil; the *__love__* of money is the root of all evil. 1 Timothy 6:10 – *For the love of money is the root of all evil: which while some coveted after, they have erred from the faith, and pierced themselves through with many sorrows.*
- You are not God's child unless you accept His son Jesus! Other than that you are simply God's creation – not His child. John 8:44 – *Ye are of [your] father the devil, and the lusts of your father ye will do. He was a murderer from the beginning, and abode not in the truth, because there is no truth in him. When he speaketh a lie, he speaketh of his own: for he is a liar, and the father of it.*
- People do not perish for a lack of knowledge alone, they perish because they have no vision; they *__die__* because they have no knowledge. Proverbs 29:18 - *Where [there is] no vision, the people perish: but he that keeper the 'law', happy [is] he.* Hosea 4:6 - *My people are destroyed for lack of knowledge: because thou hast rejected __knowledge__, I will also reject thee, that thou shalt be no priest to me: seeing thou hast forgotten the 'law' of thy God, I will also forget thy children.*

We are free from the penalty that is imposed by the 'law' (eternal death) through the 'Law of the Spirit of Life'. We cannot, however, trample the 'blood' of Christ underfoot. This means that God is watching; that the saints do not adopt the philosophy of the Sadducee. We cannot believe that after Jesus did all that He did, we have the right to live any kind of way that we want too. We are to take the gift that God gave us seriously enough not to disrespect it! Jesus sweated blood and tears; literally. for us to have the opportunity that God has given us out of His love for His creation.

> *"How much __more__ shall the blood of Christ, who through the eternal Spirit offered himself without spot to God, purge your conscience from dead works to serve the living God?"*

Hebrews 9:14

Finally, there is free will and this however, gives us the power of choice; the opportunity to obey the law or to disobey it.

If we choose to transgress the 'law' of God, then we must accept the fact that the rules and consequences were set into place before He created man. Why do you think that Satan got thrown out of heaven? Heaven and Earth will pass away, but the 'Word' of God will never pass away. He will make a new heaven and a new earth, but He will never make a new 'law'; this is His Word!

Law#20: "The Law of Judgment"

> *"__Behold__, I stand at the door, and knock: if any man hear my voice, and open the door, I will come in to him, and will sup with him, and he with me. To him that overcome will I grant to sit with me in my throne, even as I also overcame, and am set down with my Father in His throne. He that hath an ear, let him hear what the Spirit saith unto the churches."*

Revelation 3:20

This is the spiritual law that tells of a new day and age where all of the physical laws will be changed. This is the Law of Judgment!

This last law will be enforced in every dimension and in every realm both prior to, during, and after the return of Christ. It will be made clear that God is, has and always will be the point of reference to

146

and for everything in the universe. He will be the zenith of harmony between the mind and spirit of mankind. The third dimension will cohabit ate with the fourth dimension as God originally intended when He created Adam. This is what we see in scriptures. [God speaketh once, yeah twice....] *For God speaketh once, yea twice, yet man perceived it not.*

Job 33:14

And they heard the voice of the LORD God walking in the garden in the cool of the day: and Adam and his wife hid themselves from the presence of the LORD God amongst the trees of the garden.

Genesis 3:8

And after six days Jesus takeout with him Peter, and James, and John, and leaden them up into an high mountain apart by themselves: and he was transfigured before them.

Mark 9:2

Enoch walked with God and God took him as well as Elijah. [Two further witnesses] Adam walked with God in the cool of the day and Jesus was transformed in front of Peter, John and James.

Finally, the fourth will know the peace and tranquility as it did before the rebellion of Satan. First however, there must be '*judgment*'.

Judgment is always prerequisite or fulfillment of carrying out the whole letter of the law. Without putting the terms of the law into action, there can be no fulfillment of the law. As we have previously stated, God's Word will not return to Him *void*; so it stands to reason that the action required by the 'law'; whether judgment or blessing, must be carried forth. Without this, there can be no 'law', there can only be the '*implication*' of morality and truth. Isn't this where Satan has gotten us today? Today, whether mankind acknowledges God or not, God is the absolute!

Jesus tells us in Revelation that the earth will come into a time that might be considered a 'war tribunal'. This will be a time when the earth will begin to experience God's accusations against mankind's behavior. What people don't understand across that board is that it will not be God standing in condemnation of man, but rather man's actions being weighed against him according to the 'law' that God has set into place. The only way that any man can escape this is by accepting the free gift of 'life' that God has afforded every man through His son Jesus. Let me say this; while there is the Law of the 'Spirit of Life', it only tells us what to do to obtain life. No law could effectuate or offer to us 'life'.

> *"[Is] the law then against the promises of God? God forbid: for if there had been a law given which could have given life, verily righteousness should have been by the law."*

Galatians 3:21

During this time of judgment, the book of Revelation tells us that there will be 'seven seals' opened prior to the opening of the Book of Life. These 'seven seals' correspond to the 'seven trumpets' and the 'seven vials' of wrath that we read about throughout Jesus' *revelation* to John on Pat mos.

The Law of Judgment is that there shall be an end to what we now know and have come to believe as 'reality'. How much will remain of this present creation is unknown. Scripture says that the heaven and the earth will pass away and that there will be no more sea. My thought is that the framework shall remain; or perhaps an ideology of what we have known yet completely transformed and completely new.

> *"Where wast thou when I laid the foundations of the earth? Declare, if thou hast understanding. Who hath laid the measures thereof, if thou know est? Or who hath stretched the line upon it? Whereupon are the foundations thereof fastened? Or who laid the corner stone thereof..."*

Job 38:4-**6**

I know that myself as a builder, you don't necessarily need to destroy the entire structure. If you have the foundation and the structure can already be in place; then the building may require a major facelift, but the entire building need not be destroyed. Who knows; God is fully capable of doing either. He will destroy the third dimensional body and present us with a new house.

Trust me when I tell you that I completely love these verses in Job. Before I wrote these books that God gave me on Spiritual Warfare; I was a Contractor who owned my own construction company. So when God speaks about measures and foundations and corner stones; it is completely within the grasp of my understanding as a builder. I also have a certain love for the fact that God chose to place His son under the care of a 'carpenter' because He is the original and true carpenter. (My apologies Dear Reader, but I simply had to express that!)

In any case, the earth will be destroyed by fire *this* time. That speaks of a *complete* purging! The heaven and the earth will be remade and the curse will be lifted. Satan will finally have to reckon with the Law of Judgment! He will be judged and found to be in treason against the Kingdom of Heaven and his sentence will be eternity in the lake that is burning with fire and brimstone. [Watch the movie 'Knowing' to see one of the only; or from my standpoint; theatrical Hollywood movies that has ever realistically come anywhere close to the biblical truth of end-time prophecy.]

Likewise will the heavenly host, following Satan and all of humanity, that have not accepted God's pardon through Jesus. This is known as the second death. Look at it this way; when enemies of the state need to be housed, there is a jail to hold them. This place is hell! There is no escaping from hell and just like a jail, the inmates will stay there until they are sentenced by the judge. Then they must be moved from the jail or 'holding cell' to the penitentiary where they will serve out their sentence. It is amazing to me that God has already seen and knows who will _not_ accept His pardon for sins...For this reason; He has designed hell to get bigger!

> ***Therefore hell hath <u>enlarged herself, and opened her mouth</u> <u>without measure</u>:** and their glory, and their multitude, and their pomp, and he that rejoice, shall descend into it.*

Isaiah 5:14

On the day that those that are charged, with crimes against the state, are brought before the white throne; there will be *NO* opportunity for explanation or excuses. This is also a trick that the enemy has injected into the sinners mind. They believe that they are not so bad and that God will understand. They believe that they will plead their case; they believe that the verdict could never be what the 'law' has already decreed it to be. Our legal system has a penalty for each and every crime; accidental and purposed. Those that have not been specifically spelled out fall into some category of the ones that have been; even if an earthly judge has to do a little more homework to render a verdict and pronounce a sentence, the crime will be dealt with.

The devil or adversary (Satan/Lucifer), the beast, the false prophet, and all those that have not accepted Christ Jesus and those that have stood in opposition to him shall be cast into the lake of fire. The only case, that any of them will have is the opportunity to plead, is the fact that Jesus is King of Kings and Lord of Lords! Amen!

Judgment is the fulfillment of the 'law' and this, in and of itself, is a standard. The consequences of *not* meeting the requirements of the law, or being emancipated from it, cause us to be subject to the penalties associated with it. When God renders His judgment on creation once again, we can expect for it to be final. We can expect a complete and total renovation.

This is actually the way that a super-power operates during wartime. When a country is in opposition to world interests; posing a threat to world peace, or has committed war crimes against humanity; then that super-power will step in to rectify the situation. Afterward the insurgent country is made to submit to the 'super-power'. This means that that entire nation has been determined to no longer be a threat. That nation has been nullified concerning it's capabilities to impose a threat. The super-power can pull back its forces and its soldiers can return home to their country and their families for some long overdue R&R (Rest and Relaxation). Satan will be removed from power; Jesus has already retrieved the keys from to the enemies P.O.W. (prisoners of war) camp. The earth will be under a new 'divine' constitution! The saints of God, that have believed in and accepted the shed blood of Jesus Christ unto salvation, will rule and judge! The new heaven and the new earth will be occupied by the people of God!

> *"He will swallow up death in victory; and the Lord GOD will wipe away tears from off all faces; and the rebuke of his people shall he take away from off all the earth: for the LORD hath spoken [it]."*

Isaiah 25:8

> *"For the Lamb which is in the midst of the throne shall feed them, and shall lead them unto living fountains of waters: and God shall wipe away all tears from their eyes."*

Revelation 7:17

> *"And God shall wipe away all tears from their eyes; and there shall be no more death, neither sorrow, nor crying, neither shall there be any more pain: for the former things are passed away."*

Revelation 21:4

Notes And Reflections For The Reader:

Notes And Reflections For The Reader:

The Hierarchy

The players in the game

Why do we even have a hierarchy and what is it?

In the military there are ranks that have been set up to: establish order, insure success, and build cohesiveness within the force. That idea stems from every other basic principle that mankind ever has or will have – God!

God has created us in His likeness and in His image; so it stands to reason that we should also '*think*' like Him and carry out our activities in much the same fashion as He would. The problem with man is that we choose to erase and are attempting to erase God's blueprint within us and claim the credit for God's ideas. Satan knows this and what he does is assist in helping man to establish a basis for excluding the creator from the equation.

A private in the military does not understand things in the same way that a 5-star general understands things. The private does not know the intricacies that work behind the scenes to get each mission accomplished. He does not know where to place troops, when to go into unfamiliar territory, or how to negotiate the terms of surrender of say a despot or dictator. A soldier knows and is expected to do the job that he has been trained for and how to work with the soldiers that he has trained with.

When I read Genesis for the first time, I always wondered what verse 2:1 meant. At first I assumed that when it said 'host' that it was talking about just the *things* that God had created. For some reason the word 'host' kept haunting me; so I looked it up.

Thus the heavens and the earth were finished, and all the <u>host</u> of them.

Genesis 2:1

Webster's describes 'host', in one way, as a multitude or great number of persons or things. It also describes 'host' as an army. Okay, that could not be all that there was to it. So I looked in the Strong's Concordance for the original Hebrew definition to see what God meant when He told Moses that the 'host' were finished and set in place. I then asked myself. "Why would God need to set 'heavenly army' into place on an earth that He just created and that He was proud of? Look at this scripture:

"And he said unto them, I beheld Satan as lightning fall from heaven."

Luke 10:18

We need to realize that Satan was cast *out* of heaven; he lost his position and his place. He did not however lose his power or his abilities as a 4th dimensional (spiritual) being. We find out in Job 1:7 that Satan was on earth!

When Satan was cast out he took 1/3 of the angels in heaven with him. It is reasonable to assume that God set a guard in place to protect His creation. So when we read that the heavens and the earth were finished and all of the host of them; we can say that the heavenly army was in place and remains in place until the 'war counsel' convenes to sentence the traitors of the 'Kingdom' of God. Scripture tells us in 1 Corinthians 6:3 that we will 'judge' angels. Judge them for what? The angels that remain in heaven have no need of judgment, but the ones that have lost their place in heaven along with Satan; they need to be set straight. We will judge them according to the Word of God; according to what they have done *concerning* and *upon* the earth; and according to how they have come up against God's creation as a whole. Some things must be looked at as man did not find out certain information on his own. Some things must be looked at from the stand point of spiritual beings have placed some things in *our* path to further their own agenda.

So in our military we have everything from 5 star generals to privates and everything in-between. We don't know much about how God has set things in order concerning His army, save what scripture tells us. I have done some deeper digging into studies that claim to know more, but it is true wisdom to remain grounded before researching things with which the enemy can lead us astray.

In scripture we are told about:

- **Archangels** – The first in political rank and power; highest order of angel; like five star generals.
- **Angels** – lowest order of angels; like privates in the military.
- **Principalities** – Princes over nations and countries and the affairs of man. Ephesians 6:12
- **Powers** – Having power over certain places and or things... Ephesians 6:12
- **Dominions** – Having '*dominion*' over certain areas of their particular expertise...
- **Sycophant** – (Wheels or Thrones) [God's Justice and Authority] – Ezekiel 10:17 & Colossians 1:16
- **Cherubim** – (Protectors, Guardians) – Genesis 3:24, Ezekiel 10:17-20 & 1 Kings 6:23-28
- **Seraphic** – Care takers of God's throne and are in continuous praise Isaiah 6:1-7
- **Spiritual Wickedness in High Places** - Ephesians 6:12
- **The Rulers of the Darkness of this world** - Ephesians 6:12

With all of this going on, we need to view some of this from the Hebrew (original text) what was being communicated. The Heb. Word for **_host_** is: Tswana and it translates soldiers prepared for war. So the heavens and the earth were finished and the *soldiers prepared for war* were set into place. So the hierarchy or order was set into place before Adam and Eve's transgression in Eden. God's foreknowledge moved Him to prepare for what was to come within the temporal time frame six thousand years later.

So who is it that we are fighting? Amongst those deceived in heaven by Satan, were a great number of differing ranked angels that would have normally been submissive to Satan's authority under God and in their heavenly ranks. If he was a 5 star general in heaven, then he had an entire group of different ranking angels that were under him from lieutenants, captains, corporals, officers, and on down to privates.

Our war is *not* against flesh and blood or better put, temporal things; it is however against these spiritual beings. We know that we cannot prevail against them. They are older than us, smarter than us, stronger than us and exist on a different realm than we do. For these reasons God has stepped in from on high with His army ready and set into place; all we need do is be obedient.

There are a great many scriptures that allow us to know that our God will fight for us, does and always will! God is already prepared, all we have to do is be obedient and shut up (or hold our peace); however you choose to say it?

> *"The LORD shall __fight for you__, and ye shall hold your peace."*

> Exodus 14:14

> *"The LORD your God which goth before you, he shall __fight for you__, according to all that he did for you in Egypt before your eyes..."*

> Deuteronomy 1:30

> *"Ye shall not fear them: for the LORD your God he shall __fight for you__."*

> Deuteronomy 3:22

> *"For the LORD your God [is] he that goth with you, to __fight for you__ against your enemies, to save you."*

> Deuteronomy 20:4

> *"Ye shall not [need] to fight in this [battle]: set yourselves, stand ye [still], and see the salvation of the LORD with you, O Judah and Jerusalem: fear not, nor be dismayed; to morrow go out against them: for the LORD [will be] with you."*

> 2 Chronicles 20:17

When we have this many scriptures that tell us to stand still and that our God will fight for us; we begin to understand the value of obedience and silence. All Joshua had to do was march around the city walls thirteen times; all Moses had to do was keep his hands up or hold his staff up; all Gideon had to do was light the candles and blow the horns; all Jesus had to do was keep quiet and let them crucify him and so on. When God is fighting for you, what can we do? It's like calling your father or your older brother to take care of the bully.

The Hierarchy is God's created angels that are no longer playing on God's team. They are former beings of authority and power that no longer desire to be under the direction of their creator. These beings have been removed from their positions and their places. In today's military terms we would say that they are receiving an Article 15 or bring dishonorably discharged ire. non-judicial punishment. Later; and God has already ordained and decreed this; there *will* be a Court Marshall.

Article 15 excuses one from active duty with an air of having lost not only their military responsibilities, but their honor.

I have tried to envision what the Lake of Fire would be like and I simply cannot. All that I can write Dear Reader is that I would not be able to take it! The lake that burns with fire and brimstone eternally must be a different kind of lake indeed. Brimstone literally comes from the Old Norse **Bannister** meaning 'Burning Stone' or 'Stone of Fire'; rather another name for **sulfur**. What kind of fire and burning stones could never be quenched; never die out? What kind of fire could burn a spiritual being and cause them pain for eternity?

The closest comparison that I have is a YouTube video of NASCAR driver Rick Mars and his mechanic engulfed in what is called an 'alcohol fire'. The flames are invisible to everyone, but the effects are not. We have to be realistic and admit that there are some things that, whether we know about them or not, they exist and cannot be swept under the rug or ignored. Scary to say the least!

I tell anyone that I have the opportunity to minister too, for the most part; the average man will never have to deal with certain members of the spiritual hierarchy. Archangels, Thrones, Dominions, Powers, Principalities, etc. have things set up so that their agenda is already in place. It is a government and like a government there are certain things that need to take place before you can move up the food chain. If you need the governor, then you must first contact the councilman for your district, and then the mayor, and then the senator and *then* the governor. The private never skips through the chain of command and deals directly with the general, however the general can instruct a private as he sees fit and *anyone* that is under his command.

Satan does not need to deal with average individual unless they are a person of influence, money, power or someone that has the ability to change the world scene. I am quite sure that he is grooming whoever will be the Anti-Christ, The Beast and the False Prophet. There is already enough technology in place where it would be very easy to demonstrate signs and wonders, make the *image* of the beast talk and people worship that image. Japanese technology already has robots in place that mimic human beings in every way.

The who's who doesn't matter as much as we may like to believe; we are not the ones fighting the battle. It does however make difference as far as being knowledgeable so that we know what to ask God for and how our prayers should be directed. We cannot expect God to fight our battles for us if we don't know what and where to point for Him to help. Sure He knows, but we have an accountability of our own as well!

Notes And Reflections For The Reader:

Notes And Reflections For The Reader:

Location

Where the Enemy Dwells

Where are our enemies? Everywhere! It's like what one of my favorite movies says; "The agents are no one and everyone" That is very true because we must contend with the fact that scripture tells us that we entertain angels unaware and also those forces can and do *influence* everyone. The only way that we stand any sort of chance and know how to mount a defensive is by knowing the Word of God and by staying alert. There is never an instance where the Christians fail-safe system is never on yellow-alert. When it comes to winning this race, it should always be on red-alert.

Satan will attack your mind first because that is where the battle begins. He will let us bask in the glory of our salvation for a moment and then wait for the fire to cool down. "Oh so you have accepted Christ as your Savior?, but can you be obedient and keep it going?" "Are you willing to hold up your end of the bargain or go through the trouble of finding out what your end of the Bargain actually is?" "Are you willing to suffer what you say you believe?"

Yes, Satan has your Christian walk mapped out as well! His goal is to turn you into a *double-agent* and use you to pull other saints away from the 'Kingdom' or others that would follow you into thinking that they can live any way they want and still enter the 'Kingdom'. It may surprise you who actually has the belief that they are going to rest in the Glory of God while they are still doing their own thing here on earth. God will hold you accountable. That is why Exodus 20:7 says: ***"Thou shalt not take the name of the LORD thy God in vain; for the LORD will not hold him guiltless that takeout his name in vain."***

Since Christ's name is above every other name that God has placed before man; then as a Christian, which means *follower of Christ*, and we are claiming that title and not living up to it or trying, then we have already broken that commandment. Remember Jesus said that He did not come to do away with the 'law' but to fulfill it. Jesus also says that not one *jot* or *tittle* shall pass away from the 'law'. (**Jot** and **Tittle** are the marks in the Hebrew alphabet that are like crossing the English 'T's' or dotting the 'I's' or commas or periods.) God says that debt you must pay because He won't hold you guiltless.

Satan will attack your mind first and your new found walk with Christ. He will then attack your family. Why your family? Your family is the closest thing to you. "He or She seems like they are in it to win it; let's try his wife or her husband." The scriptures tell us in Ephesians 6:12 that we are not wrestling against 'flesh and blood'. The word is 'wrestling' not fighting. We are only _wrestling_; the fight is not ours, but the Lord's. If we get caught up into trying to fight as opposed to understanding the wrestling aspect, then we will not only lose before we get our feet squarely planted, but there will be casualties of war that are on our account balance.

It will get **bad**, but God only requires us to stand still and hold our peace. Our spouses will not act right, our children will not act right, our friends and co-workers will not act right, as a matter of fact, Satan will also use the average person in the gas station or in the convenience store to push our buttons. God will allow this to test us and prove us so that when we do get to the 'Kingdom' we will be good stewards over the reward that He has paid so much for us to possess.

The enemy wants your life! This is the importance of reading your bible and allowing God to write His Word on your heart. It is so that when the enemy comes in the same way as he did with Jesus; with all of his offers and tricks, we can simply 'stand' and recite the Word of God back to him. Jesus never lifted a finger; He simply reminded Satan of what God had already said. This is why the scripture says of itself:

"All scripture [is] given by inspiration of God, and [is] profitable for doctrine, for reproof, for correction, for instruction in righteousness."

2 Timothy 3:16

Make no mistake, our enemy is **bold**. From his standpoint what does he have to fear from us? Christ's sacrifice; that's what. Satan was the 'anointed cherub that coverlet'; created beautiful and perfect. I believe that it is a misnomer to continue with the idea that Satan was in charge of some heavenly choir. The bible does not say that. The bible speaks about how Lucifer was created only in terms of his physical *attributes*; his appearance. They are however <u>spiritual</u>.

His job was to *cover* or *protect* the throne of God. Go back and see what we have already listed as the jobs or duties of those that are in this spiritual hierarchy. As a cherub, he was a 'protector' and this means that all of the military intelligence, all of the power and all of the abilities were perfected in him. It only says in God's Word that he was cast out. As we see that Satan is made of certain jewels and that he is made of musical instruments, he was most assuredly a *reflection* of God's grace and beauty.

How art thou fallen from heaven, O Lucifer, son of the morning! how art thou cut down to the ground, which didst weaken the nations! For thou hast said in thine heart, I will ascend into heaven, I will exalt my throne above the stars of God: I will sit also upon the mount of the congregation, in the sides of the north: I will ascend above the heights of the clouds; I will be like the most High. 15 Yet thou shalt be brought down to hell, to the sides of the pit. They that see thee shall narrowly look upon thee, and consider thee, saying, Is this the man that made the earth to tremble, that did shake kingdoms;

Isaiah 14:12-16

Moreover the word of the LORD came unto me, saying, Son of man, take up a lamentation upon the king of Cyrus, and say unto him, Thus saith the Lord GOD; Thou sealest up the sum, full of wisdom, and perfect in beauty. Thou hast been in Eden the garden of God; every precious stone was thy covering, the sardines, topaz, and the diamond, the beryl, the onyx, and the jasper, the sapphire, the emerald, and the carbuncle, and gold: the workmanship of thy tablets and of thy pipes was prepared in thee in the day that thou wast created.

Ezekiel 28: 11 - 13

[This is what is known in scripture as a 'double reference' or 'dual reference' since we know that the king of Cyrus was not the anointed cherub that covered God's thrown and he was not designed the way that this scripture is telling us.]

Something that struck me as ironic was the fact that he had the freedom to walk up and down in the midst of the stones of fire in heaven around God's thrown. When Satan has been judged, God will bring the fire out from the middle of *him* and it will burn him to ashes for eternity. It's like God is saying, *"You wanted my spot in the midst of the stones of fire? Here you are; you can have them forever; your new duty is to be the catalyst that keeps those stones burning for the Lake of Fire for all of eternity."* We have just pointed out that sulfur or brimstone is known as the 'burning stone' or the 'stone of fire'.

"Thou hast defiled thy sanctuaries by the multitude of thine iniquities, by the iniquity of thy traffic; therefore will I bring forth a fire from the midst of thee, it shall devour thee, and I will bring thee to ashes upon the earth in the sight of all them that behold thee."

Ezekiel 28:18

We understand that this is what is known in scripture as a *'double reference'*. Ezekiel is prophesying about two separate beings with the same character; the prince of Cyrus and Satan. The reference is about both, but only one is a spiritual being and can have this particular spiritual punishment executed on him.

Think about how Satan spoke to God when he went back to heaven with the other angels to give an account. He debated with and challenged God about Job. He has made it his goal to destroy God's creation and take as much of mankind to the lake if fire as he can before God executes His final judgment. It is my opinion that an 'attempt' at repentance might have been a better tactic. I do not know, but it seems like that may have been worth a shot especially after having been that close to God and *knowing* as much about God as he does? Just food for thought.

So again, where are these 4thdmensional beings? When scripture speaks about familiar spirits, these are spirits that are very close to us. With their intelligence and abilities, they catalog every detail about us and utilize those details against us. What you like to eat and drink may become tools for obesity. What you like watch on television may turn into a 'doorway' for their doctrine. What you like in a man or woman may be a way for him to pull you away from your faith. What we like as far as recreation may be a way for them to insert that into God's time alone with you and so on.

Satan will make it *seem* like he is everywhere, but with an army of 1/3 of an innumerable amount of angels that were cast out of heaven with him, he can make it **seem** that way. They attack our minds to the extent that they know what too and when too whisper and make suggestions to our minds. They know how to excite our flesh and make us believe that we are still in God's grace. They know how to send their agents into our lives and give us choices and alternatives that we may or may not seek God concerning the right answers so that a good Godly decision can be made. They study and know our character. They are close to us every step of the way during our walk. What else do they have to do while they await judgment? They keep following the same leader that led them away from safety and security in heaven and apparently their loyalty extends to the very gates of hell.

They are always watching and always plotting their next move according to their orders. They are fulfilling Satan's plans to the very letter. They are helping him to enlarge hell to the point that, by the time the end comes, there will be a flow of spirits cast into the lake of fire unlike any that there has ever been in any other portion of creation. You might say the flood of Noah, but there weren't seven billion people on the planet at that time. Human souls will pour into hell by the billions. That doesn't sound nice, but neither I nor God ever said that this would be a pretty picture.

Definitely don't take my word for anything hat you read or hear! I got to the point where I am able to write about what I know by number one reading and number two listening to people that held the truth close to them and respected God's word as such. As far as reading, Brian Nichols told me in college that, *"Anything that you ever wanted to know about <u>anything</u>; someone has already written about it."* That was just two college students having casual conversation, but it was so simple and profound that I made it paramount in my thinking and I never forgot it.

Here is an excerpt from God Issuer:

An African proverb says, "When elephants fight, the grass always loses." In the realm of spiritual warfare, Christians are the "grass": "our struggle is not against flesh and blood, but against the rulers, against the authorities, against the powers of this dark world and against the spiritual forces of evil in the heavenly realms" (Ephesians 6:12).

For further reading you may go to this website for the complete article:

http://www.godissues.org/what-are-demons/

I like this because it confirms a lot of what I have already been writing in these pages Dear Reader.

Notes And Reflections For The Reader:

Notes And Reflections For The Reader:

Doorways

What and Where to Guard

God has created doorways into our minds and spirits. Mankind is not a closed or locked building; we are God's temple. As a temple, we are to open our doors at the appropriate times and allow those things bearing the correct identification to come in and be entertained by Jesus the host of the banquet. We have invited Him into our lives to take up residence and make Himself at home as our **Lord**. We must begin to treat him as such if we are to maintain the hope of having residence with **His** Father for eternity.

> *"In my Father's house are <u>many mansions</u>: if [it were] not [so], I would have told you. I go to prepare a place for you."*

John 14:2

The word mansions does not mean '*mansions*' in the sense that we think of *large* houses here on earth, but rather dwelling places. Jesus is saying, "*In my Father's house are many dwelling places, positions or habitations.*" My thought is that since an innumerable amount of angels lost their positions in heaven, God will fill this void with those that accept His son. The 3rd dimensional realm will coexist with the 4th dimensional realm the way that God initially intended it. Jesus has returned to prepare our places!

Sin is the chief doorway that the enemy uses to infiltrate what would have been mankind's first line of defense post creation. Scripture tells us that all sin falls into three categories and three only. This seems overly simple, but how many corn fields can be planted from what is produced by a single kernel of corn? Had Adam and Eve not sinned, then mankind would have kept the doorways into his spirit unified with God and eventually gained *all* that God had intended to give him.

All sins fall into the categories of: the *lust* of the eyes; the *lust* of the flesh or the *pride* of life. Satan used all three of these to deceive Eve in Eden.

> *And when the woman <u>saw</u> that the tree [was] <u>good for food,</u> and that it [was] <u>pleasant to the eyes</u>, and a tree <u>to be desired to make [one] wise</u>, she took of the fruit thereof, and did eat, and gave also unto her husband with her; and he did eat.*

Genesis 3:6

Eve saw the tree and also that it was pleasant to the eyes. What Satan did was direct attention to the tree and then impress upon her how beautiful the tree and its fruit were. Eve got a double dose of *eye* candy. I always teach that we lust after what we commonly see on a regular basis. What we like to take into our eye doorway is always an opportunity for our enemies to cause us problems. It is not by chance that the saying goes, *"The eyes are the windows to the soul."* Like a window, the eyes can operate in two ways. The eyes can reflect our emotions from inside of our temples and tell the story of what is happening on the inside. Likewise, the outside world can *peer* into our eyes or present something *to* our eyes that can influence what goes on within the temple.

The eyes or our **visual** or **optic** doorway is what the enemy uses for fornication, adultery, theft, covetousness and any crime against God's law that can stimulate our desire to obtain something that we have not earned correctly. This doorway is one that we *can* close, but with it closed it remains difficult to function on this third dimensional realm. People that do not have sight prove to us everyday that it is still possible, but difficult. The eye is a very intricate mechanism. It can see closeness and distance; central and peripheral; it can see and translate correctly, to our brains, things that are upside down *and* backward. The main reason that the enemy uses this doorway so prolifically is because of its ability transfer information directly to our souls. The right or wrong thing presented to our eyes can create thoughts that we may then need to differentiate between our own, the world's or the enemy's. Our eyes take pictures and present them to our brains for storage faster than we have developed the technology to measure. This is not a task that the average person will add to their list of many worries, but it is important if we want to have the testimony of being one that stood.

Paul tells us how to 'stand' in **Ephesians 6:13 & 14**:

> *"Wherefore take unto you the whole Armour of God; that ye may be able to with<u>stand</u> in the evil day, and having done all, to <u>stand</u>. <u>Stand</u> therefore, having your loins girt about with truth, and having on the breastplate of righteousness..."*

He tells us how to stand up *against* and how to do all that we have to do to stand. He also says stand this way and with these *spiritual* weapons. Why are they spiritual weapons?

> *("For the weapons of our warfare [are] not carnal, but mighty <u>through</u> God to the pulling down of strong holds...")*

> 2 Corinthians 10:4

We are not supposed to engage the enemy on his territory, but rather hold the territory that we already have and endure hardness like a 'good soldier'. God is doing the fighting and our weapons are so that we are not 'standing' on the battlefield defenseless and naked.

Our ears or our **auditory** senses are also doorways into our minds. It is one of the doorways that we cannot close physically or mentally. What we allow into our ears goes directly into a portion of our minds that makes it nearly impossible to defend. This is why music is so influential. When we here certain music, it bypasses our 'frontal lobe' and enters our mind directly before we have the ability or a way to stop it. Think about how the media uses commercials and music in unison to sell products or influence our psyche. Once certain 'jingles' get into our minds through our ears, we can then recite the whole commercial. I am not talking about for the time frame that the commercial runs its course, but for *years* afterward.

Think about how just twenty short years ago there were stipulations by the FCC about what could and could not be broadcast over the airways. It is like scripture says, "A little leaven, Leavenworth the whole lump!" What the enemy did was take words that had alternate meanings and slide them in a little at a time. Then he took people that looked younger than they were and made the public view them as children using adult language and placed them into adult roles. Then he used real child actors and placed them into situations where the public could understand their dilemmas and their rationale for using such strong language. Then he implanted it into our minds through implications and through comedy, movies and finally television, The implications and inferences placed us in the mindset of being able to look at the forbidden from more than one angle. Once we began to become comfortable with what we were hearing and had a way to rationalize and turn a blind eye to it, he had us hooked.

We began to say, *"Oh that's just a bad kid,"* or *"That child has issues."* We began to look at things from the standpoint of, *"He/She shouldn't have said that, but it WAS funny."* *"This or that is a real life situation because I know someone that went through the same thing."* Satan still allows the warning labels; the 'illicit lyrics' labels on music, but who actually goes to the store to buy music with their children? We cannot protect our children's ear doorways when they must go to school with other children whose parents have a different God view than we do or when bus drivers are using music to pacify those that are on the bus so that they can do their job effectively.

Our ears have been designed to transmit information to our minds *in* our sleep. Think about the way that some companies sell language tapes that have been designed to teach us a different language while we are asleep. Think about hypnotists who speak to their subjects while they are in a state of hypnosis or light sleep. Think about the mentality of our children when they wake up, after they have fallen asleep with earphones in their ears, listening to some *pop star* or *rapper* preach and minister **their** worldview to our children while they are supposed to be resting.

Technology has gotten out of control because we have not placed any checks or balances into place. The scary part is that technology is getting smaller and smaller daily. At some point we will not even know who is connected to some outside source while they are standing directly in front of us. The enemy has found the way to slip into our minds through a doorway that we are not able to easily guard.

What about our noses? The only way that we have to guard this doorway is to hold our breath, wear some type of protection or move away from anything that is attempting to infiltrate our bodies through this doorway. A woman will wear perfume that stimulates our smelling sense. This mimics *pheromones*, which are odors that stimulate the desire that God has given us to procreate with the opposite sex. Our noses also alert us to potential dangers such as fire because we are able to smell something that is burning. We can be *calmed* by smelling certain scents that have been designed to give us peace or even put us to sleep.

The sense of smell is called the **olfactory** sense. This system, like all of our senses is connected to our nervous system. When one of our five senses is stimulated, it can affect our entire body. The sense of smell can alert us to danger, welcome familiar company, things that can be desirable or undesirable, and it can induce something into our cardiovascular system and/or blood stream. I believe that the enemy's goal once having infiltrated this doorway is always to tamper with our blood. Think of the millions that are killed by chemical agents that are designed to be breathed. The military's of different countries use these types of weapons against their enemies and sometimes their own people.

"Before I continue with 'Doorways', does it not stand to reason that Satan knows or has taken the time to educate himself on the intricacies of how man is made? Satan knows how we are made better than we will ever have a chance to discover or uncover." He will never know what God knows, but he knows more than we can ever imagine. In Genesis Chapter 4, Satan thought that he had cut off the bloodline of Jesus by inspiring Cain to kill Abel. In Genesis Chapter 6, Satan tried to cut off the bloodline of Christ a second

time by trying to inject it with the sin nature of 'Fallen Angels'. And yet again in Exodus when the Hebrew male children were cast into the river. Only the males were killed because there were other plans for the female children that were born. The life is in the blood as the scripture tells us and it is the shed blood of Christ that makes atonement for our sins.

It is more important than we care to delve into how really important the blood is.

> *"...And he said, "What hast thou done? The voice of thy brother's blood crieth unto me from the ground."*

Genesis 4:10

> *And it came to pass, because the midwives feared God, that he made them houses. And Pharaoh charged all his people, saying, Every son that is born ye shall cast into the river, and every daughter ye shall save alive.*

Exodus 1:21

> *"For the life of the flesh [is] in the blood: and I have given it to you upon the altar to make an atonement for your souls: for it [is] the blood [that] maketh an atonement for the soul."*

Leviticus 17:11

> *Then Jesus said unto them, "Verily, verily, I say unto you, Except ye eat the flesh of the Son of man, and drink his blood, ye have no life in you."*

John 6:53

Think about the drunkard or the drug addict; the way that the drug enters into their body is either through the nose, the mouth, or the skin. We will talk about the skin in a moment, but no matter the doorway, it finds its way into the blood. After it has found its way into the blood, our defenses are down and the enemy's influence is almost unstoppable. Drugs and alcohol enter the bloodstream and give the user an 'altered' sense of reality for a time. That span of time is enough to take that person out of a normally rational state of mind and place him into an altered state. If the person that is affected by either one of these does not possess a rational way of thinking, the enemy will capitalize on the collateral damage that is incurred to those associated with or in close proximity too that person.

Satan attacks the blood because the life is in the blood. He attempted to taint the blood of the Savior because he knew what God was saying in Genesis 3:15. God promised a Savior that would come through a human woman that would defeat him (Satan). Jesus' death on the cross was the beginning of God's NEW Testament to mankind!

Think about it as a will and testament. We have Will's that are read upon someone's death. The person that dies is referred to as the 'Testator' and what is read during the legal proceedings is known as the 'Testator's' *last* 'Will and Testament'. In past times it was necessary for blood to be shed in order that the 'Will' be effectual. This adds a whole different spin to why Jesus needed to die on the cross and why we have separated the Bible into two portions called God's Old Testament and God's New Testament.

A testament also tells us which party's shall be the beneficiaries of the testator's final Will and who shall be excluded. This is the reason that the enemy seeks to infiltrate our 'doorways' and steal what our Savior has left for us according to God's **New** Testament.

So ask yourself why so many young people are gravitating towards inhalants as a form of drug? This leads Satan directly into the part of the human body that will allow him to enter not only the bloodstream, but the mind. Our sinus passage leads from our nose directly into our brain and filters what we breathe to the rest of our body through the lungs. Satan's goal is to storm our temples and seat himself on the throne therein; just like he tried in heaven. Look at scripture and the things that Jesus says about His body; how if they destroyed

His temple He would raise it up again in three days. Then research the twenty-four elders and how they correspond to the human rib cage; the sea of glass and how that corresponds to the pericardium; water around the human heart and the thundering and lightnings and how that corresponds to the four chambers of the heart and the four gospels. [*credit given to Michael Haggard of Bethe Church in Fests Missouri for these teachings and more*]

Our taste 'doorway' is one that Satan can manipulate very easily. What we want to taste can depend on what it looks like, what it smells like and what it feels like to our mouths. We will get to our sense of touch momentarily as well, but our sense of taste can incorporate other 'doorways'. We might not look at this 'doorway' as being very important, but when we look at what is arguably the greatest country that has ever existed on this planet and the degree of obesity from children to adults; we are forced to change our thinking. America is the land of excess and having more than what you could possibly use; it is also the land of waste. I have watched people that have visited from other countries go into an All-You-Can-Eat restaurant and become astounded. I have spoken with them and heard them explain the degree of difficulty that they and their families must go through just to get the portion of the food that we throw away.

What Americans resort to in order to preserve this way of life is actually causing more problems than it will ever solve. Preservatives, flavoring, coloring, and even non-edible items that have become a part of our diets, is shortening our lifespan. Look at all of the cooking shows that have made it to cable. (The *FOOD Network* is one of my favorite channels, but I still see the waste, the excess and the pride that is involved.) There does not seem to be anything wrong with the different types of food that are being presented; does it? Remember, if you give the enemy a rope he will want to be a cowboy and you are the bronco that he will be trying to break. He will take you where you do not want to go, involve you where you do not want to be involved and keep you longer than you want to stay.

Our sense of taste is a delicate doorway and involves not only our inner bowels, but it must pass over the tongue that is the key to our speech. How often has something that was too hot or too spicy prompted a response from another part of your body? If Satan can get you to eat what he wants you too eat or not eat certain things that are good for you, then he is making progress.

God has pointed out, in His Word, that the 'doorway' of our mouth is very important to Him. It does not have to do simply with taste. Out of this 'doorway' comes blessings and cursing and this is because it is linked to our tongues. This is where the gift of speech comes from and what confirms that we are created in God's image and likeness. This is the doorway that Jesus used to heal the sick; tell the lame to rise and walk; open blind eyes; calm the storm and bring Lazarus forth from the grave. Is it a wonder that Satan used this doorway to trick Adam and Eve into bringing the curse of sin on humanity? Of course it was the sin of disobedience that brought sin upon mankind, but the 'doorways' that the enemy used was how he executed his plan. Presenting the tree to the eye was not the problem. Coaxing Eve into actually placing the fruit into her mouth 'doorway' was!

Our sense of **touch** is the last 'doorway' that we will speak about. Every part of our physical being is attached to this doorway. It permeates us both internally and externally. Some areas are more sensitive than others, but is related to the biggest organ of our bodies and we don't think of it this way – our skin.

Our skin is sensitive to heat, cold, roughness, smoothness, sharpness, softness, rigidity, and a whole host of other things that directly affect our other 'doorways'. If a grain of sand gets into our eye then it can basically stop us in our tracks. If the temperature outside is too hot or too cold, then it can quicken or impede our movement. If we are touched a certain way it can attract us or repel us. Touch is the way that God has set aside for some of His most basic gifts. This is the 'doorway' that God used with Adam and Eve, but had to step away from after man sinned. Sin cannot dwell in the presence of God. Touch is a part of *fellowship* and *relationship*; these are the reasons that man was created.

Jesus encouraged Thomas to touch Him and handle Him after the cross.

"Then saith he to Thomas, reach hither thy finger, and behold my hands; and reach hither thy hand, and thrust [it] into my side: and be not faithless, but believing."

John 20:27

Thomas' touch is what led to his ultimate belief and increased his faith to the point where he was willing to *die* for what he had handled with his own hands. God understands what this 'doorway' means to man. It is the way we are soothed, comforted, relaxed, encouraged, and much more. It is a 'doorway' that God has created so that we are able to experience the sensation of who He is more readily and that is 'LOVE'!

Our most intimate experience with our fellow human being comes through this 'doorway' and it is through this 'doorway' that Satan seeks to destroy humanity. He will dull how this 'doorway' will operate; pervert how we utilize this 'doorway', or make it so that this 'doorway' is abused. Satan has turned his focus toward this 'doorway' extensively in these end times. The restraints on sex have been removed and the world stage has broken out of the gates with lightening speed.

What *is* restrained or prohibited today as far as sex is concerned? Homosexuality has grown to epic proportions in the last 20 years; group sex is common nowadays; having sex with the under aged has names and titles that have become common place in the English vernacular, pedophilia has become a household topic; sexual crimes with both men and women have become the norm with persons who have issues in their adult life; bestiality is not identified as such anymore; and mankind has gotten to a point where thrill seeking rules the day. The enemy has basically turned America into a modern day Sodom and Gomorrah and the powers that be are endorsing it to say the least.

Satan has kicked this 'doorway' wide open, in this day and age. The only way that I have been able too come to terms with any of what is considered 'normal', in today's world, is to remind myself that what I am seeing, hearing and reading about on a daily basis is what God has already pointed out in His Word that these *would* be the 'doorways' attacked in the last days. I can't, however, help but still be shocked on a regular! I cringe about the things that my children are going through and have yet to go through.

Our children are a lot smarter and sharper nowadays than when we were their age. They are intelligent beyond their years and able to think and multitask seven times faster than we could at their age. Look at the video games that they play or the way that they pick up on the latest technology. By the time that the next technological advance hits the market, they are waiting and have studied how to utilize it before we the parents can actually afford it. The introduction of the 'information age' has catapulted our youth into areas where their young 'doorways' are wide open.

We, as good stewards, have to teach them how to *stand* for holiness in a world that has been *tailor* made to make them *fall*. We have to do our very best to train them in the areas in which the enemy will attack them. Above all else, thy must be shown, as well as our letting them know, that God is alive; He has created them for a purpose and He cares.

Notes And Reflections For The Reader:

Notes And Reflections For The Reader:

Our Strategy

Plan of Action

Training should be the first goal for those who come to Christ. A good shepherd will place a new member of their flock around members that have been faithful, trustworthy, loyal, and have the necessary experience and Christian character, that can be easily recognized. We must choose a shepherd that will place us around other members of their flock that understand and are submissive to them as shepherd and that have remained teachable. These members must follow their shepherd as that shepherd is led to greener pastures; over hills; through valleys; by still waters; and be willing to follow him over mountains and rocky terrain if required. Our strategy depends entirely upon our ability to make '*good*' decisions concerning '*how*' we are going to walk our walk.

When Jesus was gathering the twelve, He chose them according to what He saw *in* them; whether or not they were able to be taught; and if they would be committed to gathering other people to the flock. Jesus did not force Himself upon any of them, but rather allowed them to make their own decisions concerning the direction in which *He* was already going. He simply made His offer and kept going. This is something that we have to understand; something that we have to decide. We must ask ourselves if we are capable of seeing the trees or will we live our lives focused on the forest?

Like the disciples, the first part of our plan of action must include us placing our minds into the right perspective. We must ask ourselves the question of whether or not we are willing to let go of the world *or* will we try to drag it behind us. The disciples gave up their entire way of life and everything that they had ever known to follow Jesus. We must be *that* compelling when we share the gospel. Our witness should be something that will persuade the average man to follow Christ; something that, when presented, is so attractive and rational that they will, at the very least, want to ask themselves the questions, **"...should I... and what if...?"**

We must outline and correctly represent the 'hope' that *we* have and that we desire for them to share with us and others. We have to show the worldly minded man a way that they have never seriously considered. Once we have planted that seed, we have done what the Lord has asked us to do. Any further work on our part will come in after they have made their informed decision. The unsaved need to know, before they start on Christ's path, that we have left the world that we know and have been a part of, behind! We cannot present too them that we are perfect, but that we are moving toward perfection daily and purposefully. They must understand that we have chosen our path and only offer them the opportunity to walk along side us in the same direction. We have to let them know that we have understood that we are on a different path; we are seeking to please God; that we are soldiers; and that we have an eternal hope.

> **"No man that Warren entanglement himself with the affairs of [this] life; that he may please him who hath chosen him to be a soldier."**

> 2 Timothy 2:4

They also need to know that we cannot walk in the same direction together unless we are willing to have the same goal.

> **"Can two walk together, except they be agreed?"**

> Amos 3:3

That is all we need to worry about in the beginning. Our strategy should never be to leap right into the midst of battle. Our strategy should *begin* and *stay* that we are always in the mindset of learning. We are to stay teachable! I continue to stress this point because the Word tells us that once we think that we have got it; it I at that point that the enemy will trip us up and make us fall.

"Study to shew thyself approved unto God, a workman that needeth not to be ashamed, rightly dividing the word of truth."

2 Timothy 2:15

A follower of Christ can never forget that we are to study in order to receive God's approval and never have to worry about being ashamed. People that have other spiritual views are usually able to run circles around the Christian that is unread in his own faith. Do not think that those that are on the enemies side don't know this as well. They attack Christianity daily through every venue that the enemy has at his disposal. Persons that profess Jesus are easily exposed concerning this one simple scripture – **STUDY**!

I watched a popular entertainer actually take the time out of his schedule to fly his hand in the face of God. Can I say that he did a good job? I would never say that he did a good job challenging God, but he did a good job in showing the body of Christ that we have become far too easy for the enemy to pick us apart and shame us. Does it make any sense for a soldier not to know that he is a soldier? Is a country at war aware that they are at war? No; to my first question and Yes; to my second. All soldiers should know that they are soldiers; what their country's expectations of them as soldiers are; how to perform their part for their division; and how to fight and improvise in the time of war. Any country at war, knows that it is at war. When the bombs fell on Hiroshima and Nagasaki, those people definitely knew they were at war. When America started to move into Afghanistan, Kuwait, Iran and Iraq; those Middle Eastern countries knew they were at war. Christians have to wake up and recognize that Satan has declared *war* on Christianity; on God's Kingdom; and on God!

Knowing is half the battle or Tevet Noyce!

Knowledge is power all by itself. The two greatest tricks that Satan has are: Getting the world to believe that he doesn't exist and misdirection. Accepting Christ often nullifies the first trick, but misdirection can deceive anyone; even the very astute. This is a magician's trick. "Watch my left hand and do not pay attention to my right hand." This is how Satan gets us to fight the wrong battles, in the wrong places and always at the wrong times.

The enemy will tell us that our husband did this, our wife did that, our children are doing this, our boss is impossible, the man at the bank did not do his job correctly, that person is not driving as he/she should and it just persists and persists. We are to be conformed to the image of Christ and have His mindset.

> *"I beseech you therefore, brethren, by the mercies of God, that ye present your bodies a living sacrifice, holy, acceptable unto God, [which is] your reasonable service. And be not conformed to this world: but be ye transformed by the renewing of your mind, that ye may prove what [is] that good, and acceptable, and perfect, will of God."*

Romans 12:1 **& 2**

I would also ask, Dear Reader, if you would do your own reading of Philippians 2:5-16 which tells us the exact mindset and thinking that we should have. Too often we do not take the simplest of statements, yet very 'profound', into consideration. WWJD – What *Would* Jesus Do? Whether we are right or wrong about what we think, it is undeniable that Jesus was a breed apart. His walk was undeniable; His life a matter of historic record worldwide and anyone in disagreement really has to rely on imagination and distorting the truth to read something else into His life story.

Our strategy really hinges on *God's* strategy and it is just that simple. A general that cannot depend on the solders that are under his command may as well draw up plans for surrender before the war is under way. The Word tells us that, "obedience is better than sacrifice."

When we look up the word 'sacrifice' in Strong's Concordance we see that what Samuel is telling Saul is that it is better for him to have been *obedient* rather than to sacrifice animals. However, when we look up sacrifice in Webster's Dictionary we find an interesting synonym. Among the synonymous words that are there for sacrifice is the word *surrender*. From that standpoint, it reads, **"...obedience is better than <u>surrender.</u>"**

That speaks volumes directly too and fits our current study. The General and the Captain of the Host would rather we be *obedient* to their orders rather than surrender to the other side. They know what the outcome of surrender will mean for us. We would end up being imprisoned as a prisoner of war and eventually killed without the hope of hostage exchange. Jesus has already gone into the enemy's camp once and rescued the P.O.W. once and He will <u>**not**</u> do it again.

> **Revelation 1:18 I am he that liverish, and was dead; and, behold, I am alive for evermore, Amen; and have the keys of hell and of death.**

Once we have joined the shepherd and are being obedient, we must wait. The shepherd is led by his connection to the owner of the sheep. As the shepherd watches us with the flock, He will determine our place amongst the flock. We should never seek positioning or strive to be recognized; the shepherd knows where we are needed and where we would best fit into His flock. If we are the type of sheep that the other sheep will follow, He will place us in the lead. If we are the type of sheep that are adept at helping other sheep come into the flock, He will assign us to that position and so forth. Some things the shepherd wants us to take initiative with, but it will never be anything that will pull us or others away from His watchful eye or satisfy our own agenda. It will never be anything that elevates us to a position that will be above being a sheep; no matter how good of a sheep that we are. I am using the shepherd/sheep as an analogy, but the thinking must be that *we* are considered as sheep and *Jesus* or the pastor, as being led by Jesus; is *the* true shepherd.

The five 'fold ministry' is generally considered to be a list of the ministry positions that Jesus has given to the church.

> *"And he gave some, <u>apostles</u>; and some, <u>prophets</u>; and some, <u>evangelists</u>; and some, <u>pastors</u> and <u>teachers</u>; For the perfecting of the saints, for the work of the ministry, for the edifying of the body of Christ: Till we all come in the unity of the faith, and of the knowledge of the Son of God, unto a perfect man, unto the measure of the stature of the fullness of Christ:"*

Ephesians 4:11-13

The positioning of the sheepfold is for the edifying and betterment of the body. We could call it our MOS – (Military Operations Specialist(y) – or our job in the military).

- An **apostle** is someone that is sent and is therefore an emissary or missionary.
- A **prophet** is someone that speaks for God through divine inspiration. To prophecy means to speak God's word.
- An **evangelist** is a minister or 'preacher' of the gospel who travels from place to place as an itinerant; as on a circuit. Someone who's sole job is to spread the gospel.
- A **pastor** is someone who acts as someone that has been charged to lead a particular body or house of believers.
- A **teacher** is just that; someone who teaches and trains members of the body.

I must say this Dear Reader. If you belong to a church that has changed a good godly recognizable name that; one that let people know that they are members of the body of Christ and what they believe, then contemplate why? Too many churches are adopting names that have numbers as their titles. This in my opinion so that the enemy will know where the saints are when he comes in like a flood and is usually on the mega church side of the tax bracket. This makes it simple and easy for Satan to identify saints, family and friends as well as areas they live in and their jobs etc... Also, these numbers correspond to occult or mystery practices/religions in the secular world. They will always find a scripture to smooth the edges and make their name change palatable. C3 says that this pastor has chosen the same numbers that correspond to Christ's age upon death and the number of bones in our spinal columns in which each joint is fit together. 15 speaks to the five fold ministry supposedly, but it also speaks to the Wicca pentagram or five pointed star. Their logos tell on them as well.

[My humble opinion]

Our strategy again should always be to do our very best for the 'captain' who has placed his life on the line for His men. It should always be the Forest Ump attitude of gong back to save 'Bubbly' and as many men as there are that are *trying* to make it out of the bush or jungle of the world. We should always want company on our walk down this road and while we are on this path while following our 'Captain'.

The next key to our strategy is to learn and become proficient in communication. If we do not learn how to press forward through learning the communication of our country, then the enemy will cut us off from our squad and flank us. He will corner us when he knows that there is no help coming or that our squadron will have to search for us in the jungle before it can send any backup.

We must learn the prayer that Jesus taught us, but understand that it is so much deeper than what we initially read in scripture or the way it is preached and interpreted. When He tells us to say, "<u>Our Father</u>..." He is letting us know that we have become heirs and joint heirs with Him through adoption. ***Our Father*** is <u>personal</u> and moves God because one of *His* children is trying to get His attention. The way that Jesus said it was, "Abba Father..."; Abba being 'Daddy'. "...<u>Which art in Heaven</u>..." Jesus is showing us both *who* and *where* to direct our prayers. He is pointing us to the One True and Only God; the maker of all that is and toward His dwelling place which is the highest heaven. "...*<u>Hallowed</u>* <u>be thy name</u>..." He is establishing that as a son; ***the*** Son; He recognizes who His Father is, what His Father represents and that His Father is worthy of the titles associated with Him. *Hallowed* means: holy or different, venerated, honored and sacred, among other forms deserving of the ultimate respect, etc...

Some members of the flock have been blessed with the ability to speak to our commander in another language and some to even be able to interpret that language. This is the gift of 'tongues' and the gift of 'interpretation of tongues'. Those blessed with these gifts are on special assignment because the Word says that not everyone is given these gifts. 1 Corinthians 14:22 tells us that speaking in tongues is for a sign to them that do **_not_** believe. It is for a sign because it will be in another language (earthly language) that the person who understands it will take notice of because the person speaking obviously did not know it before. This is the way that it was manifest in the book of Acts when the Holy Spirit was given to the 120 in he upper room. Speaking in tongues is not necessarily for those that are already believers. Think about it this way; when a soldier needs to speak in code, he does so because he does not want the enemy to understand what he is saying. The other soldiers have not had cryptology (code and cipher systems) as a part of their MOS. [Read 1 Corinthians chapter 14 and see how the enemy has stepped in and made this gift ineffectual in today's church. Anytime that someone speaks in tongues in a public setting, there is supposed to be someone there with the complimenting gift of interpretation or the troops are being confused. I have had this happen to someone that I brought to church and it scared them because it was babel.]

The only other time that we are to use this gift is to edify ourselves and let the Holy Spirit speak for us with <u>words that we cannot say</u>.

> *"Likewise the Spirit also helper our infirmities: for we know not what we should pray for as we ought: but the Spirit itself maketh intercession for us with groaning which cannot be uttered."*

Romans 8:26

The enemy is a master strategist and, as such, he will exploit every opportunity to bog down the troops and inflict casualties. He *cannot* understand our secret prayer communication when the Spirit speaks to the Father, so what he will do is inject confusion into it and prevent the soldiers from being able to get a clear grasp of what their squad is supposed to be doing. If the communication is sketchy the troops cannot perform their duties efficiently. If the troops cannot perform their tasks efficiently, what can be an advantage can become a disadvantage.

When we study warfare, we see that a great deal of time and effort goes into planning. What the layperson may take for granted will not be overlooked by a person in charge of planning out a war. Every possible scenario is taken into consideration, mapped out and met with a counter plan. This is where our trust and faith weigh heavy on us. We will not be in the 'war room' when the orders are given to send out the troops. We are not a part of the decision making process. We are soldiers and we are to endure and stand!

> *"And if a man also strive for mysteries, [yet] is he not crowned, except he strive <u>lawfully</u>. The husbandman that labored must be first partaker of the fruits."*

2 Timothy 2:5 **& 6**

Every man does not strive for mastery, in what they are aspiring to do, but then we should ask ourselves whether or not we intend to *grow* in our profession. Again we see the 'law' insuring that we are not deceived into thinking that we can be in the presence of God by doing things our own way. Timothy tells us that we will not be recognized as having passed certain tests unless we do things the right way; God's way.

So what's next? Now that we are learning and growing in Christ the enemy will definitely step up his attack and God will allow him to test us or try us. Every trial, tribulation and test is designed to make us into the soldier that God has designed us to be. It is designed to get us closer to our purpose; closer to what God has designed us to be. What we have to make certain of is that we do not despise the testing. The testing is for our benefit and we must always remember that. We cannot afford to be a 'halfway saint', 'middle of the road saint', or a 'carnal Christian'; we have to run this race to win. Only those that do will receive the prize of the high calling in Christ Jesus.

"*I press toward the mark for the <u>prize</u> of the high calling of God in Christ Jesus."*

Philippians 3:14

The next step is PRESS! We have to press past everyone who desires to stay in the world; past those that are standing in our way; past those that would try and hinder or stop us; past those that are only willing to go only but so far; and past those that are even running as fast as we are. Our goal is to win without any doubt! Every part of our strategy must speak of the fact that we are soldiers and that we are on duty. This is why God sent so many back, during the Israelite journey, who went to war with Gideon. The only soldiers that God wanted were the ones that wanted to fight and the ones that acted like soldiers. He still wants the same thing today. All that we experience and all that we endure and go through here on earth will prove us for when we get to heaven. I am not writing about or preaching works, but we will not go to the 'Kingdom' with the same flaws that we currently have. We will not disobey orders and make it and we will not do things our own way and make it. We are being 'Kingdom Prepared' now; 'Kingdom Trained' now!

The Word of God is our strategy and obedience is the implementation. Some plans simply work out better when we stick to them. They work if we trust in and have faith in our commander; in our leader. Some plans work if the soldiers are not spending their time looking for morale boosters; a good leader knows when morale is waning. The plan will work if we believe and do not doubt.

Notes And Reflections For The Reader:

Notes And Reflections For The Reader:

Engaging the Enemy

The Master's Walk;
Through Jesus' Eyes

To engage an enemy that is bigger than you, smarter than you, and more intelligent than you means that the strategies of the one who can defeat him must be followed to the letter. The goal is to be *transformed* instead of *conformed* and to renew our mind so that we have the same mind that Christ does. That is not 'brainwashing' as some comedians and opponents of God may try to persuade the world that Christianity is. No Dear Reader; it is simply called **_agreement_**.

Jesus never engaged the enemy in any other way than *controlled or meek*. Jesus was always in control of himself; in control of His thinking and actions. Did He have the power? Yes. Did He have a motive to vanquish Satan? Yes. Could He have made an example of His enemies? Yes. Yet, everything that Jesus did was in meekness; a demonstration of power under control.

When Satan attacked Jesus in the wilderness, Jesus' response was the Word of God, the Word of God, and the Word of God! When Jesus was in Gethsemane and the soldiers asked him who He was; clearly intending to do him harm; He simply said, "I AM he." [They backed up and fell to the ground. This is one of my favorite scriptures because it is a demonstration of His power, but not meant to be offensive or retaliatory.] When the synagogue heads intended to stone Mary, Jesus simply wrote in the sand and said, *"He who is without sin, cast the first stone."* When He was being interrogated by Pontiffs Pilate He simply said, *"Thou sanest."* I could go on and on about how Jesus met with the opposition from Satan and also from man. The Master definitely has shown us a lesson that needs to be learned; a lesson that I am practicing during the course of writing this book – "Silence is Golden".

It is golden in the sense of being *valuable*. It is golden in the sense of being *powerful*. It is golden n the sense of being *effective*. Everything does not need to be addressed and every attack does not have to be met with force. Sometimes the best offense is to flow with the enemy's power and use it against him.

There is a martial art called Meet **Kane Do,** founded by Bruce Lee, which teaches this technique. [I am not a martial arts fan other than the fact that I enjoy the movies. Satan can turn almost anything into something that man can put in place of God, but He will always mix it with some truth so that it can be accepted.] The thought process behind this technique is: "The Style without a Style".

Jesus only acted in a way that could be considered aggressive one time. It is what can be called 'Righteous Anger'. He was rightfully offended by the moneychangers disrespecting His Fathers house and He let them know it. God's Word does not teach us to be emotionless; it rather teaches us to have a right, realistic perspective and how to deal with our humanity in a 'Kingdom' fashion. God gets angered by things as well, but it is the 'Kingdom' mindset that keeps Him from destroying mankind. We see His anger kindled with mankind during the flood. We see it kindled with Sodom and Gomorrah. We also see it kindled with His own people after the exodus from Egypt. Was God wrong to be angry? No. He was also restrained by the fact that He saved eight people during the flood; He saved three people of Lot's household; and He listened to Moses when Moses reasoned with Him concerning Israel and He did not destroy them in the wilderness.

The Masters walk; Jesus' journey on earth was probably similar to most young people of that day. He had the same trials and tribulations as did all of His people. He had family issues that needed to be addressed. He had siblings to contend with and He had to grow and learn like every other human person in history. We need to focus on the fact that Satan turned up the heat on Jesus at the point when His ministry was beginning to take shape.

The Holy Spirit drove Him into the desert, where He was tempted by Satan for forty days. Satan knows human weaknesses and so he attacked Jesus on those fronts. When Jesus was faced with catering to the flesh, He prevailed. When He was faced with catering to the ego, He prevailed. And when He was faced with contradicting God's Word and being disobedient, He prevailed. He exemplified every correct response to Satan's attacks that anyone, including His Father, could have expected. This is how we are to fight this battle. Smarter than us or not, Satan is not smarter than God's Word or He would still be heaven doing what he was created to do.

The Master's walk can be painful to us. It will cause us to battle our flesh on a daily basis because the flesh is against God and wants to dominate our spirits. Paul is telling us that we have to run this race the same way that Jesus ran it because He has given us HOPE!

> *"I protest by your rejoicing which I have in Christ Jesus our Lord, <u>I die daily</u>. If after the manner of men I have fought with beasts at Ephesus, what advantageous it me, if the dead rise not? Let us eat and drink; for to morrow we die. Be not deceived: evil communications corrupt good manners. Awake to righteousness, and sin not; for some have not the knowledge of God: I speak [this] to your shame."*

1 Corinthians 15:31-34

Our hope is in the fact that Jesus conquered death and, in this hope, we *can* win this race. Paul reminds us that we are walking this path daily! He has to fight with his own flesh daily; he has to die to it daily. He has remembered and is also encouraging us to remember…

> *"…That <u>no flesh </u>should glory in His presence."*

1 Corinthians 1:29

> *"Because the carnal mind [is] <u>enmity against God</u>: for it is not subject to the law of God, neither indeed can be."*

Romans 8:7

> *'...And that he might reconcile both unto God in one body*
> *by the cross, <u>having slain the enmity thereby</u>."*

Ephesians 2:16

> *"Ye adulterers and adulteresses, know ye not that the*
> *friendship of the world is <u>enmity with God</u>? Whosoever*
> *therefore will be a friend of the world is the enemy of God."*

James 4:4

It became easier for the Master to accept His walk when He came to terms with fact that the flesh was only that; flesh. It did not become easier for him to walk His walk, but rather easier for Him to understand *why* He had to walk it.

We are to become a mirror image of our Savior? So that when the enemy comes up against us he will think twice. Satan should see so much of Jesus in us that it will make him apprehensive about wanting to attack us. The glory of God should permeate or beings and give every demon, that is on assignment from Satan, a reason to doubt their captains orders.

How did Jesus see things? What was His outlook from a human perspective? Those questions are impossible to answer adequately. I am fairly certain that He did not think it was a big deal to read the scripture in the synagogue when He was twelve. I'm sure He did not think it strange to speak with the elders, during that same trip with His earthly parents, leaving Egypt. I believe that Jesus' calling manifested itself in part in His thirties and came to fruition after being baptized.

By the time He was baptized and fasting in the wilderness, He was prepared. He was a grown man. He had studied to show Himself approved and His knowledge was undeniable because He was able to converse with adults that surpassed Him in age and in study. He had gained the favor of the elders of the day because they knew His parents. He most definitely had the favor of His Father in heaven.

"And Jesus increased in wisdom and stature, and in favour with God and man."

Luke 2:52

Now we must understand the 'testing' phase. I have said that Jesus was fully prepared by the time that the enemy began his initial attacks. This initial attack is called *'counter force'* in military terminology. This technique attacks the enemy's arsenal and resources while the attacking force remains able to survive any type of retaliation.

Satan attacked Jesus' foretold assignment from the beginning. In Genesis 3:15, God speaks to the fact that Satan will be allowed to 'bruise' Jesus' heal, but Jesus would 'bruise' Satan's head. The Hebrew word is: shutdown **(shoo)** - meaning to snap at; to break; to overwhelm. Satan's first attempt to destroy Jesus' bloodline was also in Genesis when he introduced Cain to murder. Able was the chosen one to bring the messiah's bloodline into the earth. Afterward, Seth became the son that would carry the bloodline. Satan tries again in Genesis 6, when he attempts to taint the bloodline with his army of fallen angels. The result, as I have stated prior, was the flood of Noah's day as the whole earth was purged by water. Satan then attempts to erase the bloodline in Egypt as every male child is killed under pharaoh and again with Herod in the same fashion. Adolph Hitler seeks to eliminate the entire race with the ideology that he can bring back the Atlantes race in Marilyn Ferguson's book 'the Age of Aquarius'.

After failing this number of times, Satan attacks Jesus directly when the Holy Spirit descended upon Him, after His baptism by John. Since the previous attacks failed, he was forced to come at Jesus from a different angle. He attacks Jesus' credibility amongst those at the wedding and His mother steps in to tell the men to listen to Him. Satan next attacks Jesus' credibility with the authorities of that day, who had positions in 'ministry'.

Jesus often had to prevent the enemy from destroying, those who should have been, *valuable resources*. The Pharisees and the

Sadducee were men that knew the Word of God and were entrusted to teaching that Word to God's chosen people. This was a group of seventy men that were on a council dedicated to nothing else but studying and promoting the Word of God every day of their lives. Called the Sanhedrin. Paul was so entrenched in this group that he claimed to be a Pharisee of the Pharisees; ire. the best of the best!

We will have to face this exact same attack during the course of our walk. When we have made our decision to follow Christ; dedicated ourselves to being in church and in bible study weekly; are in our right positions and are on our way to being elevated in God's service; that is exactly where the next attack will come in. Satan will attack God's work.

When the military is on the battlefield and certain ranking officers are recognized, they become targets. The idea is to disrupt the opposing army's chain of command and personnel as a *valuable resource* to their enemy's ability to wage effective warfare. Satan will attack what you love about God and the area where God has placed you; the area in which you want to serve God.

In these last days, let us simply look at the rate in which the proclaimed men and women of God are being destroyed. This is also a way that the enemy has engaged in destroying God's *valuable resources*. This attack hinders the faith of those that are already following Christ and prevents others from wanting to follow. It also gives those that are aspiring to move into certain leadership positions, the incentive to mislead the troops. If they believe that the troops are 'less than' or gullible, then they will abuse them and use them for the wrong purposes. If the Pharisees and Sadducee were not doing what they were supposed to be doing with the people of God, then it may have been the same scenario that we are seeing today. The men of God are supposed to be officers in God's military. Now we see them abusing the troops by misusing their money; engaging in sexual misconduct; not teaching them correctly; and generally weakening the human army of God. One of the things that Jesus may have written in the sand, when the men wanted to stone Mary, were the names of those that had already been with her. The 'Captain of the Army' may have been chastising those that should have been leading other soldiers. (Just food for thought.)

Remember, God has assigned us to be His hands and feet on the earth. We are the ones that are supposed to take the gospel [Good News] and run with it the way that Jesus trained the disciples. If the enemy destroys the *validity* of this resource, He will have accomplished at least the part of his plan that destroys a portion of Gods elect. This is what I call the 'Salted Earth' plan.

Satan will always *pervert* the plans of God if he is allowed. While salt is a preservative and Jesus uses it as a teaching tool to instruct the disciples. Satan will use it in just the opposite way the same way that the Romans did too Carthage. Jesus said:

> **"Ye are the salt of the earth: but if the salt have lost his savor, wherewith shall it be salted? It is thenceforth good for nothing, but to be cast out, and to be trodden under foot of men."**

> Matthew 5:13

Jesus is pointing out ***purpose***! He is telling the disciples that they are to be like 'salt'; a preservative in the earth. The reverse of God's idea for salt is that when, a city was defeated in war, the conquering force would raze the buildings, burn what was still standing and sew salt into the earth so that nothing could be grown. This made the earth uninhabitable and unproductive. This is what Satan is trying to accomplish with God's people. If he can salt us before we can produce fruit for God, then the evangelistic battle has been lost. We see that Satan has already razed the cities by bringing society to the point where everything is allowable. Satan is burning what remains standing and is destroying what used to be considered a refuge in the churches. When this is complete, the earth, which is mankind, will be 'salted'. We will become unable to produce fruit and nothing will grow for the 'Kingdom'.

There comes a point when you have to wonder, "How?" How did Jesus do it? He was here on earth, in the flesh and had the same human issues as we do. What did His human life look like through His eyes?

> *"For we have not an high priest which cannot be touched with the feeling of our infirmities; but was in all points tempted like as [we are, yet] without sin."*

> Hebrews 4:15

He took not only His portion, but allowed God to lay on His shoulders everyone's portion; past, present and future. [His portion being that He was encased in flesh] Jesus was probably in utter pain by seeing what He had created come to such a diminished state of chaos. What He was experiencing was the exact opposite of what He had created.

As a contractor, I have created some very attractive changes in people's homes. That was one of the things that drew me to the profession; to be able to see the home-owner's vision and meet and surpass their expectations. Nothing broke my heart more than to complete a job and see that the very same home-owner, who thought the time, work, and effort, that went into the project was worth so little to them, that they simply allowed it to waste away or be destroyed.

He suffered what He suffered because of love! Love for His creation and the simple fact that it would break His heart to see it destroyed by Satan. He knew Satan and He knew His own creation, so He took the abuse; He took the rebuke; He took what had always been abhorrent to His character. He, who could _never_ die, died worse than anyone had _ever_ died or ever could die.

When we attempt to look at things through the eyes of Jesus, we are overwhelmed with 'love'. It is easy to wonder, "How?" It would be because you had an *investment*; it is something that you would have poured yourself into. This is why the enemy has attacked humanity on this front. Satan has devalued mankind in man's own mind by minimizing creation. If mankind views creation from the standpoint of evolution, then it is very easy to see why our value system for ourselves has all but disappeared. If we are deceived into believing that we are the product of randomness and chance, then life has no ultimate meaning. Jesus does not see His creation in this way; nor would I. It means something when you take the time out to figure out what needs to happen; how it can happen; how it will work and envision the finished product. God, Jesus, and the Holy Spirit poured themselves into the creation of mankind. In fact, it was their best work and to have a rebellious, prideful, disobedient child want to destroy it because he could not get his way… God simply is not going to allow this.

We can only begin to see things from this perspective. We can never understand it in totality, but we can touch it because God has recreated Himself in our beings. We can touch it because we were created to be _able_ to touch it; wonder about it; try to imagine it and think about it; to think, *"What kind of love is this?"* We will spend eternity with Jesus still trying to figure out what marvelous love He had for His creation too. To do what He did and to create everything that we will see and know once we are with Him. The only thing that I can say is, **"Maratha's –** *Even so come quickly Lord!"*

Notes And Reflections For The Reader:

Notes And Reflections For The Reader:

Big Picture, Little Vision

A Fork in the Road

God's purpose for us is *extraordinary*. God's purpose for us is God sized! His Word tells us this and if we dig into it we will see that He still has His way for us to fulfill that purpose. He has it mapped out; He has it planned; and He has it in *progress*. The problem is that because we cannot see it; because we have not been a part of the planning; and do not know the end result other than what He tells us in His Word; our vision tends to be small.

This is where the fork in the road in life comes in. Jesus asked the disciples if they were going to leave when times got tough; when there was a fork in the road. Peter answered correctly and I am striving toward that same answer.

> *"And he said, therefore said I unto you, that no man can come unto me, except it were given unto him of my Father. From that [time] many of his disciples went back, and walked no more with him. Then said Jesus unto the twelve, Will ye also go away? Then Simon Peter answered him, Lord, to whom shall we go? Thou hast the words of eternal life. And we believe and are sure that thou art that Christ, the Son of the living God."*

John 6:65-**69**

This is the response of someone that is persuaded and has made up his mind that he will not be moved from his position. The disciples that turned back had a *'little'* vision. This is what happens when you *hear* what is being said, but you aren't really paying *attention*. There is a reason why it is called paying attention; it cost you something. You will find that people that you may *think* have the same vision as you and are *acting* like they are walking the same path as you; have simply walked with you for the loaves and the fish. This is a hurtful revelation, but it is a real one. Some people, like Satan and his followers, can be *in the presence* of God and have no *relationship* with Him.

How could you have the position of guarding the throne of 'God' and be so disconnected from His presence that He would push you away; cast you out?

Our vision must line up with God's vision. He is pointing toward the end of the road; all we have to do is turn our heads and look in the direction that He is pointing. For those that do not:

> *"But he that shall <u>endure</u> unto the end, <u>the same shall be saved."</u>*

> Matthew 24:13

> *"And ye shall be hated of all [men] for my name's sake: but he that shall <u>endure</u> unto the end, the same shall be saved."*

> Mark 13:13

> *"Behold, we count them happy which <u>endure</u>. Ye have heard of the patience of Job, and have seen the end of the Lord; that the Lord is very pitiful, and of tender mercy."*

> James 5:11

> *"These all died in faith, not having received the promises, but having seen them afar off, and were persuaded of [them], and embraced [them], and confessed that they were strangers and pilgrims on the earth."*

> Hebrews 11:13

This scripture in Hebrews tells us of the patriarchs that died with their heads pointed in the direction that God was pointing. This tells us that their vision was '*huge*' because Jesus had not yet come. To be able to have the testimony that your faith withstood the test on the mere word that a promise was *coming* is incredible. Jesus *has* come and almost all of what was prophesied of Him *has* come to pass. Much that God has foretold would happen in the last days is happening now. So what is our excuse? Why are their still those whose vision is very small?

My god-daughter was amazed when I showed her pictures from the Hubble Telescope. She had never had anyone point out to her that what I showed her was an actual phenomenon that could be seen in outer space. She was amazed at the colors, the shapes, and the fact that there was movement and things that were changing and taking form so far away from all that she had imagined. She had a difficult time wrapping her mind around all that I was able to tell her and present to her about simply the sun and the moon that we see every day. My question to her was simple, "*Why did God create all of these things if no one was ever meant to see and experience them?*" This blew her mind because she was starting to realize that, until that point, her vision had been 'small'. This sparked the beginning of a barrage of questions that led to more questions and still more questions. All of her questions, however, did not revolve around what the Hubble Telescope was sending back to earth. There were questions about God; questions about God's Word; questions about Jesus; questions about man's finite reality as opposed to God's infinite existence; questions about how she fit into the equation and so on. The blinders had come off and she was beginning to look in the direction that God was pointing. God was saying to her spirit at that moment, "*Your God-Father is showing you all that I have created for you to see and experience; go in the direction that he is going! What you never considered possible is not only possible, but I would love to show it to you personally.*"

The scary thing about other people's vision is that the reverse is also very true. Some people would like to keep their blinders on. They do not want their vision expanded; they do not want to turn their heads.

Turning their heads would mean that they have an option about the direction that they can go. Having the blinders removed would mean that they are able to see more than they are willing to process and this requires that decisions be made. Some people want to keep the blinders on so that they can continue to walk in the direction of the crowd. Some people do not want their vision expanded because this would make them accountable to what they are currently choosing not to be accountable for. So what happens is that we come to a *fork* in the road while we are walking through life. Some will go right and some will go left. What needs to be pointed out is that no matter which direction you choose, God is only looking in one direction.

A fork in the road means that there are decisions to be made. We may *want* that decision to be made by someone else, but we have been given free-will. If God wanted robots that He could tell do this or do that, then He could have made us that way. He *could* pull us in the direction that He would like us to go, but He knows that we would complain that He is hurting our arm. God could *turn* our heads so that we would be looking at what He wants to show us, but we would say He is hurting our neck. The way He did it was to open His arms on the cross and let us make our own decision!

The fork in the road also means that the direction we choose to go in will take us to a destination that already exists. The problem is that there are very few side roads along the way and very little opportunity to change direction. It is like trying to turn your car around on a very narrow back road where there are no street lights. It is very hard to change direction when you have blinders on. It is very hard to see the forest when you are staring at how many trees there are.

We are now living in an age where the enemy is telling man that all roads lead to Rome. This may have been true when Rome owned all of the roads, but Satan is the God of this world and there is only *one* way to get to Rome. We cannot be on the road to La Vegas and expect to end up in Rome. This is when we have missed the *big picture*. This is when we have moved into an area of self deception. God has placed signs all along the path too which He is pointing, but some people choose to believe that they already know the way because they have heard someone talk about Rome. It does not work that way no matter what the enemy has programmed into your GPS.

Satan wants to keep your vision *small* so that he can hide the *big picture* from you. He would like for you to keep the blinders on and to keep you following the crowd. Once he has succeeded in this, then he can use his soldiers to direct the flow of traffic. He will send the wrong information to your GPS and play *his* music the whole time that you believe that you are on your way to Rome.

It's sad actually; we don't even question the little voice on the GPS because we have been trained to follow directions without giving them a second thought. When those that thought that they were on their way to Rome get to their destination they will only be able to say one thing, *"Hey, This isn't Rome!"* Then what?

Notes And Reflections For The Reader:

Notes And Reflections For The Reader:

Casualties of War

P.O.W.'s, M.I.A.'s and Refugees

P.O.W.'s are Prisoners of War. They are people that have accepted the sacrifice of Christ, but who, for whatever reason, have not stayed the course. Perhaps it is because they are holding onto something that God wants them to let go of. Perhaps their focus is not on God and Satan is magnifying the thing that they are focusing on. For whatever reason, they have become prisoners. They move around as the enemy dictates; they are eating what the enemy is feeding them; they are drinking his dirty water and they are on his time schedule in life.

This is not their desire, but they are not strong enough to persevere or think of a way to contact help. At some point they will begin to believe that escape is impossible. They will begin to give up hope that a rescue is on the way. They will become accustomed to and will have gotten used to being a prisoner. They will not be able to see any other way except the enemy's way.

This way of thinking is called 'Stockholm Syndrome'. In psychology, **Stockholm Syndrome** is a term used to describe a real paradoxical psychological phenomenon wherein hostages express empathy and have positive feelings towards their captors; sometimes to the point of defending them. These feelings are generally considered irrational in light of the danger or risk endured by the victims, who essentially mistake a lack of abuse from their captors for an act of kindness.

This is exactly what Satan wants. He would love for the prisoners of war to begin to see things his way. When someone gets used to or has been trained into using the back door, even when there is *no* back door, their mentality will no longer allow them to accept that reality. They will in fact demand that there be a back door for them to utilize.

This type of thinking is very difficult to address and requires caution to maneuver. The rational has become non-existent and their mentality has become trapped in stasis. The ability to reason has been lost. The only thing that makes sense is what they have come to believe about their captors. Rescue becomes more difficult and more dangerous for the rescue team.

A prisoner of war, that has changed sides mentally, has become a danger to himself and to the other captives. Does the rescue party give up? No. The rescue party holds out hope. That hope lies in the belief that the prisoner can be restored. We see in god's Word that this is exactly the scenario that the father of the prodigal son faced. That son, who was raised the same as his older brother, was drawn away by the lure of the enemy. He became convinced that there was more outside of the gates of his father's house and ventured out on his own into enemy territory. I am quite sure that initially he was having the time of his life, but he was being deceived and could not see it. At some point, the party ended and where he found himself was in a place where they kept pigs. He had what I will call "a moment of clarity." All it takes is for that prisoner to be correctly stimulated in an area that will turn their thinking ever so slightly in the direction of the road that lies behind them. In the prodigal son's case, it was his taste 'doorway' that was entered by God. He was awakened for a moment and was able to remind himself that what he was eating was garbage. The taste of that garbage was enough to stimulate his memory of better food at his father's house. It was enough to get him to think that even the servants; the lowest of those that were in his father's house; were not eating garbage. This reminded him of the meals that he did have at his father's house. Which in turn reminded him of how he received that food; how he ate that food in comfort; how the servants treated him as a 'son'. That moment of clarity was enough *stimulation* to provoke *motivation*. The decision was always his as he begins to recognize, and so he gets up! The prisoner does not have to know how he will return to reality; they only need the restored desire to do so. The prodigal son finds himself approaching his fathers house to find that his father has not abandoned the 'hope' that he would have that moment of clarity; the 'hope' that he would remember his father and who *he* was.

This is what God wants from the prisoners of war. He wants them to clear their minds and grab hold of that moment of clarity. He wants them to remember that they have a brother at home and that they will be well treated; that the door has *always* been open; that they are a member of the family and they are still welcome home.

Read **Luke 15:11-24** to get a clearer picture of the prodigal son; it will speak volumes about how the enemy wants us on *his* battlefield; the battleground.

The M.I.A.'s are those that are missing in action. They are those that have fought alongside us and have gotten lost or have been deceived into wandering too close to enemy lines. The largest problem is that the military does not know where they are and neither do they. A prisoner's whereabouts are known; they are in the enemy's camp; in the enemy's territory. The soldier missing in action could be in the jungle, in a cave, or in the bush. They are trying to figure out what led them to the point that they have been separated from their unit.

The missing soldiers still recognize that the war is going on, but they do not recognize where they are and how to rejoin their unit. They are lost and must rely on all of their training and survival skills to get them back to a place where they can get back into the battle.

We lose our way when we are reliant upon our own skills and abilities and are ignoring the leading of our captain. For the Christian soldier; this usually happens when we believe that we have arrived. It happens when we believe that we have met the mark and think we know all that there is to know. It happens when the enemy has deceived us into becoming *prideful*.

> **"Wherefore let him that <u>thinker</u> he standee take heed lest he fall."**

> 1 Corinthians 10:12

215

See then that ye walk circumspectly, not as fools, but as wise,

Ephesians 5:15

Take heed means to *be careful* and *listen.* Circumspectly means to always be *looking around;* ever aware of your position and your surroundings. When special units go into a military zone to execute a mission, they have prepared themselves to deal with all kinds of counter attacks, enemy resistance, the territory and the terrain and how to maneuver around and through civilians. They must use all of their skills to accomplish the mission at hand. They must be quiet; they must know how to communicate covertly; they must know what the plan is; how to execute it and how to get out when done. It is when someone in the unit acts outside of their 'specialty' or believes that they do not have to function as a part of the team, that not only the mission becomes jeopardized, but also the unit. If a soldier sees a sniper and sees a way to attack; his response should not be to leave the unit and go the back way to attempt to neutralize the sniper alone. By the time he has climbed to the snipers position, he will find that the enemy has allowed the sniper to be seen in order to lure one of our soldiers away from the unit. The soldier that has moved on his own accord is now missing and presumed to be either: captured, M.I.A. or K.I.A. (Killed in Action).

That soldier was deceived into thinking that he was able to *stand* and deal with the situation by himself. The idea in spiritual warfare is that this soldier only thinks that he knows how to handle the situation and how to rectify it. He is not taking heed to his captain, his unit or his training and now no one knows what's happened to him.

The way that we can avoid this type of occurrence in our unit is found in 1 Thessalonians chapter five.

"And we beseech you, brethren, to know them which labor among you, and are over you in the Lord, and admonish you..."

Thessalonians 5:12

How can we go onto a mission that is dangerous and not know who we are to be relying on; what their capabilities are; or their personality and character? This is the reason why units are trained to do things together; why they are taught together; why they run scenarios together and even why they bunk together. It's all about 'relationship'. If I have no relationship with you, how do I know that I can count on you or you on me when we reach that fork in the road? How do I know you will try to prevent my capture so I do not become a prisoner of war or that you would come looking for me should I go missing? Without a relationship between us, I will never feel safe.

I am not certain, if there can be considered to be, actual 'refugees' in the 'Kingdom'. God can supply and will supply our needs above that we could ever ask or envision.

"Now unto him that is able to do <u>exceeding abundantly</u> above <u>all</u> that we <u>ask</u> or <u>think</u>, according to the power that worketh in us..."

Ephesians 3:20

There are, however refugees here on earth. When a pastor misleads the sheep or is caught in sin; when a person of influence and power, that has been trusted with God's word, misuses his position or is fleecing the sheep; refugees are created. The flock has no where to turn. The flock feels betrayed. The flock becomes disheartened and dismayed. In scripture this is known as a stumbling block.

"But ye are departed out of the way; ye have caused many to stumble at the law; ye have corrupted the covenant of Levi, saith the LORD of hosts."

Malachi 2:8

"And a <u>stone of stumbling</u>, and <u>a rock of offense</u>, [even to them] which stumble at the word, being disobedient: hereunto also <u>they were appointed</u>."

1 Peter 2:8

We see in the book of Malachi that refugees are created when people depart out of the way of the Lord; when they stop being obedient and do not follow their captains orders. In 1 Peter, we are told that they are a stone of stumbling and a rock of offense. The person who causes someone in the 'Kingdom' to be a refugee has offended that soldier and caused them to stumble. In other words, they have become what we call in construction a 'trip hazard'. This occurs when a certain flooring is being laid and/or something remains that can catch your shoe and cause you to trip. (An uneven edge or something that is supposed to create a smooth transition between rooms can become a trip hazard if not installed properly.) This is what the leaders of God's people are becoming in these end times. The draw of the world has sunk its teeth into the church and the leaders are leading God's people in the wrong direction. The problem comes in when there are hurting people in the church and they are seeking truth. This type of problem escalates when the people are not reading their own Word; not studying to *show* they have been approved by God. They are ending up exactly like the Word says that they will end up – **ashamed!**

The fault is twofold. It will fall on the soldiers head because he was instructed to *read* his manual [B.I.B.L.E. – Basic Instructions Before Leaving Earth] and it will fall on the leaders head because they have crippled the military finesse of the army. To have refugees from the 'Kingdom' of God is a shame! A refugee is usually someone whose city, country or homeland has been decimated by war and the citizens no longer have a home. This does not sound like our God or His 'Kingdom'. What we will find is that, while there are citizens of the 'Kingdom of Heaven' here on the earth; they will become refugees when they do not feel safe in their embassy or if it has been removed. These are the times when those that have been entrusted with God's Word are selling their souls for what the scripture calls filthy lucre.

A pastor is in charge of training forces to band out and rescue the prisoners of war; search for the soldiers that are missing; and definitely not create refugees. There is no such scripture in God's Word where a pastor or someone called of God has never retired in scripture. The word ___**retire**___ only appears twice in scripture and the word retie*(ed)* only appears twice. In neither of those four places does it carry the idea that we have in America; and in no place did anyone that was called to step up or down in office leave without having God place their equivalent in place to lead. 2 Samuel 11:15 and Jeremiah 4:6 plus 2 Samuel 20:22 and Judges 20:39. These terms in scripture are for those that are being forced to quit and those that have been given temporary leave of their duties for a time to rest.

I am amazed at two phenomenon. The first is the shear size of these mega-churches today. They are able to hold thousands upon thousands of people and one wonders, "Where is the relationship that we see in the book of Acts when the hundred and twenty were all in one place, on one accord and had all things in common? I make fun of the sheer simplicity of this true and real fact;

> *"Then shall they deliver you up to be afflicted, and shall kill you: and ye shall be hated of all nations for my name's sake."*

Matthew 24:9

> *"The father shall be divided against the son, and the son against the father; the mother against the daughter, and the daughter against the mother; the mother in law against*

> **her daughter in law, and the daughter in law against her mother in law."**

Luke 12:53

When these two scriptures come to fruition and are upon us; when the world wants to eliminate the followers of Christ; everyone will be in one place and Christians will be very easy to find. When the enemy begins his final assault on the followers of Christ, those that have been in churches all of their lives; and have been reared in the house of God, with their families; these supposed saints will begin to turn against one another. God will begin to separate the wheat from the tares and those that many believed were in our army will turn their backs on the faith. They will begin to show their true colors and the enemy will show up at the mega-church, on Sunday morning, with his followers and begin to remove those that are still professing Christ. Does this seem far fetched or is it worth examining? If I were planning a military attack on a certain group of people, then I would attack on a day and in a place where I knew my enemy was sure to be.

The second thing is that so many shepherds have forsaken the Word of God and turned their calling into a business. They have either turned their calling into a 501C3 or forsaken it for what the world is offering. I was also amazed at how many churches were closing down and melding their long time members with other larger churches. Amazed at the fact that the preaching that was coming across the pulpit was not Christ and him crucified, but rather all that the church *offered, was* offering and *would be* offering. The interest in saving souls and making disciples has faded in many of today's churches. It has become an afterthought to hold onto the true and older saints and their pocketbooks. The flock has become a paycheck to line the shepherds pocket and build a bigger building to grow the 'flock' and bring in more money.

Anytime that there was a relationship between the members of the body, and the Word of God was being preached from the pulpit, God grew the church. It was really just that simple! When you give people Christ, they get so much more than they bargained for. They get the love of Christ; they gain a sense of belonging; they form Godly relationships; they are encouraged; they find a sense of purpose and they are fed.

> *"And for me, that utterance may be given unto me, that I may open my mouth boldly, to make known the mystery of the gospel,*
>
> *For which I am an <u>ambassador</u> in bonds: that therein I may speak boldly, as I ought to speak."*

Ephesians 6:19,20

There is never a reason for there to be a 'refugee' in the 'Kingdom of God' or here on earth as a citizen of God's Kingdom. We are not only soldiers in God's army, but we are ambassadors for Christ. The church is our embassy. The church should and must remain a haven for not only God's people; but for the people who belong to that countries embassies and anyone that is a refugee from he enemy camp and is seeking asylum.

Notes And Reflections For The Reader:

Notes And Reflections For The Reader:

Enough to be Dangerous

People that know God's Word

I am just now beginning to realize and understand this subject. I have run into it quite often in recent years. On the battlefield, these people can blend in and imitate God's soldiers. They can appear to be working toward the furtherance of the 'Kingdom', but have an ulterior motive; they have a personal agenda that they are seeking to accomplish. They should be viewed as 'moles' or 'chameleons'. These people are persons that the enemy knows have not committed themselves fully to Christ. They are people that have grown up in church, know the inner workings of the church, are comfortable participating in church activities and generally come across as good and faithful members.

> *"Beware of false prophets, which come to you in sheep's clothing, but inwardly they are ravening wolves."*

> Matthew 7:15

They will come into the church and claim to have a gift or a Word from the Lord. They will know all of the right songs; they will know all of the right steps; they will know when to stand and when to sit; but the scary part is that they will know God's Word. This is not very amazing when we realize that Satan also knows God's Word. It is that very Word of God with which Satan began his attack against Jesus. It stands to reason that he would also send his soldiers into God's house with the very same tactic.

Therefore it is no great thing if his ministers also be transformed as the ministers of righteousness; whose end shall be according to their works.

2 Corinthians 11:15

These people know enough of the Word of God to be dangerous to those that are serious about their walk. They are deceptive and often cause confusion in the house of God and among God's people. They are hard to distinguish because they have all of the right credentials; all of the proper papers. They navigate between borders very easily and draw little suspicion. They are especially problematic for new soldiers. The captain is trying to train them and they are receiving mixed signals from other soldiers who have supposedly been in the Lord's service for much longer.

They have not being taught that a "...*little leaven Leavenworth the whole lump.*" They are being misled into thinking that they can still participate in the things of the world instead of being taught to grow in grace. They are struggling to differentiate between what is allowable for a soldier and what is taboo. They form relationships with these 'moles' and mimic their behavior; they begin to learn how to 'play church'.

Many times they will come into the church with the gifts and talents that God has created in every man; mix these with their worldly talents and soon hey are inducted into a leadership role in the church. They are being looked at as a valuable asset to assist the church in its growth. They know the talk and often can walk the walk, but the question will always remain, "*Do they have fruit?*" The Word of God tells us two things that will help prevent these types of people from scattering the flock.

"For every tree is known by his own fruit. For of thorns men do not gather figs, nor of a bramble bush gather they grapes."

Luke 6:44

225

> *"Beloved, believe not every spirit, but try the spirits whether they are of God: because many false prophets are gone out into the world."*

> 1John 4:1

As soldiers we should have a standard that has been set and will be enforced for anyone wanting to join our ranks. Everyone should have the opportunity to come in, but the older soldiers should be looking to see if they are fruitful and their spirits should be being tried by the shepherd of the house and the elders.

Satan has infiltrated the House of God. We can see an example of this in the book of Revelation.

> *"I know thy works, and where thou swellest, [even] where Satan's seat [is]: and thou goldest fast my name, and hast not denied my faith, even in those days wherein Antipas [was] my faithful martyr, who was slain among you, where Satan dwelleth."*

> Revelation 2:13

This scripture has always fascinated me. Jesus is telling the church at Pergolas that He has an issue with them. He is pointing out that there are those, *in* the church, that have the doctrine of Salaam who taught the children of Israel to follow the things of the world rather than the things of God. Salaam was a man of God; he knew God's Word and he was trusted even by people who were not God's people. His reputation had preceded him and his gifts were in demand. What he did was defy God's Word by being disobedient. God told Salaam not to curse Israel, so what Salaam did was trick Israel into cursing themselves by going against God's Word.

Jesus is also telling the Pergolas church that He is displeased with those who are practicing the doctrine of the Nicolas. This sect held the practice of unrestrained indulgence in secularism and was very closely related to the sinful nature that God found in Jezebel, who claimed herself a prophetess. They were also known for their indifference for life and the practice of excessive overindulgence in the pleasures of the flesh.

We are seeing that Jesus is recognizing certain character flaws *within* this church and He is pointing out that Satan has his very own *seat*.

> *"But I have a few things against thee, because thou hast there them that hold the doctrine of <u>Salaam</u>, who taught Balzac to cast a stumbling block before the children of Israel, to eat things sacrificed unto idols, and to commit fornication. So hast thou also them that hold the doctrine of the <u>Nicolas</u>, which thing I hate. Repent; or else I will come unto thee quickly, and will fight against them with the sword of my mouth."*

Revelation 2:14-**16**

Nice means ruler and *laity* or *laity* is the church or body of believers. So *Nicolas* are those that rule over or enslave God's people. They make 'filthy lucre' of God's merchandise. Salaam knew enough of the Word of God to be dangerous to God's people. Salaam apparently had his own agenda. Nicholas, whom it is said is the founder of the Nicolas that Jesus hates, was actually one of the original seven deacons named in the book of Acts. He was a proselyte to the church, but he also had his own agenda.

> *"And the saying pleased the whole multitude: and they chose Stephen, a man full of faith and of the Holy Ghost, and Philip, and Pro chorus, and Nicaragua, and Timon, and Parmesan, and <u>Nicolas </u>a proselyte of Antioch:"*

Act 6:5

Jesus is pointing out that he hates the character of these types of people because their character lines up so closely to Satan's character. They were at some point close enough to God to have positions in the body and been deemed worthy, but they betrayed that *trust*. Trust has been researched as one of, if not the, main reasons for divorce in today's society. When trust is broken within the institution of marriage, there is seldom a way back. God at certain points in scripture; is ready to divorce His bride Israel, but He loves Israel enough to remain married to them. Jesus is also showing us a different way in that the scripture tells men that we are to love our wives as Christ loves His bride; the church.

> *"Husbands, <u>love</u> your wives, even as Christ also loved the church, and gave himself for it;"*

Ephesians 5:25

We have to come to terms that in any relationship there are expectations on both sides. Simply because one party has the greater ability to perform certain responsibilities, does not mean that the expectations of the other party's obligations are non existent. Each party is expected to fulfill their obligations to the very ***best*** of their abilities. This is how trust is built and how a stronger bond in any relationship is formed. How much more a relationship with our creator?

Frankly I am scared by anyone that thinks so little of God's Word that they are willing to know it and still fly their fist in His face. This is a dangerous undertaking to say the least. Mankind has wondered so far away from the base camp that God has set into place that there should be no wonder why He is going to purge the world a second time with fire!

Water leaves things behind; the earth can thrive and exist in water; water is a key element in what forms the blue marble that we exist upon. Fire, however, has a destructive and purging property that leaves nothing behind. Impurities are removed from gold, silver and other metals with fire. Fire is an ironic end for anyone that has comes up against God's will. He is cleaning out the impurities of sin and making everything clean.

"But the heavens and the earth, which are now, <u>by the same Word</u>, are kept in store, reserved unto <u>fire</u> against the Day of Judgment and perdition of ungodly men."

2 Peter 3:7

God's Word does and always has kept everything in store. It has kept the wheels turning exactly the way that God wants the wheels to turn. God will not let anything or anyone stand against His Son/Word. I have three and I would give everything that I have and everything hat I am to either one of them and I am *not* God. It was a sacrifice of love that sent Jesus to the cross and was something that God does not take lightly. Jesus is the LOGOS; the living Word so God will never allow Him to be abused again.

Anyone who knows God's Word and has become a hindrance to His people is essentially aiding God's enemy Satan. That is why they all share Satan's fate. They will be cast into the Lake of Fire, which is an eternal punishment for those that know enough of God's Word to be *'dangerous'*.

Notes And Reflections For The Reader:

Notes And Reflections For The Reader:

Standing

Securing Territory

We may be asked of God to do the unthinkable. It is only unthinkable because we would have never thought to allow ourselves to go through whatever God is allowing us to go through. You might not think that standing is that difficult; trust me it will bring very close to death. You will have to rely on every ounce of your being and every scripture that you have ever read. You will have to sink yourself into scriptures that you have *never* read. You will have to find other interpretations and other people that have a different viewpoint than you do. You will have to endure what seems impossible and when you get close to the end of that, you will have to endure some more.

We do not know how long Job was afflicted and we do not hear of Paul having ever getting rid of the thorn in his flesh. We don't know how Sampson felt to be betrayed by the woman he loved and we don't know how he suffered having his eyes plucked out and being made to work as an animal. We do know that they stood. We know that they stood through everything that God allowed and they made it into the pages of history with their testimony.

When we are going through the standing process, God will prove us and make our calling an election sure. There will be times when it seems like God is allowing the enemy to throw everything *and* the kitchen sink at us. We will say, "God WHY?" God will then say to you, "Why NOT?"

Only God knows how He has created us and what testing and trials He has designed us to endure. Only He knows what our enemies are truly attempting to destroy us *with* and what He **has** and **is** protecting us *from*. This is one of the things that I am anticipating on finding out when I get to the 'Kingdom'. I really want God to show me just how may bullets that He has allowed me to dodge while I was here on earth. Certain swords we may never know that we have been protected from. Some things we can see for ourselves like avoiding accidents and being in the right place at the right time when something has just happened and we were *just* there. We can bless God for the things themselves we know, but what about the things that He has shielded us from that we could <u>not</u> see and did <u>not</u> know about?

The standing process will also tell you more about yourself than you ever knew. This process will allow you to see that you *can* take one more step when you thought the next one would make you fall. It will allow you to raise your shield at times you thought the enemy would crush you. This process will show you strengths in yourself that you did not know you had and filter out the weaknesses. It will draw you closer to God than you ever anticipated and forge a newer different kind of relationship.

You will find out just how great your faith is, in this process and how much it has grown from the small measure that He first gave you. You will see that the mustard seed has grown into a very large tree.

It is like a grain of mustard seed, which, when it is sown in the earth, is less than all the seeds that be in the earth:

Mark 4:31

When you have to stand you will be in a place like the children of Israel were; a desert place. Did you ever wonder why the Lord's Prayer asks, *"Give us this day our daily bread..."*? Did you ever wonder why the Israelites were only allowed to gather *manna* enough for one day? It was because God is trying to make us <u>dependent</u> on Him daily! Once we think that we have it all together, we will forsake the relationship and become targets for the enemy. Once we have forsaken the relationship, the other party has nothing to rely on; has nothing to trust in. This is why we must strive to be Abraham's and Moses'. They were considered to be friends with God; not acquaintances, ***friends***! There is a difference! This is one of the things that I would <u>very</u> much like to hear God express to me in the 'Kingdom', *"Well done my good and faithful **friend**!"*

Standing is not so easy to do when you're on the battlefield. When you see other soldiers getting shot or taking abuse; you want to do something; anything. We have to force ourselves to remember that we have not yet bled a drop in this battle.

"Ye have not yet resisted unto blood, striving against sin."

Hebrews 12:4

What we are to do is rely on God as Jehovah-Nisei (The Lord Our Banner) and raise our flag high against sin; against all of the sin that Satan throws at us. That is the only way he's coming; through sin and temptation. On rare occasions God will allow him to touch our bodies like he did with Job, but we also have to take into account that we are not keeping our temples. The first one is God's discretion on whether or not He has designed you or me to endure that kind of war. The second one falls squarely on our shoulders.

The offensive weapons that God gives us seem very non-lethal, but we are supposed to be standing and allowing God to fight our battles – I spoke about this earlier. While they seem non-lethal, they are effective to pulling down and nullifying the enemy's arsenal. Those weapons allow the heavenly host to operate, the way that God has designed them to operate, and gives them permission to move on the offensive for us. One thing that we do not want to do is keep our hedge of protection on the defensive all the time. I can imagine them saying, *"John you just don't get it..." "We're here and we could move on your behalf if you just do this, or pray in this way..."* I have asked God to forgive me for wearing His angels out and asked Him to ask them to forgive me as well. When you don't know; you just don't know. You have to think in terms of, *"What could be going on in a world that I cannot see?"*

"And Elisha prayed, and said, LORD, I pray thee, open his eyes, that he may see. And the LORD opened the eyes of the

young man; and he saw: and, behold, <u>the mountain [was]</u>
<u>*full of horses and chariots of fire round about Elisha.*</u>"

2 Kings 6:17

Elisha was certainly surprised that God had so many of the host of
heaven set into place around him. We should remember this simple
thing when we are really coming to the point in our standing that
is causing us to fear and doubt what God has already assured us of:

"And he answered, Fear not: for they that [be] with us [are]
more than they that [be] with them."

2 Kings 6:16

God wants us to relax and rely on Him. Yes, Yes, I definitely know
how difficult that is; trust me I do; it is something that God knows
too. It is also another reason for the standing process. God is teaching
you to trust Him and showing us how BIG He 'really' is. If God didn't
teach us to stand, then we would go through life trying to keep Him
in a (<u>*your name here*</u>) box and keep a 'little vision' instead of being
able to see the 'big picture'.

In the military, you are taught to stand your ground. You are taught
to keep the territory that you have already conquered and secure it. In
this way your fellow soldiers; your army can keep pressing forward
and making progress. This is how to: advance on the enemy camp;
destroy his strongholds; rescue prisoners; save refugees; find those
that have been lost on the enemy's side of the line and reclaim the
land that the enemy thought to reign. God is fighting the battle; we
have to stand still and be patient enough to see His salvation. The
first territory that needs to e secured, however, is us!

Notes And Reflections For The Reader:

Notes And Reflections For The Reader:

The Visionaries

Re-Thinking the Church

Does the church need to be re-thought? If a machine that has been created, to serve a certain purpose, is not functioning according to that purpose; then that machine needs to be adjusted. The creator of that machine has given us the machine, as well as given us the instruction manual for the machine. We know that the creator is not located in our part of the world, so the instruction manual is our best option until the creator returns and we can get Him to put His expertise to work. Since we have no idea when the creator will return, we need to open the manual and flip to the section that says 'church'.

> *Take heed therefore unto yourselves, and to all the flock, over the which the Holy Ghost hath made you overseers, to feed the church of God, which he hath purchased with his own blood.*

Acts 20:28

> *"And when the day of Pentecost was fully come, they were all with <u>one accord in one place</u>."*

Act 2:1

Diagram 1: Assemble the pieces of the church in one place before trying to reassemble this machine.

We can see from the instruction manual that there were one hundred and twenty pieces that were set aside in one place before the electricity of the Holy Spirit was plugged in to start the machine working. Everyone was in one place and on one accord. The disciples were joined together in the upper room and everything that Jesus had taught during His training course was prepared to be tested.

<u>Diagram 2:</u> Assemble the machine (Replace any pieces that may have been lost or damaged during shipping)

The first thing the disciples did was replace the part that was missing so that the machine would work the way that the creator intended. They replaced Judas' 'piece' with a better component; Matthias. Then the machine was ready to be assembled. When the machine was assembled and all of the pieces were in place, God turned the *power* on! The machine was operational.

<u>Diagram 3:</u> This machine will draw all men to Christ

This machine will give, all that use it, the power to bring men, women, and children to Christ. It will be a refuge for those that do not have a safe place. It will be a place where people can learn a different way to live. It will be a place where people can experience, miracles, healing, find hope and have their needs met.

<u>Diagram 4:</u> This machine will be the prototype for other machines that will be created to achieve the same purpose; as the maker has seen fit.

[WARNING: Use this machine wisely because the parts have to be ordered from God and the power will be slowly turned off when this machine is taken back to the factory to be serviced.]

Okay, that was my attempt at a little levity, but I believe it paints an adequate picture that can illustrate the fact that God has designed the 'machine' of the church to work in a certain way. It is clear, however, in scripture, that the Holy Spirit is *allowing* some things to occur, for a time, and then He (The Holy Spirit) will be taken out of the way. When He is removed, the Anti-Christ shall be revealed and all hell will break loose here on earth.

The Holy Spirit is in place now because Jesus promised us a 'Comforter' to keep us and to be a lighthouse for us during this time when iniquity has already been allowed to have its way. I have already stated that it is in our day and age that the great apostasy spoken about in 2 Thessalonians 2:3 can already be seen.

> *"Let no man deceive you by any means: for [that day shall not come], except there come a falling away first, and that man of sin be revealed, the son of perdition;"*

2 Thessalonians 2:3

Everything is upside-down, inside-out and backwards in today's world. People don't seem to care anymore about themselves or anyone else for that matter. Now is not the time to be faint of heart or wanting to turn back. God's Word cannot return to Him void, so we must rely on the fact that His Word has gone out and we *will* see results when they return to Him.

The mindset of today seems to be either that man has stopped believing in God *or* they have forgotten that He is also a God of WRATH! Yes God is longsuffering, but there comes a time when He has to rain fire and brimstone because He is just *that* angry. He says, in His Word, that His Spirit will not continue to fight with man because we are men and He is God.

> *"And the LORD said, <u>My spirit shall not always strive with man</u>, for that he also [is] flesh: yet his days shall be an hundred and twenty years."*

Genesis 6:3

God says this just before He floods the earth in Genesis chapter six. It is a very broad statement which means that it does not only apply to the deluge of Noah's time, but it is a landmark point where God is telling man that things have changed!

> *"And now ye know what withholding that he might be revealed in his time. For the mystery of iniquity doth*

240

already work: only he who now letterer [will let], <u>until he</u>
<u>be taken out of the way</u>."

2 Thessalonians 2:6-7

The machine needs to be adjusted to compensate for the fact that the power is being turned back a little at a time. The things that the church has allowed into its doors and turned a blind eye toward are causing the 'machine' to break down. The 'machine' was designed to do very specific work and that work can be seen in the fact that it has been the most successful 'machine' ever created in the history of man. Approximately two billion persons in the world identify with Christianity as their faith. This is one third of the world's population with the other two thirds identifying with other belief systems. I would say that God's 'machine' has worked out very well.

Sidenote: I would also say that two thirds of thirds of the world's populace of believers; living, dead and yet to be born; about makes up for the one third of the angels that lost their habitation in heaven. - Selah

And his tail drew the third part of the stars of heaven, and did cast them to the earth: and the dragon stood before the woman which was ready to be delivered, for to devour her child as soon as it was born.

Revelation 12:4

It is possible to adjust the 'machine', but we have to go back to the instruction manual. It may be an exercise in futility to get today's man to have all things in common, but it is not impossible. All things in common simply means that we need to *re-purpose* having the mind of Christ in our *daily* thought process.

What needs to be done is educate the older saints to the fact that the world's mentality has changed with the advent of the internet, computers and technology. Not that I am trying to thrust the older generation into the computer age, but bring them up to speed on what has happened and how they can adjust their ministries accordingly. The church cannot continue to operate the same way that it did fifty years ago and expect to survive. It cannot speak to today's young people in the same way that they were spoken to when they were young. It cannot function outside of every thing that is attracting our youth and hope to maintain their interest. Things have changed! We are not to conform to the way that the world and worldliness is alluring man, but we must be inventive, savvy, and imaginative in the way that we draw souls to the 'Kingdom'.

We have to create venues that will make people want to pay attention and turn their cell phones and tablets off without having to be told. We have to have Christian events that make people want to attend and bring their friends. We have to make the hope that we have real and tangible and obtainable to the world. We have to be more attractive than Satan.

One thing that I despise is the fact that the church feels like it has to make its agenda correspond to Satan's agenda. We should be able to out think him on at least this level. Everything that Satan is using is something that he copied or stole from God, so how much more would God bless us with witty ideas that Satan doesn't know about?

Wisdom crieth without; she utterer her voice in the streets:

Proverbs 1:20

"I wisdom dwell with prudence, and find out knowledge of witty inventions."

Proverbs 8:12

Wisdom is something that God will not withhold from us and it will find and give us knowledge of clever new ideas. Can we copy Satan's blueprints and hope that they will benefit the 'Kingdom' of God? Can we introduce a foreign manufacturer's 'metric' system or 'core math' into our 'standard' system 'machine'?

(This is a problem that builders and mechanics often face when trying to replace or repair something that is worn out or damaged. What they try to do is reinvent a new system that seems like it will work and then re-teach the populace their method. Then all wonder why the machine is not working properly)

Our strategy has to be 'fluid'. We have to assess our audience quickly and trust God to change our strategy according to what He wants sewn into His people. If this calls for a change from a message that was intended for an older listener, then we must incorporate the fact that there may be younger members listening. If the message has been tailored for a younger crowd and there are older saints in attendance, then we must be respectful of what they are accustomed to hearing and seeing. This may sound difficult, but when we have the mind of Christ and are led by His Spirit, everything can come together in uniformity to accomplish God's ultimate purpose. The 'machine' has been designed to adjust itself when these situations arise. I have seen it done in Kenya when I was slated to bring messages alongside of a pastor that I was to be an armor bearer too. Our messages lined up exactly perfectly because of His Spirit. It seemed as if we had worked together to utter what we had spoken.

Remember in the book of Acts; there was a language barrier. The 'machine' eradicated that situation very quickly by tearing down the language barrier and incorporating people that may not have otherwise listened to the gospel message. The scripture says that when the Holy Spirit came, it came in the form of 'cloven' tongues. This was an indication of two *separate* languages; with one language you could draw people in the <u>natural</u> and with one you could speak to God directly in the <u>spiritual</u>. This allowed people that were from different walks of life and spoke different languages to spread the gospel throughout their different cities, countries and throughout the world. This also allowed the disciples to get what God wanted them to be a part of in the first place. Jesus died to tear down the '*middle wall of partition*'; He died to tear down the wall that was separating man from his Creator. Beforehand, man was separated from God and had no way or hope of fellowship with Him. What we are seeing was

God beginning to draw close to man again or allowing man to enter into His presence.

> **"Praising God, and having favour with all the people. And the Lord added to the church daily such as should be saved."**

Act 2:47

When the 'machine' is running smoothly, God is the one that will bring the people into the sheepfold. When it is not, people will come; they will stay for a while; and then they will leave and try the next machine. There is no substance in a church that is struggling to accomplish a goal that is not a part of God's agenda. People will stay at a mega-church because they want to be affiliated with the churches name; affiliated with its charismatic pastor; or because they are still searching for a way to fill that sense of wanting to belong; to be apart of something bigger than themselves.

As people come into the church, the leaders must *already* know that God has designed every person with a 'hole' inside of them that can only be filled with Him. The pastors job; the churches job is to lead them in a direction where they can form their *own* relationship with God and allow Him to fill that void. The people that come to the church must be taught that we are members of a body and we all must perform our part or the body doesn't operate properly; the 'machine' in essence breaks down.

> **From whom the whole body fitly joined together and compacted by that which every joint supplier, according to the effectual working in the measure of every part, maketh increase of the body unto the edifying of itself in love.**

Ephesians 4:16

In the book of Acts, the disciples continued together; ate together; prayed together and ministered the gospel together. They were all on one accord in this regard. It is not like they gave up their daily lives or ceased to do the things that were acquainted with day to day living;

244

it was simply that they had the same goal. This is like any well oiled 'machine', when all of the parts are in place and operating properly, the 'machine' can do what it was designed to do.

Many times the church gets bogged down in a certain way of thinking and does not know how to break free. This is when the members become known as the 'frozen chosen'. They have been chosen to be a part of the machine, but they have become a frozen *cog* or *wheel* that is supposed to be operating smoothly.

They are essentially preventing the other components from being effective and hindering the entire 'machine' from working properly. They don't want to do anything differently. They are used to and were raised to rotate left and cannot see rotating right. They are used to a certain 'order' of service and cannot change to allow God to take over and have service in His way. They have become used to sitting in certain place and parking in a certain place. They have become stuck in a routine and it simply is not working anymore!

The 'Deacon Board' should not have to be consulted on every single event, activity, or dilemma that is going on at or in the church. The 'Usher Board' days of marching in have passed and cannot be received by today's generation. Sticking to the notes that you have taken to prepare a sermon may or may not be what God has planned. These things <u>can</u> exist to some degree, but when we "*...let this mind be in us that was also in Christ"*; we could take so much of the weight of the 'machine' off of ourselves and off of the people and let the 'machine' do what it was designed to do.

Let this mind be in you, which was also in Christ Jesus:

Philippians 2:5

Too much of the church mentality is trapped in tradition! This is the problem that the Catholic Church is having. They have not changed the style of hat or clothing that the Pope, priests, and nuns have been wearing in a thousand years. Do we honestly think that we can get the young people to respect that when all of their role models are

245

wearing something completely different? I'm not saying that we should imitate the world, only that we should have a newer, fresher more attractive style that speaks to *our* differences and at the same time sets a Godly standard. (No, I do not know how it can be done Dear Reader, but I can say that, *we* have not tried.)

I believe that if all of the designers in the industry recognized that there was a market in mainstream for a potential 2 billion clientele it might sway them to produce some different styles. Instead of the younger generation doing everything in their power to keep up with current trends, their parents would buy into the market as well. We should place as much time and effort into getting our venue out into the forefront as Satan; then we may find that we have allowed far too much to slip through the cracks. We could have been a lot more effective for the 'Kingdom'. This is of course excluding what mainstream has done with marketing different pastoral clothing to the general public.

We have to turn ourselves into 'visionaries'. Not the visionaries that see the next church project or that see the new building fund or that can only see the vision that the pastor has that he says that God has given him. The pastor's vision for his part of the 'machine' should be confirmation to the members of the church and not revelation. This is what the book of Acts means by *all* were in the same place and on one accord.

How did we get so far off track? We have become lazy! We stopped paying attention and that is what the enemy wanted us to do. His plan was to water down the gospel (Good News); to water down the message that the way back Tree of Life had been opened. The 'machine' was designed to get this message out to the world. This is why the 'machine' must continue to operate in a functional way until it is time for the designer to come and take it back to the factory for its scheduled maintenance.

This is something that we *can* do; *should* do; and that is *necessary* for us to do, in these last days. We should have a clear account when the creator of the 'machine' comes back and asks us have we been performing the scheduled maintenance. "Did you change and replace the parts that were not functioning properly? Did you use the lines of communication that I set into place to call the twenty four hour maintenance hotline? Did you take care of **_my_** 'machine'?"

Notes And Reflections For The Reader:

Notes And Reflections For The Reader:

More Is Required

Men Want More Than God

"But he that knew not, and did commit things worthy of stripes, shall be beaten with few [stripes]. For unto whomsoever much is given, of him shall be much required: and to whom men have committed much, of him they will ask the more."

Luke 12:48

There is always accountability! We may try to erase it from the equation or bury it in our minds, but this does *not* change the reality that the facts still remain the ***facts***! We are always accountable for what we know and for our actions, whether we want to acknowledge this or not. Knowledge *is* power and either you are using it correctly or you are misusing it. The problem comes in when people listen to your misdirection or your error in perception. They are now at risk because you have acquired the knowledge and you are not sharing it correctly or at all.

When you have knowledge and it is not divulged appropriately; when it is held and not dissimulated, you do a disservice to yourself and to others. Knowledge expressed at the proper time, place and fashion may save someone's life. If a new employee is not given the appropriate direction and protocol for the correct response during a fire, then how will they escape, help save others to escape or survive themselves?

"No man, when he hath lighted a candle, putteth [it] in a secret place, neither under a bushel, but on a candlestick, that they which come in may see the light."

Luke 11:33

250

The light is _knowledge_! When we have acquired knowledge, it is meant to be shared and given to everyone so that others can have it, at the very least, the benefit of being informed. It is never meant to be hidden or held, but revealed and shown like the light of a candle.

As a people that have been given the greatest gift that humanity has ever known; we owe a debt to mankind to make sure that we share the good news and our eternal fortune.

> *Now to him that is of power to establish you according to my gospel, and the preaching of Jesus Christ, according to the revelation of <u>the mystery, which was kept secret since the world began.</u>*

Romans 16:25

> *And for me, that utterance may be given unto me, that I may open my mouth boldly, <u>to make known the mystery of the gospel.</u>*

Ephesians 6:19

The good news of God sending humanity a Savior was never meant to be kept a secret. God has desired for His plans to be made accessible to everyone on planet earth. Since God has offered us so much through His Son Jesus, we have an accountability factor that really cannot be overlooked or dismissed. How can we expect so great a gift without there being any repayment on our part? What has always struck me as incredible about this particular scripture is the fact that men will require more from you than God will. God has His requirements and He should because He's God. It is easy to understand that if someone is given a great deal, a great deal will be expected of them, but for man to require more is startling.

Think about it, when you do something for someone, they will look at you a lot differently than God. God looks at us from the perspective of knowing more about you than you know about yourself. He looks at you from the standpoint of **knowledge**; from the standpoint of knowing how and why He created you. Man will always look at us from the standpoint of what we can do for him/her. Even in marriage, that is worldly as opposed to *God-Centered*, there is the selfish factor of each person feeling as if they will benefit in some way from the other. In today's society, people are not marrying solely for *love*; marriage has become a business arrangement or an arrangement for convenience.

God has His requirements for mankind and they are absent from the carnal idealism's of men. God's requisites for us embody only those things that can be accounted *reasonable* and *just* for a Creator and Father. Man's requirements only mimic Gods and always go far beyond what we are able to perform and/or deliver. God's requirements are for *our* best, while man's requirements are for *man's* best. God's requirements are for *our* ultimate development and improvement, while man's requirements are for man's success and accomplishment only.

The similarity lies in the fact that the punishment for not meeting the prerequisites of either bears a resemblance. For both sides the punishment is according to knowledge. Man will look at a situation and desire a certain justification. The saying is that the punishment should fit the crime. God feels the same way, but is approaching it from a different perspective. He is approaching any infraction from the standpoint of love and the desire for a closer relationship with us. Included in that is **_grace_** (blessing us with what we have not earned or deserved) and **_mercy_** (not accounting to us what we actually do deserve and have coming). Man's punishment is based on what man has viewed as a deficit in his own plans and/or worldview.

We all have our own viewpoint and even our own ideas about how to progress in life. Some people make decisions that will allow them to be in position for success in the world. Others will take the road less traveled and can also achieve their goals in life. What I would like to convey Dear Reader is that if we align our will with God's will, then the journey could be so much easier. There will still be bumps in the road; there will still be tests to pass; and there will still be adversity that must be overcome. There will still be instances where we are at a crossroads, but isn't easier to be able to turn to someone that knows? Isn't easier to be able to turn to someone that has the power to get us through our difficult times and always has our best interest at heart? I do believe that when we take the viewpoint that these things are man's prerequisites and these are God's, the odds will shift in our favor when we choose God's.

To whom much is given, much is required. What should always be taken into consideration is the ***one*** doing the giving!

Notes And Reflections For The Reader:

The Cares of This World

The World Doesn't Care for You!

Falling in love with this world will end in heartbreak every single time. It does not seem fair does it? Could it possibly *ever* be fair? A person will do everything that the world requires and find out that the world has used them up and left them for the next lover. This love affair requires all of your time; it requires all of your energy; it requires your self esteem and your dignity; in short it requires the best part of you; your *youth.*

Think about Howard Hughes. There wasn't much that he did not have or ever needed and yet he died like someone who had given himself and his vitality fully to the world that he thought loved him. From an outside standpoint many of us would have traded places with him thinking that we would have done things differently. He had an uncanny business sense and enough money to make his dreams a reality. His passion was airplanes and he became a juggernaut in the aerodynamics industry, but this goal cost him his peace and soundness of mind. Women, dinner parties, servants, and all of the money he could spend could not satisfy the pull that the world had on his mind. He was continuously driven to outdo what he had previously accomplished. His drive to make a name for himself and to be the best in his field caused him to spend his final years as a recluse. The aeronautics industry changed drastically due, in large part, to the accomplishments of Howard Hughes. Now that the world had what if needed, what was the need for Howard Hughes?

It may sound strange to look at it from this standpoint, but why wouldn't we think of these things from this viewpoint? We speak in terms of '*mother* earth' and say things like, "*That 70's spirit...*"

Why would we not give the 'world' a human persona; the quality of having people *love* it? If we can look at it from this perspective, then we can grant it the ability to accept or reject what we are putting into it; the *way* that we love it.

Make no mistake; loving the things that this world has to offer is far less beneficial than you will be led to believe.

What you will see is someone that is at the pinnacle of their personal glory, making a name for themselves and therein lies the attraction for everyone else that will follow. Professional athletes prove this on a regular basis. It is just a matter of turning on the television to obtain proof.

I remember wanting to be like O.J. Simpson as a young man; I even had the Jersey. His demise was followed worldwide by the media and followed by still incident after incident. His football career was over; his wife and her boyfriend were dead; and his lifelong success and glory was erased by the very world that once loved him.

Elvis Presley, Michael Jackson and Whitney Houston have very similar stories. It is too easy for us to sit back and speak about how things could have been different. It is too easy for us to comment on the different roads that *we* would have taken, if given the same opportunities. The same world that loved Elvis Presley, 'The King', is still making millions off of his drug induced overdose his wealth, his music and his property; Graceland. The world, that loved and idolized the 'King of Pop', later villainous him as a child molester. The same world that loved Whitney watched her drug overdose destroy her beautiful voice and reported that she was dead in a fleeting television moment. The world is still profiting off of their legacies, These three people that were acclaimed pioneers; forerunners and trailblazers in the music industry; until the world had finished implementing it's own standard and they had outlived their usefulness.

What the 'world' will not tell you is that many of those who have achieved unbelievable heights and fame have 'loved' the Gods of this world. Russell Simmons, Kimono Lee Simmons, Michael Jackson,

Oozy Osborne, Marilyn Manson, The Beatles, Jim Hendricks, Janice Joplin and many, many others have sold their souls to the 'gods' of this world for fame and fortune. Very few of them are still alive, but you can research their lifestyle and mentality very easily. Most of the ones that are still alive are mere shadows of their former selves and the toll is showing visibly. Their lives have been spent.

The world will take its toll on those that love it and the price is always too high to pay. One of the main problems is that loving the world, or the gods that are behind the scenes, is in direct opposition with the One True God.

> *"Ye adulterers and adulteresses know ye not that the friendship of the world is enmity with God? Whosoever therefore will be a friend of the world is the enemy of God."*

> James 4:4

> *"Because the carnal mind [is] enmity against God: for it is not subject to the law of God, neither indeed can be."*

> Romans 8:7

> *"Love not the world, neither the things [that are] in the world. If any man love the world, the love of the Father is not in him."*

> 1 John 2:15

> *"If ye were of the world, the world would love his own: but because ye are not of the world, but I have chosen you out of the world, therefore the world hater you."*

> John 15:19

Make no errors about how you look at this subject. The world has a *persona*; whether it is the 'spirit' that is governing the age or the mentality that the general populace has; this is a love/hate relationship. The scripture says in Matthew 6:24 & Luke 16:13 that you cannot serve two masters, because you will *love* only one and you will *hate* the other one. God will not be anyone's second. He requires the number one spot and He will take offense with anyone or anything that seeks to fill it. It's like trying to work two jobs. You can love both jobs, but eventually you will burn out and begin to despise the job that *you* feel has the least benefits even though they both have the same duties.

We have all seen people that tend to get their priorities backward. They esteem the weekend higher than the week. They look forward to the weekend because of the Friday night partying; the high. Saturday is loved because of the ability to sleep in and party Saturday night. Their Sundays are loved because they have a chance to be in church around people that will pray for their Friday and Saturday. (I Hope I have not stepped on anyone's toes?) The priority is backward because the work week is what allows for any of the previous activities. The work week is what sustains the quality and standard of life, so enjoying what the world has to offer has its place. A night of bowling or a night of dinner and jazz is completely acceptable in God's sight; however I am not sure that God likes Jazz.

Look back at chapter 2, **Don Lucifero**. What happens is that Satan will pervert the thinking that would normally put our priorities into the right order. Remember that Satan will always present the exact opposite of God's plan. If I do this first, I can still do that and have fun. Prioritizing the wrong one will most certainly mean the loss of or inability to do either. I have had friends and employees that have called into work drunk or were too tired from a party to show up on time. I have friends that abuse their sick leave and personal leave to he point of not being dependable to their boss and eventually lose their jobs. Still others show up to work five or ten minutes late until it becomes recognized and a cause for chastisement and then termination. These might seem like a very small things, but think about it, in Eden, Satan only inserted one three letter word and that messed up all of humanity.

God has told us why humanity is in the situation that it is in and He expects for His children to listen. Adam surrendered the deed and title to earth in Eden and so of course Satan is going to make the world that he runs seem like one big party.

Wherein in time past ye walked according to the course of this world, according to the prince of the power of the air, the spirit that now worketh in the children of disobedience:

Ephesians 2:2

Satan will misdirect us so that we will focus on anything and everything but God. He will make it so tantalizing and attractive that we will find it hard to resist. He will compare the things of God to his own pleasures and make God's look restrictive and confining. This is a backward way of thinking when we realize that God has created everything that we have and will have in heaven and on earth. Satan is taking something that he did not create and making it appear to be *his* invention; *his* idea. Remember, we haven't even seen heaven yet!

If you ever get the impression that Christianity is boring; too confining or too restrictive, then ask yourself how much you are putting into it. Are you praising God and throwing up your hands like you were at a Jay-Z concert? Are you dancing at Christian events as hard as you do at a nightclub? Are you having as much fun interacting with your brothers and sisters at the church picnic as you are at the bar or casino? Ask yourself, *"Why is Satan so much fun?"* *"Why does the world seem to be more attractive than the eternal promise of heaven?"*

I can assure you that God loves you and has a plan for you. He is waiting for you to RSVP the invitation that He sent by way of His Son. All you have to do is say yes and He will send someone to get you when the doors open. He will even provide the food and new clothes!

"And he saith unto me, Write, Blessed [are] they which are called unto the <u>marriage supper</u> of the Lamb. And he saith unto me, These are the true sayings of God."

Revelation 19:9

"He that overcome, <u>the same shall be clothed in white raiment</u>; and I will not blot out his name out of the book of life, but I will confess his name before my Father, and before his angels."

Revelation 3:5

Notes And Reflections For The Reader:

Unmasked

What's In You Will
Come Out Of You

"Because that, when they knew God, they glorified [him] not as God, <u>neither were thankful</u>; but became vain in their imaginations, and their foolish heart was darkened."

Romans 1:21

Guess what? A *Thank You* can go a long way; further than you may think! If I do the smallest thing for you like hold the door or allow you to pull your car in front of mine, I expect a *"thank you"* at the least. I will even take, "Thanks." This is a term of recognition for the smallest effort that you put forth. It is the acknowledgment of ones endeavor to make your life that much easier. How do we think that God should feel when we are not <u>*thankful*</u> and He is GOD?

This scripture is not speaking of the supposed person that has never heard the 'good news' of Jesus the Savior. This scripture is saying that these people have known God and are not giving Him the recognition that He deserves. After all, He did create the air that they breathe everyday for free. He does wake them up morning after morning. God is asking for a *thank you* and the recognition of who He is and what He can do and has already done.

On top of the fact that these people knew God (past tense); and did not glorify Him *as* God and also were not thankful; God *allowed* their foolish hearts to be darkened. God did not darken their hearts; He only allowed what was *in* them to come *out* of them. This is what He did with Pharaoh the King of Egypt and what He shall do to this new generation of sodomites.

When this happens, it is only God taking a step back and letting them have their way. It is God not interfering with man's freewill. As I have mentioned before, God has already revealed in His Word that we have an enemy. He has given us the choice; the freewill to choose His way. When we have our mind set on doing things our own way, then He will say, "Yes! Have it your way." It is at this point that the enemy will attack in full force and assault your mind. Satan's objective is to drag as many people to hell as he can and he doesn't mind using you or me to do it. The scripture says that 'when' they *knew* God, they did not glorify Him as God. They then become vain in their imaginations. This means: hopeless, unproductive, unsuccessful, useless, futile and worthless. This is hard for me to imagine as far as someone's thinking pattern is concerned. To fail at certain things is a point in life; it is a fact. To become useless in all that you imagine or futile in everything that you think is beyond me. There is however a point in which the enemy will allow you to seem productive while making a fool of you in God's sight. The positive thoughts are now being mixed with negative ones. The ideas that could benefit you will now hinder you. Your natural attraction and magnetism with people is now placing the wrong people in your circle. Your gifts and talents are now being used in the wrong places and at the wrong times. What could be success is now destined for failure and so on. I will not place the entirety of what Paul finishes with, but please take the time to read verses 22-32 before you continue. Satan is a master at his game which is why we have to master ours.

Satan has seen that you have not recognized God and he wants to capitalize on it. He will take the fact that God has been insulted and removed your hedge of protection as his go ahead to destroy you.

A foolishly darkened heart is the least of your worries if God is not recognized and He steps away from you. We can find ourselves on a part of the road that we never knew existed. There is no light on this part of the road; there are no street signs; there don't appear to be any lanes marked and the other cars are driving a lot faster than what we *know* to be the speed limit.

What is in you is not a matter of God's doing. He has already given you His image and His likeness upon conception. The ability to choose Him is already within you as a matter of freewill. God's Word tells us that creation itself speaks of a Creator without anyone having to be told. So the problem comes down to who is in your ear? With Eve, it was Satan that was in her ear. With Cain, it was also Satan, but with a slightly different approach. After injecting sin into the equation, Satan's work becomes easier. The sin nature is now inborn with mankind because of Adam and Eve's disobedience to God. Because, when they knew God, they did not glorify Him as God or remember to thank Him. Satan's work becomes easy when he has something in us that is working *for* him.

The sin nature in us is always fighting God and wanting to pull away from or coming into obedience and submission to Him. It is this nature in man that is actually hostile toward God. This is the single thing that has been injected into our beings that is forever trying to break away from God. It is trying to take the lead before our minds and control our spirits. Obedience to God is the last thing that the fleshly, worldly sin nature wants. This is why when God knocks on the door of our hearts; we should invite Him to come in. The knocking should prompt you to understand and realize that God will not force Himself upon us. God is a gentleman and He will wait for our invitation. If we choose not to open the door then that is a completely different story.

> *But I see another law in my members, warring against the law of my mind, and bringing me into captivity to the law of sin which is in my members.*

> **Romans 7:23**

> *Because the carnal mind is enmity against God: for it is not subject to the law of God, neither indeed can be.*

> **Romans 8:7**

We already know that man is now born with a sin nature so did your parents seek God and point the way for you? Was there anyone that prayed for you when they saw you going in the wrong direction? Have you realized that you have a need for a Savior? If none of these things apply to you, then the likelihood is that you have adopted a worldly survival technique. The things that a sin nature will allow to grow in you will always be struggling to break free and be in control. Look at scripture and the different listings and categorizing of sins and see how of broad a topic this is. If we do not want to be controlled by sin; if we do not want what is innately in us to come out of us, then we need a restraint.

For the mystery of iniquity doth already work: only <u>he who now letterer [will let]</u>, until he be taken out of the way.

2 Thessalonians 2:7

Paul is telling the Thessalonians that the mystery of sin is already at work. It is only God's Holy Spirit that is restraining it, but He will be taken out of the way at some point. Dear Readers, I have already seen far more in this world than I have wanted too; I pray that we all will be in the 'Kingdom' when the Holy Spirit of God is taken out of the earth. He is still in the earth restraining sin from completely taking hold of humanity; imagine if He takes His hands completely off and lets what is in man come out? We are already living in a time where we can see that He is loosening His grip and allowing more and more as man's foolish heart is being darkened. What will be the next vain imagination that we bear witness too before we are once again living in the days of Noah? There will be no flood this time; this time it will be a lot worse than Sodom and Gomorrah.

"But the heavens and the earth, which are now, <u>by the same word are kept in store</u>, <u>reserved unto fire</u> against the day of judgment and perdition of ungodly men."

2 Peter 3:7

When the spirit of God is taken completely out of the earth there will be chaos. Man is already challenging God and giving in to sin. It is like the desire to fight for righteousness has vanished. Man has a, "*let's try it*" attitude"; that is leading to a, "*he/she got away with it* **or** *is doing it*" attitude; that is leading to an "*I don't care*" attitude that is leading us straight to hell! This world is catching on fire one with every new thought, advance in technology, latest trend or style and every new pop star. Someone has to wake up and smell the smoke.

What I would love to see in my lifetime is a *true* revival. I would like to see people in recognition of the fact that things cannot go along the way that they have. I would like to see the Biblical End Time prophecies being paid attention too. I would like to see someone take a stand the way that they did when I was growing up. Just one familiar face on the television that says, "*This isn't right.*" I do not want it to be a televangelist either. Satan has made the majority of them laughing stocks or unbelievable at best. I would like to see someone like Bill Mather have an epiphany and realize that he is now sitting in Saul's former position (Before he became the Apostle Paul) where he was persecuting and killing Christians. I would like to see the realization and love of Christ touch him to the point that he recants all of his previous pot-shots at the gospel of Christ. The saddest part about this comedic/ actor is that he is Jewish. Bill Mather has now been unmasked. Read his bio online and you may begin to understand why he hates God so much.

God says in His Word in the book of Exodus, "*This people is a stiff necked people!*" He wanted to wipe the Jews off of the planet and start again with Moses. He had already done so much for them and had shown them the awesome power of His love. Imagine the people that God chose to be *His* people are the ones causing Him the most trouble.

What is in you will surely come out of you!

Notes And Reflections For The Reader:

Home Sweet Home

What Country Do You Seek?

Where would you like to spend your vacation? When I go on vacation, there are two things that I desire above anything else. The first is that I will have peace of mind. The second is that I will be able to rest. If I can obtain *peace of mind*, then I have no doubt that rest will come easily. In my travels abroad, or even travels within the country, I have always required time where I would be able to think undisturbed and a comfortable place to rest with which I could end my day.

In my younger days it was easy to accept the gospel message, but Satan began to work on me around the age of thirteen. He began to burden me and pull on me with the cares of this world. It wasn't anything extraordinary, but he began to draw my attention to other things. I began to see girls differently, I began to get into sports and I began to hang around the wrong people. After graduation, I went to Howard University in Washington D.C. and I was truly out on my own. I was not under the umbrella of protection provided by living in a God fearing house; at least not to the degree that my accountability was being retained in the forefront of my thinking. I know now that I have a God that affords more *grace* and *mercy* than we can ever understand and a praying mother to thank for my re-entrance into the sheepfold. I had to experience a great deal before I began to recognize that I needed to repent and turn around.

It was when I began to seek God as an adult that my life began to do a 180°. I began to see in God's Word that believing in the *saving* power, of Christ's sacrifice, was the only definite way to acquire the peace that I was craving. I didn't have to do anything accept believe in what God was saying. Did I try other faiths? Yes! You might not believe how many and I gained quite a bit of knowledge during my time and studies while searching for God and His word. It was a young Christian woman that was immovable in her faith that stopped me dead in my tracks. In conversation, I began to try and convince her that my way of thinking was right and she said something very simple to me that made me rethink everything! Lisa responded to my tirade by saying, *"What difference does it make?"* At that point I basically stopped talking and I began to ask myself that very question. *"What difference did what I was talking about make? What I had learned and incorporated into my thinking did not measure up to God's word"* None! This is what is known as the simplicity of the gospel. She was not in my face, I was in hers. She was not stepping on my toes; I was attempting to step on hers. I was trying to prove *what* and to what end?

I met my beautiful wife Tammy shortly after that and began to study the *real* Word of God on a regular basis. I realized that unlike other faiths, I did not have to reach up and try to touch God; He had already reached down to touch *me* through His Son. *There* was my *peace*! Now I'm not saying that you can accept Christ and sit on your butt; not at all. What I am saying is that my residence in heaven with my creator is not *based* on anything that I will have to *do* here on earth except say YES! My eternal vacation is not determined by my worldly works.

It was these scriptures that solidified things in my mind; helped me remember what I already knew.

> *"These all died in faith, <u>not having received the promises, but having seen them afar off, and were persuaded of [them], and embraced [them], and confessed that they were strangers and pilgrims on the earth.</u> For they that say such things declare plainly that they seek a <u>country</u>. And truly, if they had been mindful of that [country] from whence they came out, they might have had opportunity to have returned. But now they desire a better [country], that is, an heavenly: wherefore God is not ashamed to be called their God: for he hath prepared for them a city."*

Hebrews 11:13-**16**

God's Word is truly correct when it tells us to, *"Raise a child in the way that he should go and when he is older he will not depart from it."* I believe that everyone will spend their time in this 'country'; the world. The question is whether or not they will choose to stay in Egypt or look for the Exodus. We have to have our time in the world, for the purpose of being able to use our free will. This is so that we can exercise our freedom of 'choice'. God is righteous and He would never take a gift back or undo His creation without offering *grace* and *mercy* first.

These patriarchs all died persuaded of the promise of a gift that they did not receive here on earth. They all understood that the country, that they were in, was not the country in which they desired to stay. They looked forward to journeying to their *true* country and were not ashamed of their real citizenship while they were abroad. They were not ashamed to be called citizens of the 'Kingdom' and therefore God was not ashamed to be called their God. These people held onto their faith and claimed their real citizenship against every difficulty that they faced in the foreign country.

God calls people out of their current situation and awaits our response to His invitation to become a citizen of His country. Many times we have become so comfortable in the country that we are in, we will not entertain the idea of visiting God's country. Some people will do the research to find out what God's country is about and then visit but return to the country from where they came. Others will decline to visit and choose to stay in the country where they are comfortable and never experience the blessings that God has in store for them. It all comes down to *'realization'*. Can you realize that there may be something better waiting for you someplace else? Do you desire something more than what you've grown accustomed too? The people that ask themselves this question will never be comfortable until they have found the answer. Their entire life is a search for what they know within themselves is their destiny or (I don't believe in this word, but I will use it...) *fate!* There is something that awaits them somewhere and they are living a life that presses toward that end.

This is what inspired the patriarchs of antiquity and what is still driving millions today. It is the **hope** that the promise of God is awaiting them in the not so distant future. We are looking for the country that God promised us and the new city in which we will live with Him in eternity.

The key to this scripture has always been an encouragement to me. It is the fact that, these all **died** '*in faith*' and did <u>not</u> receive the promise. They must have been 'persuaded' beyond doubt and without any possibility of being discouraged. This is a blessing in and of itself especially in a world where people simply do not believe in or trust anything anymore. They believed God throughout their entire lives and did *not* receive what God promised. This is dedication to what you believe in against all odds and against all persecution. To believe in something so deeply that you are willing to die not only *with*, but *for* that belief. This speaks of a devotion that you rarely find today. You may think that you have this type of dedication, but is what you are dedicated too real? Is your dedication eternal? Does the belief that you hold have the ability to change and/or improve your current lifestyle? If you are still comfortable in the country in which you reside; or if you cannot be distinguished from those around you without true faith, then you have believed a lie. Somewhere, during the course of your existence, in your current country, you have been deceived.

There must be the ability to present the evidence of what you believe determinable in some place; in some way; somewhere. Many people will say that there is not enough evidence to prove that Jesus is the Messiah or that He was and is God incarnate. Is this true? There is more evidence to prove that He <u>was</u> and <u>is</u> who He claims to be than there is to disprove it. Too often doubters would like to dismiss the facts and never show enough evidence to prove their point. There is a world wide web of research that can now be done with new evidence being found constantly. This is a fact, so since this is true, why do we not rest in the hope of the promises of God?

If 95% of the world's population believes in a higher power, then it stands to reason that an intelligent man will not find himself in the bottom five percentile. All that a person has to do is search for the truth. The Word of God will ultimately speak for itself! Once God makes Himself known to you, then the invitation has been extended, stayed and remained for better than two thousand years. We all know that death is an absolute reality for every man; this is our earthly house or tabernacle. God's promise and hope invites us to have a place in heaven with or creator for eternity.

"For we know that if our earthly house of [this] tabernacle were dissolved, we have a building of God, <u>an house not made with hands</u>, eternal in the heavens."

2 Corinthians 5:1

"But Christ being come an high priest of good things to come, by <u>a greater and more perfect tabernacle</u>, not made with hands, that is to say, not of this building."

Hebrews 9:11

God promises us a dwelling place in a new country where we will live in houses that have not been built with hands. This is our spiritual hope. The country that we are going to is a spiritual place where everything will be more perfect than where we are now. All we have to do is believe and spend a small portion of our time doing the research required to find out about this country and new 'Kingdom'. The citizenship requirements are not as detailed as we tend to think. The retirement benefits are the best. I plan to be one of the people that hold onto my faith during the course of my life. I am definitely looking forward to God's promise. From what I have read in the brochure, the country is beautiful!

Notes And Reflections For The Reader:

The "This Is What I Want" Line

The Selfish Instead of Selfless Program

This line is getting longer and longer in these last days! It is actually unbelievable that so many people are willing to place their personal needs and desires before anyone else. The world has already gravitated to Dog-Eat-Dog and there doesn't seem to be any return charity for the sake of charity. Even if the topic is the difference is between right and wrong, you may hear, *"I know, but that is not what I want!"*

This is a sad state of affairs because it doesn't consider the elderly, children, marriage, friendship, or your fellowman. The selfish mentality transcends all boundaries; all instances; and all situations. This mentality does not take the condition of others into consideration for even the slightest instance. The enemy has designed the negative response to peoples needs to be a 'knee-jerk' reaction. *"Can you? No, I'm sorry I can't!" "Will you? I would, but..." "I need... I'm in the same situation as you, but at any other time..."* The responses have already been programmed to countermand any query that will hinder this person's needs and desires.

The primary motivator is *one* persons wants, desires, and perceived needs or lack thereof. Once the enemy has planted this particular kind of seed, it takes root in man's self preservation wiring. Over time it becomes hardwired and eventually a part of a person's system. Since God designed the system, He is the only one that can disconnect the wiring. This mentality, once hardwired, will run without ever having to be updated or modified. It will automatically adjust itself to be compatible with every other system that God has hardwired in us.

It will override compassion; it will minimize the needs of others; it will attempt to file away 'love' and it will most definitely bypass any program that we attempt to open that does not upgrade. The *'selfish'* is what will run Your machine.

Luke's gospel and letter to the Greeks paints a very accurate picture of the difference between these two types of mentalities.

> *"Two men went up into the temple to pray; the one a Pharisee, and the other a publican. The Pharisee stood and prayed thus <u>with himself</u>, God, I thank thee, that I am not as other men [are], extortioners, unjust, adulterers, or even as this publican. I fast twice in the week, I give tithes of all that I possess."*

Luke 18:10-**12**

<u>THIS IS AN EXCERPT FROM BARNES AND NOBLES' COMMENTARY ON THE PHARISEE AND PUBLICAN:</u>

Stood and prayed thus with himself - Some have proposed to render this, "stood by himself" and prayed. In this way it would be characteristic of the sect of the Pharisees, who dreaded the contact of others as polluting, and who were disposed to say to all, Stand by yourselves.

For further reading you may refer to the website below to read the complete article:

http://www.ccel.org/ccel/barnes/ntnotes.vi.xviii.xi.html?device=desktop

These types of people sit on the thrones of their own hearts; they cannot give God His rightful position because they pray too and worship themselves. It is very easy for selfish people to identify anther's flaws; usually the ones that they point out mirror their own. A selfish person will always proclaim themselves to be giving people and wanting the benefit of others before they satisfy the yearnings of their own desires. This is a self deception. They will give what they have. An excess of and never to the point where they lack anything. The selfish person will never admit that they have deprived anyone else. It is too hard for them to concede to the fact that they have injured their fellowman in their actions. Their perception of themselves is always as being 'good' and within the <u>will</u> of God. It is always easy for these people to compare themselves to those persons that are clearly not in God's will; like the Pharisee did. One of their biggest ways to vindicate themselves is by using the word '***people***'. They are right that 'people' do a lot of things and get themselves into all kinds of situations, but I have never met anyone named 'people'. It is another of the enemy's tricks – **misdirection**. Other people will <u>never</u> have anything to do with what God has called YOU and I to be.

> *"Because it is written, Be ye holy; for I am holy."*

> 1 Peter 1:16

This means that God has called us to be *different* and apart like He is *different*. The selfish person has the 'tree' mentality. This is how they seek to blend into the forest; by comparing themselves to the other trees. They do not wish to be different. What they want is the option to, *"Have their cake and eat it too."* There is nothing Godly or different about this mentality as you can see from the scripture.

The publican, on the other hand, saw himself clearly; as did the thief that was crucified next to Jesus.

> *"And the publican, standing afar off, <u>would not lift up so much as [his] eyes unto heaven</u>, but smote upon his breast, saying, <u>God be merciful to me a sinner</u>. I tell you, this man went down to his house justified [rather] than the other: for every one that exalteth himself shall be abased; and he that humbles himself shall be exalted."*

> Luke 18:13-**14**

"But the other answering rebuked him, saying, Dost not thou fear God, seeing thou art in the same condemnation? And we indeed justly; for we receive the due reward of our deeds: but this man hath done nothing amiss. And he said unto Jesus, Lord, remember me when thou comets into thy kingdom. And Jesus said unto him, Verily I say unto thee, To day shalt thou be with me in paradise."

Luke 23:40-**43**

These two had *selfless* attitudes. This is what God is seeking. The publican left the temple and went home justified before God and the thief went directly to heaven that very day. The selfless attitude will cause you to give of yourself in recognition of truth and justice. A selfless person will ignore their own needs at the cost of being uncomfortable and/or hurting themselves. It will cause you to do right in the face of death. They will endure embarrassment and humility in the face of others and withstand ridicule to achieve God's purpose.

The selfless attitude is a true giving, humble spirit. It is not easy and the enemy will want you to question yourself. The enemy will water that selfish seed to see if he can nurture it to grow in your spirit. He will ask, "Why should you?" He will tell you that others are not or would not. He will coax pride to rise up and dissuade you from moving in the right direction. We should be very simple in our response to ourselves – WWJD ("What Would Jesus Do?") When we can identify the response to this question. Then we will be on the same track as the publican and the thief. We will then have the favor and blessings of God.

We really must be careful when Satan tries to download this program into our *hard drive*. This program will continually pull us away from God and turn us against everyone and everyone against us. Our lifestyle becomes a lifestyle that is focused solely on our own desires and on our own purpose. It will turn us against God as it did the first thief on the cross next to Jesus and cause us to put ourselves in God's place like the Pharisee.

If we read in the scriptures that God's commandment is that we are not to have any other God's before Him, this includes ourselves. Look at how God's wrath dealt with the gods of the Egyptians and the gods that the nations around Israel worshiped. Remember Sodom and Gomorrah and how God dealt with any sin that man committed that pulled him away from his creator?

The selfish attitude is dangerous because it incorporates all three of the categories that every sin can fall into. It consists of the lust of the eye; the lust of the flesh; *and* the pride of life at the same time. The selfish person will see what hey want, calculate that it will make them or their flesh happy and become prideful to the point of obtaining their desire. If we can recognize this, then we must also recognize that this is not God or His mentality.

Being selfish has its reward just like every other endeavor that we undertake in life. Some people get their rewards on earth, but everyone will receive a reward when they get to heaven. It really boils down to which reward line you happen to be standing in. You will find that if you get into the selfish line in heaven, you will eventually receive your eternal reward from God when you move forward in line toward the 'White Throne'. That would be the, *"This is what I want" line."*

> *"And I saw a great white throne, and him that sat on it, from whose face the earth and the heaven fled away; and there was found no place for them."*

Revelation 20:11

Notes And Reflections For The Reader:

History

I Am The Story

If I was the only man that God created and Satan desired to interfere with God's purpose for my life, He would have still sent Jesus. That is a humbling thought! It is all *God's* story, but He has chosen to make me a part of it. This is GOD; the creator of the entire universe from the biggest thing that we can see to the smallest thing that we cannot see.

The one scripture that has moved me and allowed me to hold onto my faith like no other is:

> *"Who shall separate us from the love of Christ? [shall] tribulation, or distress, or persecution, or famine, or nakedness, or peril, or sword? As it is written, For thy sake we are killed all the day long; we are accounted as sheep for the slaughter. Nay, in all these things we are more than conquerors through him that loved us. For I am <u>persuaded</u>, that neither death, nor life, nor angels, nor principalities, nor powers, nor things present, nor things to come, Nor height, nor depth, nor any other creature, shall be able to separate us from the love of God, which is in Christ Jesus our Lord."*

Romans 8:35-39

My aunt Ora-Lee in North Carolina simplified how to get from point A to point B in one very short sentence. When asked, *"How did you stay married for so long?"* she simply replied, *"**You have to make up your mind!**"* Now how simple is that? It answers the question directly and places the ball squarely back in your court. It is like anything else in life; it is *your* decision that *you* determine and live with. Being *persuaded* is the same thing.

Persuasion means:

persuade [per-Swede] verb (used with object), -persuaded, -dissuading.

1. to prevail on (a person) to do something, as by advising or urging: We could not persuade him to wait.
2. to induce to believe by appealing to reason or understanding; convince: to persuade the judge of the prisoner's innocence.
Origin:
1505–15; < Latin persuader. See per-, dissuade, suasion

Synonyms
1. urge, influence, move, entice, or impel. Persuade, induce imply influencing someone's thoughts or actions. They are used today mainly in the sense of winning over a person to a certain course of action: It was I who persuaded him to call a doctor. I induced him to do it. They differ in that <u>persuade suggests appealing more to the reason and understanding:</u> I persuaded him to go back to his wife (although it is often lightly used: Can't I persuade you to stay to supper?); induce emphasizes only the idea of successful influence, whether achieved by argument or by promise of reward: What can I say that will induce you to stay at your job? Owing to this idea of compensation, induce may be used in reference to the influence of factors as well as of persons: The prospect of a raise in salary was what induced him to stay.

For the most part, *however* you come to be persuaded, it is still a question of setting a determined course of action or of setting a direction for yourself, in your own mind. To be persuaded means that you have accepted a <u>belief</u> or a way of thinking.

After getting to this portion of my life and seeing how God has watched over me; blessed me; kept and encouraged me; supplied all of my needs and been faithful and loyal when I was not; I am **Persuaded!** I have not been convinced or swayed by any particular person or forced in any way to believe or hold the convictions that I have. I am persuaded because I have found the truth. I have studied, compared and labored over which choices to make and found that Jesus is the *only* way. I could no longer believe that the way I was living would get me any place positive. A person always knows if they are living up to God's smallest expectations or even their own. It is inherent in us because we are designed this way. Above anything else, I knew myself and I *owned* it!

After we come to the end of ourselves and recognize that our way is not working anymore, we have to be honest with ourselves and decide to make a change. Either we fall into self deception or we stop and make a 180^0 turn. Self deception is dangerous, but repentance is what will get God's attention. When my mind was made up, God took the next step. Now I had hold of something that was real and that I could sink my teeth into. I began to ask God to show me His Word more deeply and I studied it in a way that led me to dig deeper still.

I have to say that I love Paul especially because he was so ingrained in and compassionate about his belief that he excelled beyond many that were his seniors. When Paul was persuaded, he placed as much enthusiasm and zeal into his changed mindset as he did with his former. He became a man who contributed 70% to the New Testament and won countless souls to Christ where he once killed those who followed Jesus. What Paul suffered for his faith is incredible, but the above scripture sums it up. Not dying or living or spiritual things or carnal things could dissuade him from what he believed. Nothing in the past and nothing in the future or anyone that would tell him anything against Jesus could change his mind. He viewed anything standing in his way as an obstacle that was trying to separate him from God's love through His son. This is an amazingly profound statement in and of itself. What did Paul suffer in following his faith? Besides Paul's proclamation about being persuaded, Paul suffered for what he believed.

> *"__As the truth of Christ is in me, no man shall stop me__ of this boasting in the regions of Achaean.*
>
> **2 Corinthians 11:10**

Paul found the truth and was adamant about no one being able to stop him from telling everyone about it. This truth was taking him around the world and into unknown territory.

Wherefore? because I love you not? God knoweth. But what I do, that I will do, that I may cut off occasion from them which desire occasion; that <u>wherein they glory, they may be found even as we</u>. For such are false apostles, deceitful workers, transforming themselves into the apostles of Christ. And no marvel; for Satan himself is transformed into an angel of light. Therefore it is no great thing if <u>his ministers also be transformed as the ministers of righteousness;</u> whose end shall be according to their works.

He tells the church in Corinth that he loves them and that he is going to stop anyone that is attempting to hinder Jesus' message of the 'Kingdom'. If anyone was in the same position that he was in (as Saul the persecutor of the church of Christ); if anyone was in the position of being prideful, Paul was going to erase that pride and place everyone on the same level playing field.

He plainly sees this as a trick of Satan and points out the enemy's plan. Paul's comparison is to Satan's army and followers appearing as angels of light. Those that are on Satan's side will show themselves in a way that is seductive, tempting and seemingly accommodating to the present needs or desires. Paul forces them to think by stating hat it is nothing special if Satan can use men who seem to be righteous to accomplish his deception.

I say again, Let no man think me a fool; if otherwise, yet as a fool receive me, that I may boast myself a little. That which I speak, I speak [it] not after the Lord, but as it were foolishly, in this confidence of boasting. Seeing that many glory after the flesh, I will glory also. For ye suffer fools gladly, seeing ye [yourselves] are wise. For ye suffer, if a man bring you into bondage, if a man devour [you], if a man take [of you], if a man exalt himself, if a man smite you on the face. I speak as concerning reproach, as though we had been weak. Howbeit wherein soever any is bold, (I speak foolishly,) I am bold also.

Paul then begins to be very bold toward the church in Corinth. He begins to pull the foundation out from under those that believe themselves to be very high and mighty. He says that they can think what they want of him, but he asks them to look at themselves and make the comparison. This is a challenge that *persuaded* them! He is telling that he was once like them and he knows wherein their pride is based. What he is saying is that if he can do a 180^0 and be convinced to this degree, then they surely can seeing that his former position was greater than theirs. He uses himself as an example by pointing out that the things that he has been persuaded of have made him bolder than he once was. He attempts to show them that his change of heart has its pros and cons, but is ultimately worth it.

Are they Hebrews? so [am] I. Are they Israelites? so [am] I. Are they the seed of Abraham? so [am] I. Are they ministers of Christ? (I speak as a fool) I [am] more;

He knows that he is speaking to learned men. He is not trying to take anything from them, but is attempting to add something to them, but he is, however being slightly sarcastic.

> *...in labors more abundant, in stripes above measure, in prisons more frequent, in deaths oft. Of the Jews five times received I forty [stripes] save one. Thrice was I beaten with rods, once was I stoned, thrice I suffered shipwreck, a night and a day I have been in the deep; [In] journeying often, [in] perils of waters, [in] perils of robbers, [in] perils by [mine own] countrymen, [in] perils by the heathen, [in] perils in the city, [in] perils in the wilderness, [in] perils in the sea, [in] perils among false brethren; In weariness and painfulness, in watching often, in hunger and thirst, in fasting often, in cold and nakedness.*

2 Corinthians 11:27

This portion is Paul's resume of suffering. He spells out that he has done more for his new cause than anyone else. He lists that he has more scars than he can count and that he has been in prison and in danger of death more often. He states that he has been beaten 199 times and beaten with rods on three separate occasions. He was stoned and in three different boat wrecks where on one he had to to tread water for a night and a day. In his travels, he has had to face thieves and strangers and has been in danger by his own countrymen as well. Paul says that he has faced danger in the country and in the city; on dry land and at sea. He has been among people who are not who they say they are and is constantly having to look over his shoulder. Even when he is cold naked and hungry; even when he is fasting, in pain, or naked he is focused on what he believes.

Something has made an impression on Paul and is driving him to face the dangers of the world to tell others. There is no doubt that Paul suffered all of these things externally and yet he also suffered internally in his body. His greatest concern was the proclamation of the gospel message and insuring that those who had already been persuaded were encouraged to hold onto their faith.

Beside those things that are without, that which cometh upon me daily, the care of all the churches."

2 Corinthians 11:10-**28**

There are very few people that have been so convinced of their cause that they are willing to suffer all of these dangers and wrongs to establish and share their conviction. The list of these certain types of people would be very short and amongst the greatest men and women in human history. These people did not see themselves as special or extraordinary; they simply believed what they believed with an unsurpassable conviction.

Where will you find yourself in the chronicles of history? Will the things that you have fought for in this life carry on into eternity? When the world looks back at your record and life, will they remember that there was something of which you were persuaded? Will they be able to say that your story was the same as Hi Story?

Conclusion

In the end, we are all soldiers in this Christian Army or we are soldiers for the enemy. Our enemy will continue to come at us in any way that he can, but like the word says, "He will come in one way and flee seven different ways". Well that's his job so we should not be dismayed. We have to hold on to what we know about God's Word and what we don't know we have to read, research, ask questions and find out. The journey does not always get better; sometimes it gets worse! The questions we face are: "Are we committed?" "Are we willing to follow the *true* shepherd through and over any terrain that He chooses to lead us through?" "Are we willing to wage war no matter what it cost us?" "Are we willing to stand?" "Are we persuaded?"

If nothing else is true, whether we have the answers or not; whether we do everything perfectly or fall short trying; one thing is for certain, we have lived a better life here on earth than the average man. It is certain that the character traits, integrity, trustworthiness, dependability and consistency of the Christian walk are attractive to every man.

Dear Reader, this is a war and we are the soldiers. Whether we have joined the army or by some circumstance or turn of events have ended up on the 'Battlefield', we remain people that reside in a war torn land and have to endure the hardships of such a reality on a daily basis. The children that we see on television did not ask to be casualties of war. Those children did not ask to live in the country that they were born into. Those children did not make any political decisions or hate a group of people that were not like them. Those children did not ask to be hungry or homeless or without their parents. Those children, if given a choice, would choose the same lifestyle as any other child across the globe that is in a better circumstance. Those children would love their parents and siblings and grow up well fed and clean. Those children would express their love for their siblings; for their parents and grandparents and their extended family. Those children would care for the person that was hurt and crying or that would want to be cared for. Well Dear Reader, these are the lives that we all hope to lead and the world that we all would choose to live in. The reality is very far from these types of nice pictures. The reality is that we were all '**Born on the Battlefield**'!

Born on the
Battlefield
The Art of Spiritual Warfare

[The Book Signing]